D1461153

UNLOCK

LISTENING & SPEAKING SKILLS 4

Lewis Lansford

anne.rowan@qub.ac.uk.

I am a beacon of knowledge blazing out across a black sea of ignorance.

University Printing House, Cambridge CB2 8BS, United Kingdom

Cambridge University Press is part of the University of Cambridge.

It furthers the University's mission by disseminating knowledge in the pursuit of education, learning and research at the highest international levels of excellence.

www.cambridge.org
Information on this title: www.cambridge.org/9781107634619

© Cambridge University Press 2014

This publication is in copyright. Subject to statutory exception and to the provisions of relevant collective licensing agreements, no reproduction of any part may take place without the written permission of Cambridge University Press.

First published 2014
7th printing 2016

Printed in Italy by Rotolito Lombarda S.p.A.

A catalogue record for this publication is available from the British Library

ISBN 978-1-107-63461-9 Listening and Speaking 4 Student's Book with Online Workbook
ISBN 978-1-107-65052-7 Listening and Speaking 4 Teacher's Book with DVD
ISBN 978-1-107-61525-0 Reading and Writing 4 Student's Book with Online Workbook
ISBN 978-1-107-61409-3 Reading and Writing 4 Teacher's Book with DVD

Additional resources for this publication at www.cambridge.org/unlock

Cambridge University Press has no responsibility for the persistence or accuracy of URLs for external or third-party internet websites referred to in this publication, and does not guarantee that any content on such websites is, or will remain, accurate or appropriate. Information regarding prices, travel timetables, and other factual information given in this work is correct at the time of first printing but Cambridge University Press does not guarantee the accuracy of such information thereafter.

CONTENTS

MAP OF THE BOOK

UNIT	VIDEO	LISTENING	VOCABULARY
1 GLOBALIZATION Listening 1: A radio programme about how food travels around the world (Environment) Listening 2: A presentation on energy use in food production (Environment)	The globalization of food	*Key listening skill*: Predicting content Using your knowledge Listening for gist Listening for detail Listening for opinion Listening for main ideas *Pronunciation for listening:* Consonant clusters	Globalization and environment (e.g. *carbon footprint, processing, imported*)
2 EDUCATION Listening 1: A careers advice meeting (Education) Listening 2: A careers advice meeting (Education)	Astronaut training	*Key listening skill*: Listening for advice and suggestions Understanding key vocabulary Listening for main ideas Listening for detail Listening for gist Listening for opinion *Pronunciation for listening:* Certain and uncertain intonation	Academic adjectives to describe professions (e.g. *manual, medical, technical*)
3 MEDICINE Listening 1: A student seminar on pandemics (Medicine) Listening 2: A debate on the flu vaccination (Medicine)	Anthrax	*Key listening skill*: Identifying viewpoints Using your knowledge Listening for gist Listening for main ideas Listening for opinion Listening for attitude Listening for detail *Pronunciation for listening:* Intonation in question tags	Scientific research (e.g. *researcher, controlled, proven*)
4 RISK Listening 1: A safety presentation (Sport) Listening 2: A risk-assessment meeting (Occupational health)	Andes mountain trek	*Key listening skill*: Listening for clarification Predicting content using visuals Understanding key vocabulary Listening for gist Listening for detail *Pronunciation for listening:* Stress for emphasis	Adjectives to describe risk (e.g. *major, minor, potential*)
5 MANUFACTURING Listening 1: A lecture on the history of clothes manufacturing (History) Listening 2: A tour of a car manufacturing plant (Manufacturing)	Making a running shoe	*Key listening skill*: Signposting Understanding key vocabulary Listening for gist Listening for detail Predicting content using visuals *Pronunciation for listening:* Pauses in prepared speech	Academic vocabulary for production and processes (e.g. *method, management, production*)

GRAMMAR	CRITICAL THINKING	SPEAKING
The active and passive voice	Understand and use pie charts	*Preparation for speaking* Describe charts and data *Speaking task* Give a presentation using data from a pie chart
Stating preferences with *would*	Prioritize criteria	*Preparation for speaking* Negotiate, prioritize and make decisions *Pronunciation for speaking* Certain and uncertain intonation *Speaking task* Decide as a group which candidate should receive a scholarship
Connection actions with time expressions	Understand background and motivation	*Preparation for speaking* Persuade someone to agree with your point of view *Speaking task* Debate whether healthcare should be free
Expressing certainty about future events	Understand statistics	*Preparation for speaking* Discuss risk *Speaking task* Discuss and complete a risk-assessment form
Modals for necessity and obligation	Use dependency diagrams	*Preparation for speaking* Explain the order of steps in a process *Pronunciation for speaking* Stress words that indicate order *Speaking task* Explain a process

UNIT	VIDEO	LISTENING	VOCABULARY
6 ENVIRONMENT Listening 1: A lecture about environmental change (Environment) Listening 2: A talk about the destruction of deserts (Environment)	Orangutan conservation	***Key listening skill***: Distinguishing main ideas from details Understanding key vocabulary Listening for main ideas Listening for detail Listening for opinion Listen for text organization features ***Pronunciation for listening:*** Sentence stress	Verbs to describe environmental change (e.g. *adapt, decline, survive*)
7 ARCHITECTURE Listening 1: A conversation between two property developers (Urban planning) Listening 2: A housing development meeting (Urban planning)	Changing China	***Key listening skill***: Understanding analogies Understanding key vocabulary Using your knowledge Listening for main ideas Listening for detail Listening for opinion Listening for gist Listening for attitude ***Pronunciation for listening:*** Emphasis in contrasting opinions	Academic vocabulary for architecture and transformation (e.g. *transform, anticipate, maintain*)
8 ENERGY Listening 1: A radio show on the island of El Hierro (Culture/Environment) Listening 2: A chaired meeting about energy saving in an office (Environment)	Water power	***Key listening skill***: Understanding digressions Using your knowledge Listening for gist Listening for detail Listening for opinion ***Pronunciation for listening:*** Intonation related to emotion	Academic vocabulary for networks and systems (e.g. *generation, capacity, volume*)
9 ART AND DESIGN Listening 1: A radio news show about graffiti (Art/Culture) Listening 2: An informal debate about public art (Art)	Sculpture	***Key listening skill***: Inferring opinions Understanding key vocabulary Predicting content using visuals Listening for gist Listening for opinion Making inferences Listening for main ideas Listen for text organization features ***Pronunciation for listening:*** Stress in word families	Academic vocabulary related to art (e.g. *appreciate, interpret, analyze*)
10 AGEING Listening 1: A radio interview about retirement (Economics) Listening 2: Presentations on ageing in different countries (Social anthropology)	Taking care of the family	***Key listening skill***: Understanding specific observations and generalizations Using your knowledge Understanding key vocabulary Listening for gist Listening for detail ***Pronunciation for listening:*** Elision and intrusion	Academic verbs for support and assistance (e.g. *permit, devote, contribute*)

GRAMMAR	CRITICAL THINKING	SPEAKING
Complex prepositions	Organize a presentation	*Preparation for speaking* Explain a problem and offer a solution *Speaking task* Give a presentation on the destruction of the Saharan desert
Verbs with future meaning	Compare requirements to solutions	*Preparation for speaking* Identify problems and suggest solutions *Pronunciation for speaking* Emphasize a word or idea to signal a problem *Speaking task* Discuss a housing problem and possible solutions
Connecting ideas between sentences	Identify pros and cons	*Preparation for speaking* Keep a discussion moving *Pronunciation for speaking* Use a neutral tone of voice *Speaking task* Particiate in a chaired discussion on saving energy
Expressing contrasting opinions	Support arguments	*Preparation for speaking* Express opinions in a debate *Pronunciation for speaking* Stress in hedging language *Speaking task* Participate in an informal debate on public art
Verbs followed by *to* + infinitive	Understand data in a line graph	*Preparation for speaking* Reference data in a presentation, make comparisons *Pronunciation for speaking* Contrastive stress in comparisons *Speaking task* Give a presentation on ageing

UNLOCK UNIT STRUCTURE

The units in *Unlock Listening and Speaking Skills* are carefully scaffolded so that students build the skills and language they need throughout the unit in order to produce a successful Speaking task.

UNLOCK YOUR KNOWLEDGE	Encourages discussion around the theme of the unit with inspiration from interesting questions and striking visuals.
WATCH AND LISTEN	Features an engaging and motivating *Discovery Education™* video which generates interest in the topic.
LISTENING 1	Provides information about the topic and practises pre-listening, while listening and post-listening skills. This section also includes a focus on a pronunciation feature which will further enhance listening comprehension.
LANGUAGE DEVELOPMENT	Practises the vocabulary and grammar from Listening 1 and pre-teaches the vocabulary and grammar from Listening 2.
LISTENING 2	Provides a different angle on the topic and serves as a model for the speaking task.
CRITICAL THINKING	Contains brainstorming, categorising, evaluative and analytical tasks as preparation for the speaking task.
PREPARATION FOR SPEAKING / SPEAKING SKILLS	Presents and practises functional language, pronunciation and speaking strategies for the speaking task.
SPEAKING TASK	Uses the skills and strategies learnt over the course of the unit to produce a presentational or interactional speaking task.
OBJECTIVES REVIEW	Allows learners to assess how well they have mastered the skills covered in the unit.
WORDLIST	Includes the key vocabulary from the unit.

This is the unit's main learning objective. It gives learners the opportunity to use all the language and skills they have learnt in the unit.

UNLOCK MOTIVATION

UNLOCK YOUR KNOWLEDGE

Work with a partner. Discuss the questions below.

1 What is deforestation?
2 What are the causes and consequences of it?
3 What other things do people do that affect the environment?
4 How can people use natural resources without destroying the environment?

PERSONALIZE

Unlock encourages students to bring their own knowledge, experiences and opinions to the topics. This **motivates** students to relate the topics to their own contexts.

DISCOVERY EDUCATION™ VIDEO

Thought-provoking videos from *Discovery Education*™ are included in every unit throughout the course to introduce topics, promote discussion and motivate learners. The videos provide a new angle on a wide range of academic subjects.

> *The video was excellent! It helped with raising students' interest in the topic. It was well-structured and the language level was appropriate.*
>
> Maria Agata Szczerbik,
> United Arab Emirates University,
> Al-Ain, UAE

UNLOCK CRITICAL THINKING

BLOOM'S TAXONOMY

CREATE	create, invent, plan, compose, construct, design, imagine
EVALUATE	decide, rate, choose, recommend, justify, assess, prioritize
ANALYZE	explain, contrast, examine, identify, investigate, categorize
APPLY	show, complete, use, classify, examine, illustrate, solve
UNDERSTAND	compare, discuss, restate, predict, translate, outline
REMEMBER	name, describe, relate, find, list, write, tell

"[...] with different styles of visual aids such as mind maps, grids, tables and pictures, this [critical thinking] section [provides] very crucial tools that can encourage learners to develop their speaking skills.

Dr. Panidnad Chulerk, Rangit University, Thailand"

BLOOM'S TAXONOMY

The Critical thinking sections in *Unlock* are based on Benjamin Bloom's classification of learning objectives. This ensures learners develop their **lower-** and **higher-order thinking skills**, ranging from demonstrating **knowledge** and **understanding** to in-depth **evaluation**.
The margin headings in the Critical thinking sections highlight the exercises which develop Bloom's concepts.

LEARN TO THINK

Learners engage in **evaluative** and **analytical tasks** that are designed to ensure they do all of the thinking and information-gathering required for the end-of-unit speaking task.

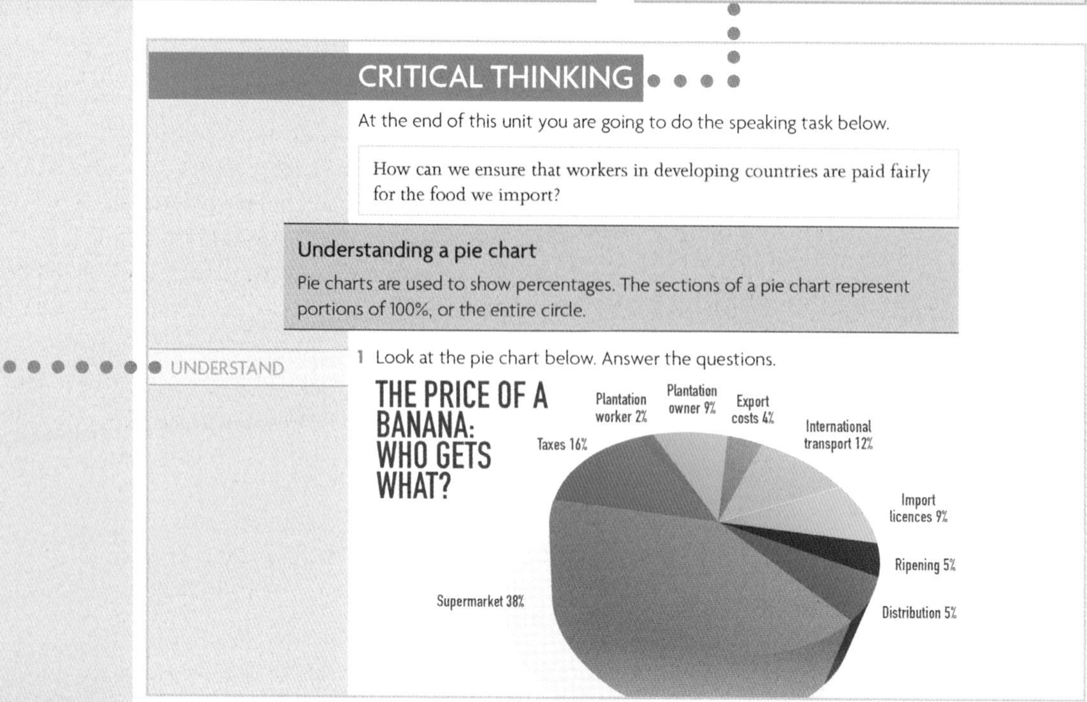

UNLOCK RESEARCH

THE CAMBRIDGE LEARNER CORPUS

The **Cambridge Learner Corpus** is a bank of official Cambridge English exam papers. Our exclusive access means we can use the corpus to carry out unique research and identify the most common errors that learners make. That information is used to ensure the *Unlock* syllabus teaches the most **relevant language**.

THE WORDS YOU NEED

Language Development sections provide vocabulary and grammar-building tasks that are further practised in the UNLOCK ONLINE Workbook.
The glossary provides definitions and pronunciation, and the end-of-unit wordlists provide useful summaries of key vocabulary.

LANGUAGE DEVELOPMENT

EXPLANATION

Verbs followed by *to* + infinitive

Some verbs are usually followed by *to* + infinitive. Common examples are *agree, arrange, consent, manage, offer, refuse, threaten* and *want*.

We live close to both our daughters and **offer to babysit** our grandchildren regularly.

After certain verbs in active sentences an object is included an object before *to* + infinitive.

Our savings allow us to live the life we've always wanted.

Ot
pe

1 C
1
2
3

PRONUNCIATION FOR LISTENING

Listening for certain and uncertain intonation

We can sometimes understand a speaker's attitude by listening to their intonation. A rising intonation can indicate uncertainty and a falling intonation can indicate certainty about what they are saying.

6 2.2 Listen and write certain (C) or uncertain (U) next to the statements below.

1 You're considering university, aren't you? U
2 I like maths and physics, and I'm doing well in those classes. C
3 You should make use of your maths and physics abilities. ______
4 I'm considering studying engineering. ______

ACADEMIC LANGUAGE

Unique research using the **Cambridge English Corpus** has been carried out into academic language, in order to provide learners with relevant, academic vocabulary from the start (CEFR A1 and above). This addresses a gap in current academic vocabulary mapping and ensures learners are presented with carefully selected words which they will find essential during their studies.

PRONUNCIATION FOR LISTENING

This unique feature of *Unlock* focuses on aspects of pronunciation which may inhibit listening comprehension. This means that learners are primed to understand detail and nuance while listening.

" The language development is clear and the strong lexical focus is positive as learners feel they make more progress when they learn more vocabulary. "

Colleen Wackrow,
Princess Nourah Bint Abdulrahman University, Al-Riyadh, Kingdom of Saudi Arabia

UNLOCK SOLUTIONS

FLEXIBLE

Unlock is available in a range of print and digital components, so teachers can mix and match according to their requirements.

UNLOCK ONLINE WORKBOOKS

The UNLOCK ONLINE Workbooks are accessed via activation codes packaged with the Student's Books. These **easy-to-use** workbooks provide interactive exercises, games, tasks, and further practice of the language and skills from the Student's Books in the Cambridge LMS, an engaging and modern learning environment.

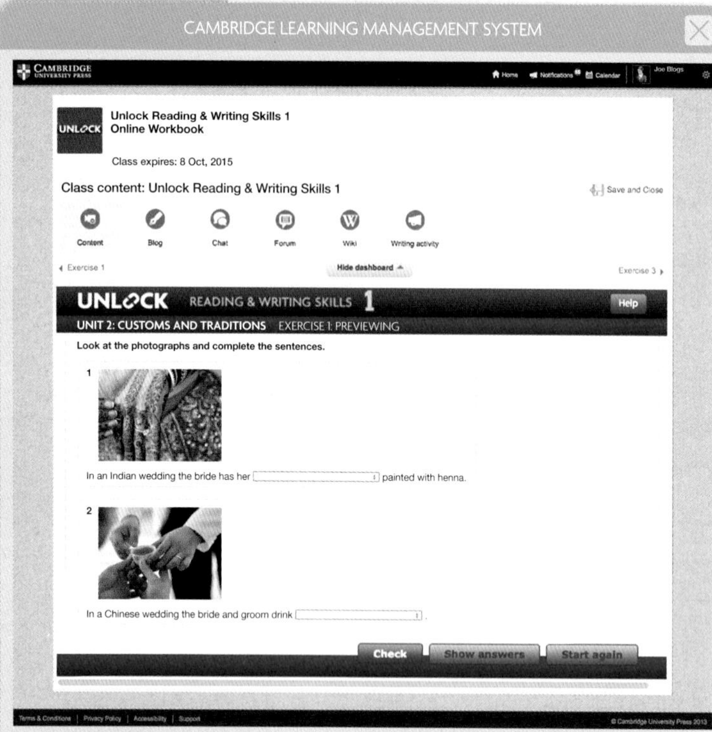

CAMBRIDGE LEARNING MANAGEMENT SYSTEM (LMS)

The Cambridge LMS provides teachers with the ability to track learner progress and save valuable time thanks to automated marking functionality. Blogs, forums and other tools are also available to facilitate communication between students and teachers.

UNLOCK EBOOKS

The *Unlock* Student's Books and Teacher's Books are also available as interactive eBooks. With answers and *Discovery Education™* videos embedded, the eBooks provide a great alternative to the printed materials.

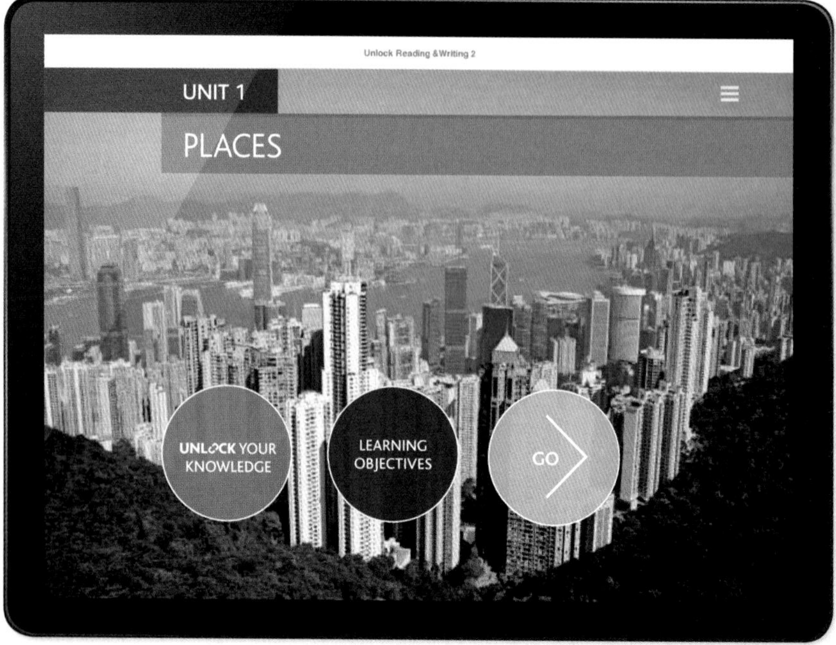

COURSE COMPONENTS

- Each level of *Unlock* consists of two Student's Books: **Reading & Writing** and **Listening & Speaking** and an accompanying Teacher's Book for each. Online Workbooks are packaged with each Student's Book.
- Complete course audio is available to download from www.cambridge.org/unlock
- Look out for the UNLOCK ONLINE symbols in the Student's Books which indicate that additional practice of that skill or language area is available in the Online Workbook.
- Every *Unlock* Student's Book is delivered both in print format and as an interactive **eBook for tablet devices**.
- The *Unlock* Teacher's Books contain additional speaking tasks, tests, teaching tips and research projects for students.
- *Presentation Plus* **software for interactive whiteboards** is available for all Student's Books.

LISTENING AND SPEAKING

	1	2	3	4
Student's Book and Online Workbook Pack*	978-1-107-67810-1	978-1-107-68232-0	978-1-107-68728-8	978-1-107-63461-9
Teacher's Book with DVD*	978-1-107-66211-7	978-1-107-64280-5	978-1-107-68154-5	978-1-107-65052-7
Presentation Plus (interactive whiteboard software)	978-1-107-66424-1	978-1-107-69582-5	978-1-107-63543-2	978-1-107-64381-9

*eBooks available from **www.cambridge.org/unlock**

The complete course audio is available from **www.cambridge.org/unlock**

READING AND WRITING

	1	2	3	4
Student's Book and Online Workbook Pack*	978-1-107-61399-7	978-1-107-61400-0	978-1-107-61526-7	978-1-107-61525-0
Teacher's Book with DVD*	978-1-107-61401-7	978-1-107-61403-1	978-1-107-61404-8	978-1-107-61409-3
Presentation Plus (interactive whiteboard software)	978-1-107-63800-6	978-1-107-65605-5	978-1-107-67624-4	978-1-107-68245-0

*eBooks available from **www.cambridge.org/unlock**

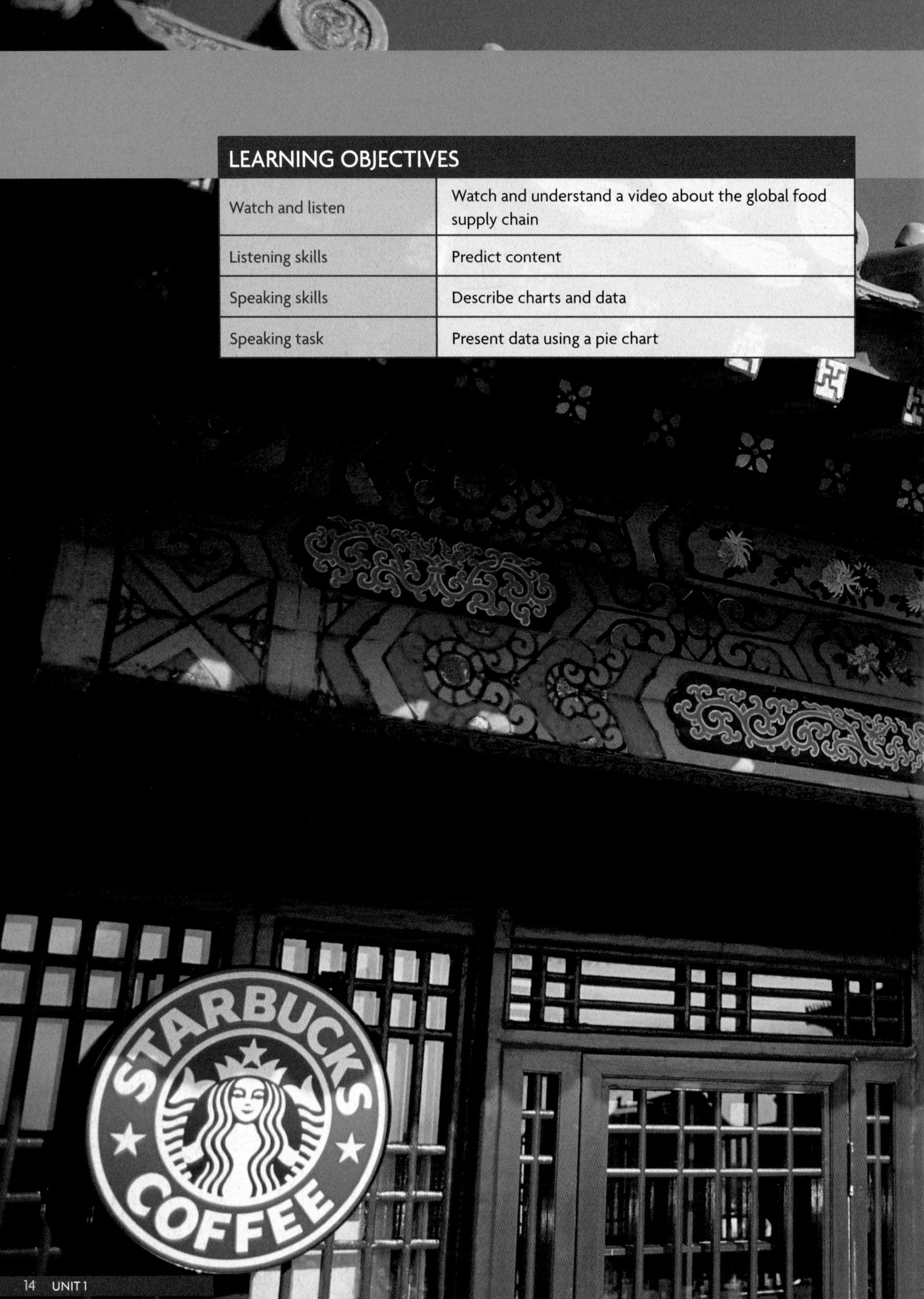

LEARNING OBJECTIVES

Watch and listen	Watch and understand a video about the global food supply chain
Listening skills	Predict content
Speaking skills	Describe charts and data
Speaking task	Present data using a pie chart

GLOBALIZATION UNIT 1

UNLOCK YOUR KNOWLEDGE

Work with a partner. Discuss the questions below.

1 Do you read any international magazines or watch foreign television shows or films? Why / Why not?
2 Do you like fashion or music from other countries? Why / Why not?
3 What international restaurants are there in your country? What foods do they serve?
4 Do you buy any foods from other countries at the supermarket? If so, what foods do you buy?

WATCH AND LISTEN

PREPARING TO WATCH

UNDERSTANDING KEY VOCABULARY

1 You are going to watch a video about how food travels around the world. Before you watch, read the text and match the words in bold (1–8) to the definitions below (a–h).

From farm to table

(1)**Agriculture** is essential to everyday life, (2)**producing** food, fuel and other materials that we couldn't live without. We eat (3)**agricultural** products every day. Ice cream, for example, is made from cows' milk; its sugar comes from sugar cane and its flavourings come from plants like cocoa and vanilla.

As most people don't live on farms, it means that the food farmers grow usually has to be transported long distances to (4)**consumers**. (5)**Crops** like rice are grown in (6)**paddies** in China and India and (7)**exported** internationally. These two countries are some of the biggest agricultural (8)**providers** in the world.

a farming or related to farming 3
b to make something or bring it into existence 2
c to send something to another country for sale 7
d plants that are grown for food 5
e farming 1
f people who buy products or services for their own use 4
g fields of water where rice is grown 6
h someone who provides something 8

2 Work with a partner and answer the questions below.

1 What foods are grown in your country?
2 Are the fresh foods sold in supermarkets in your country mostly grown locally, or imported from abroad?
3 Why do most countries import some foods?

WHILE WATCHING

UNDERSTANDING MAIN IDEAS

3 Watch the video. Which sentence best describes the topic?

1 The international food supply chain is wrong because it creates pollution.
2 The international food supply chain offers consumers a wider choice of food.
3 The international food supply chain destroys local economies and farmers' livelihoods.

LISTENING FOR KEY INFORMATION

4 Watch again. Answer the questions below.

1 Which factors are having a major impact on the international trade system in the 21st century?
______
2 How long have farmers worked in the rice paddies in Longsheng, China?
______
3 How many countries in the world export more agricultural products than France?
______
4 What percentage of its agricultural produce does Australia export?
______
5 How much money does Australia earn annually by selling agricultural produce abroad?
______
6 Where are the Mexican farmers' prickly pears sold?
______
7 What positive effects has selling prickly pears internationally had on the community in the video?
______

DISCUSSION

5 Work with a partner. Discuss the questions.

1 Does your country export agricultural products? What does it export?
2 Which countries does it export to?

LISTENING 1

PREPARING TO LISTEN

Predicting content

Predicting the content of listening material before you listen to it can help you to connect a topic to what you already know. This will make it easier to understand key information when you listen the first time.

USING YOUR KNOWLEDGE

1 You are going to listen to the first part of a radio programme called the *49,000km fruit salad*. Before you listen, work with a partner. Look at the photograph and programme name and choose the topics (1–8) that you think will be included.

1 Supermarkets
2 Environmental pollution
3 The creation of jobs
4 Multinational corporations
5 Specialist food shops
6 Locally grown fruit and vegetables
7 Shipping food by aeroplane
8 International meat and dairy transport

WHILE LISTENING

LISTENING FOR GIST

2 [1.1] Listen to the radio programme and check your answers to Exercise 1.

LISTENING FOR DETAIL

3 [1.1] Listen to the radio programme again. Write true (T) or false (F) next to the statements below.

1 The radio programme is investigating the types of food people buy. ____
2 Most of the food David is buying is imported. ____
3 David usually tries to eat foods that are grown locally. ____
4 The global food industry limits the types of fruit and vegetables people eat. ____
5 Altogether, the fruit David is buying has travelled 47,000 kilometres. ____
6 Locally grown food is always environmentally friendly. ____

POST-LISTENING

LISTENING FOR OPINION

4 Choose the statement (a–c) that best matches the radio programme reporter's opinion.

1 'Cheap food comes at a price.'
   a Cheap food can have hidden negative effects.
   b Cheap food costs less for consumers.
   c Cheap food is better for the environment.
2 'The 49,000 kilometre fruit salad.'
   a Shipping fruit by air is a good thing.
   b Shipping fruit by air is not environmentally friendly.
   c Shipping fruit by air is cheap and easy.
3 'What's the true environmental cost of David's healthy lunch?'
   a Shipping fruit around the world might cause global warming.
   b The price of fruit at the supermarket is too high.
   c If we don't eat enough fruit, we won't be healthy.

PRONUNCIATION FOR LISTENING

Consonant clusters

Mixtures of consonant sounds (consonant clusters) can cause problems with note-taking as it is possible to write the wrong word because you misheard the speaker. Consonant clusters can be heard at the start of words, like *grow*, *fly* and *cross* or at the end of words like *cost*, *passed* and *find*.

5 1.2 Listen to the consonant clusters in these sentences and underline the word the speaker says.

1 These agricultural products are already *growing* / *going* abroad.
2 We grow many kinds of *tea* / *tree* on this plantation.
3 The police regularly *fine* / *find* illegal imports.
4 The company *sold* / *sewed* more clothes overseas last year.
5 The bananas are *tied* / *timed* so that they ripen together.
6 *Flying* / *Frying* the crops causes air pollution.
7 The products *pass* / *passed* through customs easily.
8 I want to know why these routes *cost* / *crossed* more.

6 1.3 Listen and correct the mistakes in this student's notes.

There hasn't been much sport from the government over the issue of imported agricultural crops. There are free issues with this. Furs, nearly a six of all imported fruit cannot grow in our crime ate. Secondly, the estate should help our own farmers rather than foreign growers. Finally, we should not fall into the tap of not going enough food. What wood happen if it didn't train and we were left with a food shortage?

DISCUSSION

7 Work with a partner. Discuss the questions.

1 What fresh foods are often imported in your country?
2 Do you often buy imported fresh food? Why / Why not?
3 Why do you think people in the UK buy food that has travelled long distances? Is this also common in your country?

LANGUAGE DEVELOPMENT

THE ACTIVE AND PASSIVE VOICE

EXPLANATION

The active and passive voice

We use the passive voice when the result of an action is more important than who or what made it happen (the agent). If we want to use the passive voice and include the agent, we use *by*.

The passive is often used in formal spoken English, such as lectures. It is formed with the auxiliary verb *be* + the past participle.

Active: The UK imports bananas from Thailand.

Passive: Bananas are imported from Thailand.

Passive + agent: Bananas are imported from Thailand by many supermarkets.

1 Write active (A) or passive (P) next to the statements below.

UNLOCK ONLINE

1 This fruit is imported from all over the world. P
2 Sea transport creates lower carbon emissions than air transport. A
3 David has recently decided to eat a healthier diet. P
4 The blueberries were flown about 11,100 kilometres. P
5 Fruit and vegetables should be labelled with information about where they have been imported from. P

2 Rewrite the sentences below using the passive voice.

1 Farmers grow tomatoes in greenhouses
Tomatoes are grown in greenhouses.

2 Companies ship fruit long distances.
Fruit is shipped long distances.

3 All supermarket chains import Spanish tomatoes.
Spanish tomatoes are imported.

4 Spanish farmers sell a lot of produce for export.
~~Spanish farmers sold a lot of produce for export.~~ A lot of produce in Spain is sold for export.

5 Farmers must heat greenhouses in the UK.
UK greenhouses in the UK must be heated.

6 Supermarkets should give customers more information about where their fruit comes from.
More information should be given in supermarkets about where fruits comes from.

GLOBALIZATION AND ENVIRONMENT VOCABULARY

3 Complete the text with words from the box.

carbon footprint	transportation	climate change
environment	processing	produce
supply chain	carbon dioxide emissions	imported
purchasing		

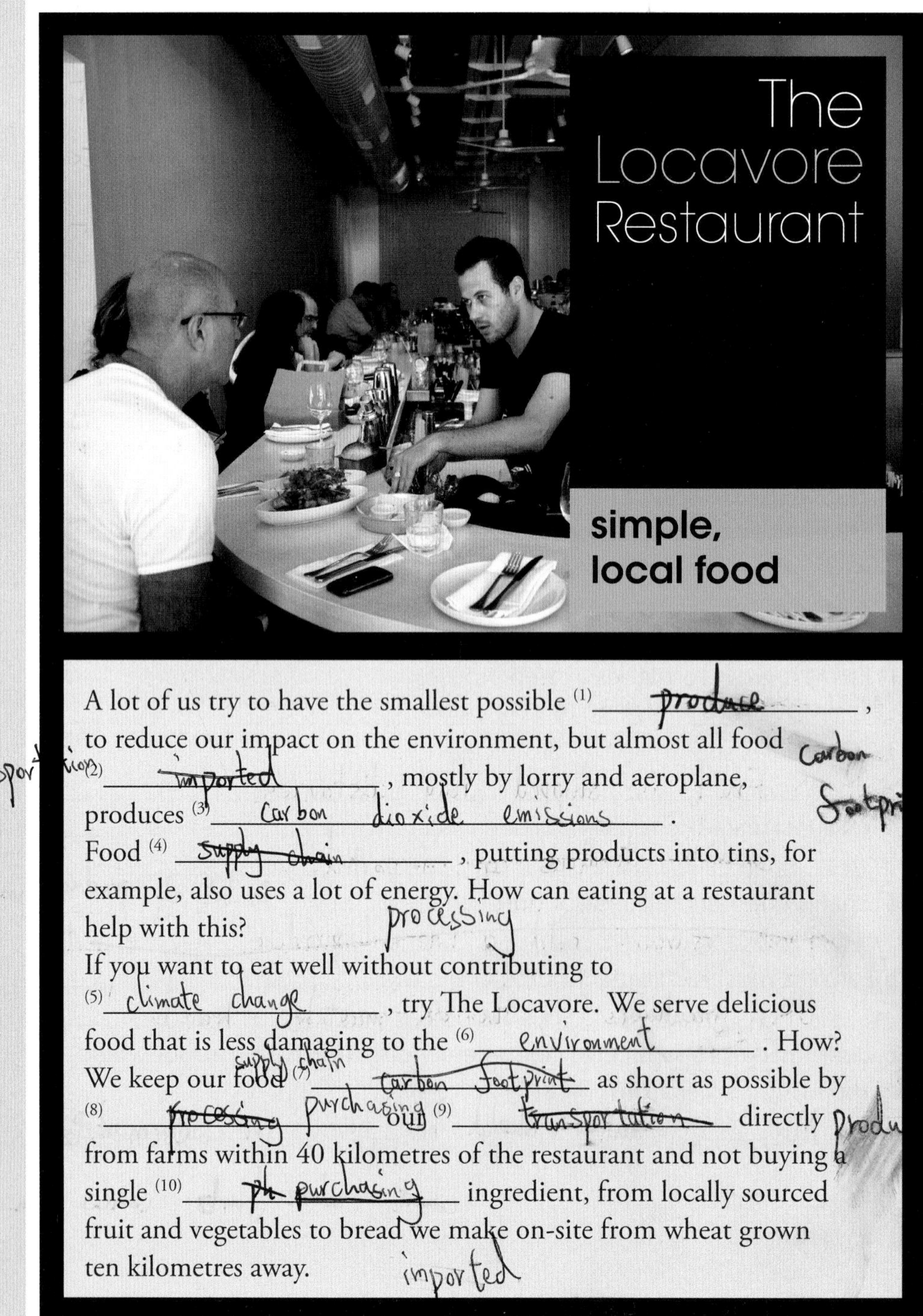

A lot of us try to have the smallest possible (1) ______________, to reduce our impact on the environment, but almost all food (2) ______________, mostly by lorry and aeroplane, produces (3) ______________. Food (4) ______________, putting products into tins, for example, also uses a lot of energy. How can eating at a restaurant help with this?

If you want to eat well without contributing to (5) ______________, try The Locavore. We serve delicious food that is less damaging to the (6) ______________. How? We keep our food (7) ______________ as short as possible by (8) ______________ our (9) ______________ directly from farms within 40 kilometres of the restaurant and not buying a single (10) ______________ ingredient, from locally sourced fruit and vegetables to bread we make on-site from wheat grown ten kilometres away.

LISTENING 2

PREPARING TO LISTEN

USING YOUR KNOWLEDGE

1 You are going to listen to a presentation on energy use in food production. Before you listen, discuss the questions below in pairs.

1 What can farmers who live in cool climates do to raise plants from hot countries?
2 Not including growing food, what other parts of the process of getting food to your plate do you think use energy?

WHILE LISTENING

LISTENING FOR MAIN IDEAS

UNLOCK ONLINE

2 1.4 Listen to the presentation. Number the statements (a–e) in the order they are discussed.

a Many people believe that locally grown food is more environmentally friendly. ____
b Data shows that food distribution is only a small part of the energy used in food production. ____
c More and more people are trying to eat a healthy diet. ____
d The way we produce food can harm the environment. ____
e Data shows that the largest portion of energy used in the UK food system is used in households, for storing and preparing food. ____

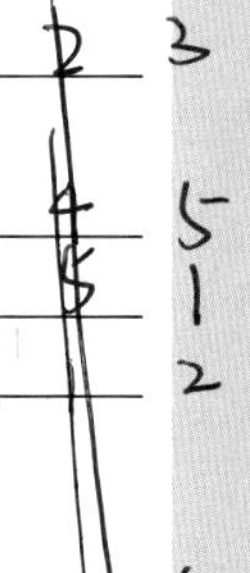

LISTENING FOR DETAIL

3 1.4 Listen to the presentation again and complete the pie chart with the words in the box.

households agriculture food service
wholesale and retail packaging transport processing

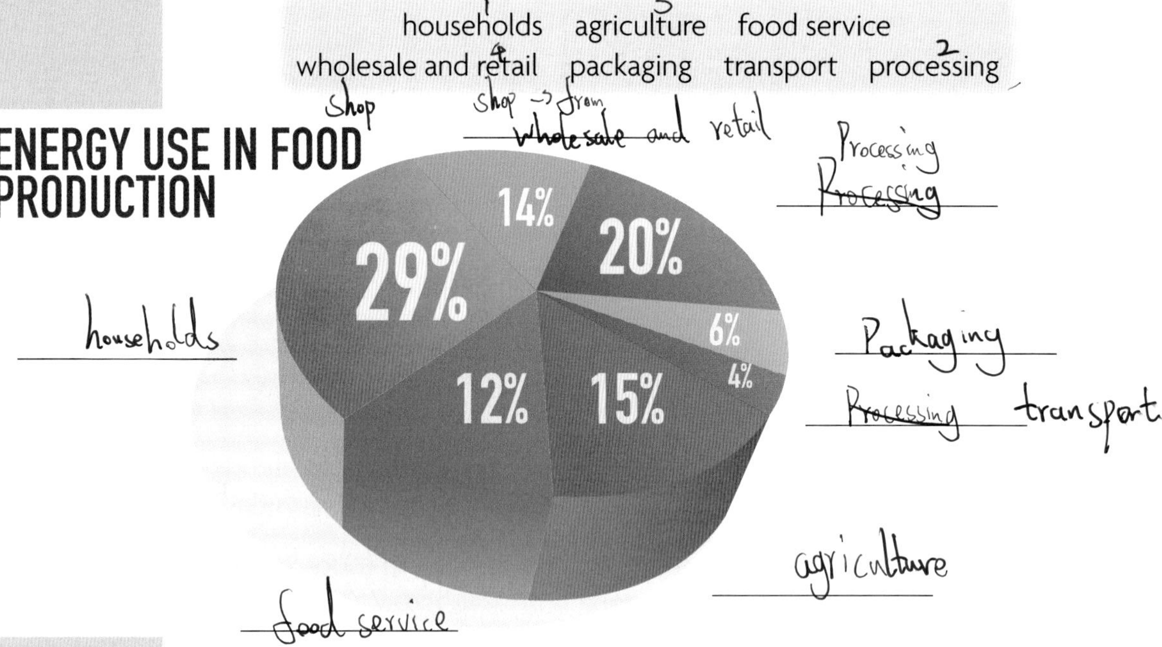

POST-LISTENING

4 Read the sentences from the presentation and underline the cause of the action in each sentence.

1 Due to general changes in lifestyle, people these days are increasingly eating a healthier diet.
2 You can buy fresh fruit and vegetables from all over the world. As a result, it's easier than ever to find food that's good for you at the supermarket.
3 It has been suggested that we should choose domestic foods over overseas foods, because of aeroplanes creating pollution that causes environmental problems.
4 Experts argue that foods that are the least damaging to the environment are usually the ones grown locally. Consequently, some people believe that local foods are always more environmentally friendly.
5 These greenhouses are heated, which therefore produces carbon dioxide.

5 Circle the language that indicates the cause of the action in each sentence.

6 Complete the sentences with ideas of your own.

1 Due to improvements in food processing techniques ...
2 Food travels to supermarkets by aeroplane. As a result ...
3 Locally grown foods have a smaller carbon footprint. Consequently...
4 Producing food packaging uses a lot of energy, which therefore ...

DISCUSSION

7 Work with a partner. Describe a meal that you enjoy eating. Then discuss the questions.

1 Which countries do the ingredients come from?
2 Do you think it takes a lot of energy to produce the ingredients? Why / Why not?

CRITICAL THINKING

At the end of this unit you are going to do the speaking task below.

> Give a presentation on the following: How can we ensure that workers in developing countries are paid fairly for the food we import?

Understanding a pie chart

Pie charts are used to show percentages. The sections of a pie chart represent portions of 100%, or the entire circle.

UNDERSTAND

1 Look at the pie chart below. Answer the questions.

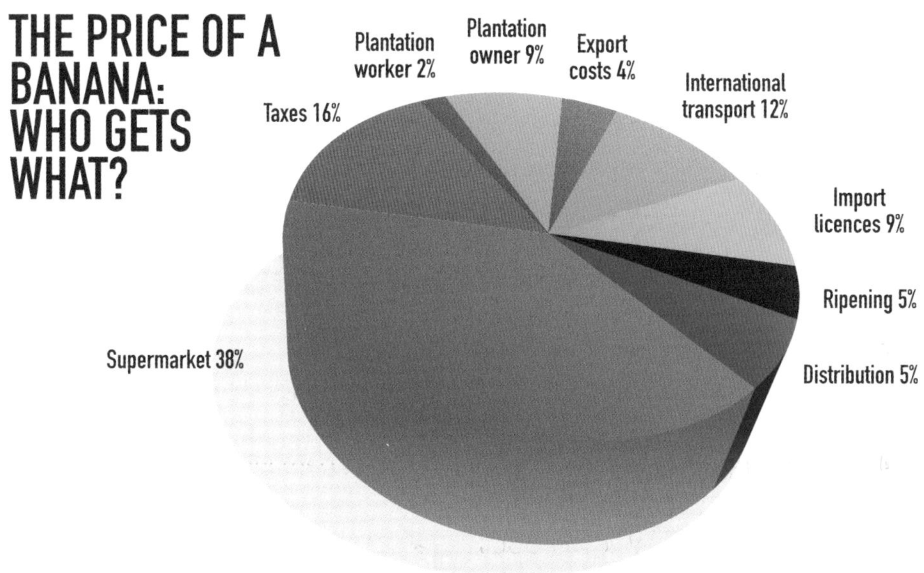

1 What does each section of the chart represent?

____

2 How many different activities does the chart present information about?

____

3 If the government reduced taxes on bananas to 10%, what would happen to the other percentages in the chart?

____

UNDERSTANDING DATA IN A PIE CHART

2 Look at the pie chart and answer the questions below.

1 What accounts for the biggest share of the price of bananas?

____

2 What accounts for the smallest share?

____

3 Which accounts for a greater share: *international transport* or *distribution*?

____

4 What share does *ripening* contribute to the price of bananas?

____

5 What total percentage do *import licences* contribute to the pie chart?

____

ANALYZING AND USING DATA IN A PIE CHART

ANALYZE

3 Does the pie chart support or contradict the following statements? Write support (S) or contradict (C).

1 The cost of transporting bananas from the plantation to the supermarket accounts for the largest share of their price. ______
2 The plantation owner does not receive a large share of the price of bananas. ______
3 Import licences contribute nearly the same amount to the price of bananas as international transport costs. ______
4 The ripening process accounts for a much bigger share of the price of bananas than the growing process. ______
5 Taxes contribute the smallest amount to the price of bananas. ______
6 Supermarket costs are usually more than half of the price of bananas. ______

4 Work with a partner and answer the questions below.

1 Why might supermarket costs contribute so much to the price of bananas?

____

2 Why might the cost of growing bananas contribute so little?

____

3 Why might plantation owners receive much more than workers?

____

4 If governments reduced the cost of import licences, what effect would it probably have on the supermarket section in the pie chart? Why?

____

5 If plantation workers received twice as much money per banana, what effect would it probably have on the overall price of bananas? Why?

____

SPEAKING

PREPARATION FOR SPEAKING

Presenting data

Charts present data in a way that makes it easy to understand. When giving a presentation, you can use charts to explain information that supports your point of view. You can make best use of the information by drawing general and specific conclusions from it, using figures such as fractions or percentages to describe it, and listing points and conclusions you make using sequential language.

1 Complete the introduction to the presentation below using the words and phrases from the box.

would like to show | a lot of discussion | look at | many people believe | they say | others have pointed out | consider | I'd like to talk about

(1)________________ where your money goes when you buy a cup of coffee. There has been (2)________________ in the media recently about fair prices for the people in countries who grow crops like coffee. (3)________________ that it's not right that a cup of coffee can cost £3 or more, of which the farmers only get a few pennies. However, (4)________________ that the coffee beans are only one part of the cost of supplying a cup of coffee. (5)________________ that the other ingredients, such as milk and sugar, are also a big part of the cost of a cup of coffee. However, I (6)________________ that in a typical coffee house, the ingredients are only a small part of the overall cost. Let's (7)________________ some data. If you (8)________________ the information on this chart …

2 1.5 Listen and check your answers to Exercise 1.

DESCRIBING A PIE CHART

3 Look at the pie chart for the price of a cup of coffee in the UK below and complete the sentences with the words from the box.

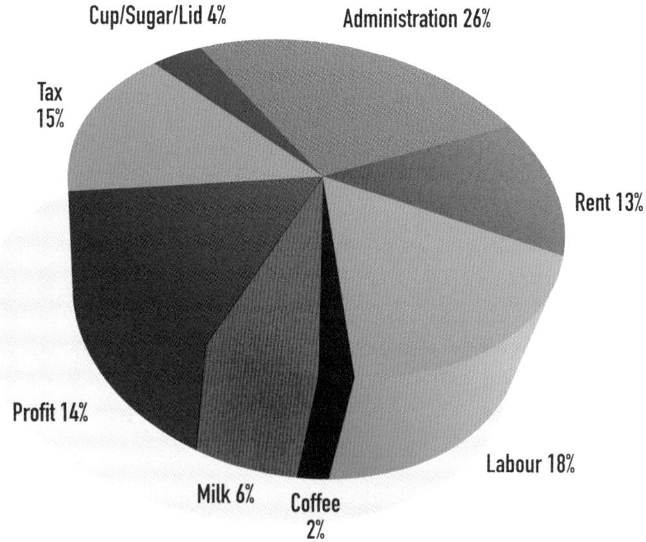

The largest part	accounts for	Three parts are related to
each make up	a total of	more than a quarter of
they make up		

1 ______________ of the cost is administration, at 26%. That's ______________ the cost per cup.
2 Labour ______________ 18% of the cost.
3 Tax, profit, and rent ______________ about 14% of the cost, or ______________ 42% of the price of your cup of coffee.
4 ______________ the product you take away – milk at 6%, the cup, sugar and lid at 4% and the coffee itself at 2%. Together, ______________ 12% of the price you pay.

DRAWING CONCLUSIONS FROM DATA

4 1.6 Listen to the next part of the presentation and number the expressions (a–g) in the order you hear them.

a As you can see ... ____
b This pie chart shows ... ____
c You'll notice that ... ____
d Finally, I'd like to draw your attention to ... ____
e Next ... ____
f Firstly ... ____
g Secondly ... ____

5 Match the sentence halves.

1 You can see that in a typical cup of coffee,
2 This data shows that the raw ingredients only
3 This means that it may be possible
4 Looking at the chart, we can conclude
5 In summary, the data shows that the two biggest

a account for 12% of the price you pay. ____
b parts of the cost of a cup of coffee are administration and labour. ____
c that we could pay coffee farmers a lot more for coffee beans, and coffee drinkers wouldn't notice the difference. ____
d to increase the price we pay for raw materials without significantly raising the cost of a cup of coffee. ____
e the milk can cost three times as much as the coffee itself. ____

SPEAKING TASK

Give a presentation on the following: How can we ensure that workers in developing countries are paid fairly for the food we import?

PREPARE

1 Work with a partner and choose one of the statements below. You are going to give a presentation agreeing or disagreeing with it.

1 Food producers and exporters should be responsible for helping workers in developing countries get a fair deal.
2 Governments in importing countries should take the lead in sharing their income from the food trade with workers in developing countries.
3 Consumers should put pressure on supermarkets and distributors to do more for workers in developing countries.

2 Look at the pie chart from the Critical thinking section on page 25 and the statement you have chosen for your presentation. Answer the questions below.

1 Which segments of the chart relate to your statement?
2 What data evidence is there in the pie chart that supports your view?
3 What data evidence in the pie chart contradicts your view?

PRACTISE

3 Using the information in the chart, organize your points in the order you want to speak about them. Remember to put the most important points first and support your points with data. Remember to use language from the Preparation for speaking section in your points.

4 Write notes and a conclusion to help you organize your presentation.

5 Practise the presentation with your partner. Remember to use language from the Preparation for speaking section to organize your talk and present data.

6 Work with a new partner. Take turns to give your presentation.

TASK CHECKLIST	✔
Did you set the context in the introduction?	
Did you describe the pie chart?	
Did you support your view with data?	
Did you draw a conclusion supported by the pie chart?	

OBJECTIVES REVIEW

I can ...

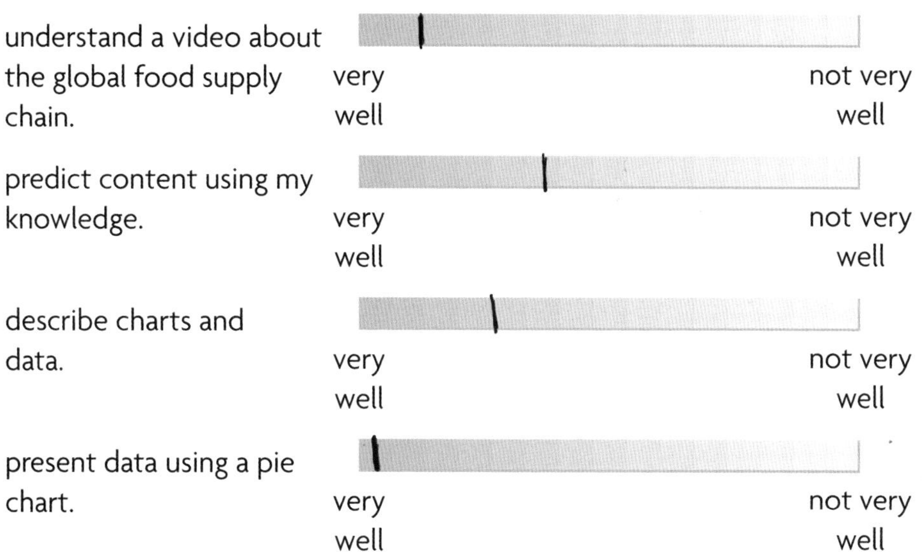
understand a video about the global food supply chain.
very well
not very well
predict content using my knowledge.
very well
not very well
describe charts and data.
very well
not very well
present data using a pie chart.
very well
not very well

WORDLIST

UNIT VOCABULARY	ACADEMIC VOCABULARY
carbon dioxide emissions (n)	agricultural (adv)
carbon footprint (n)	agriculture (n)
climate change (n)	consumer (n)
crop (n)	environment (n)
imported (adj)	export (v)
provider (n)	processing (n)
rice paddy (n)	produce (n)
supply chain (n)	produce (v)
	purchase (v)
	transportation (n)

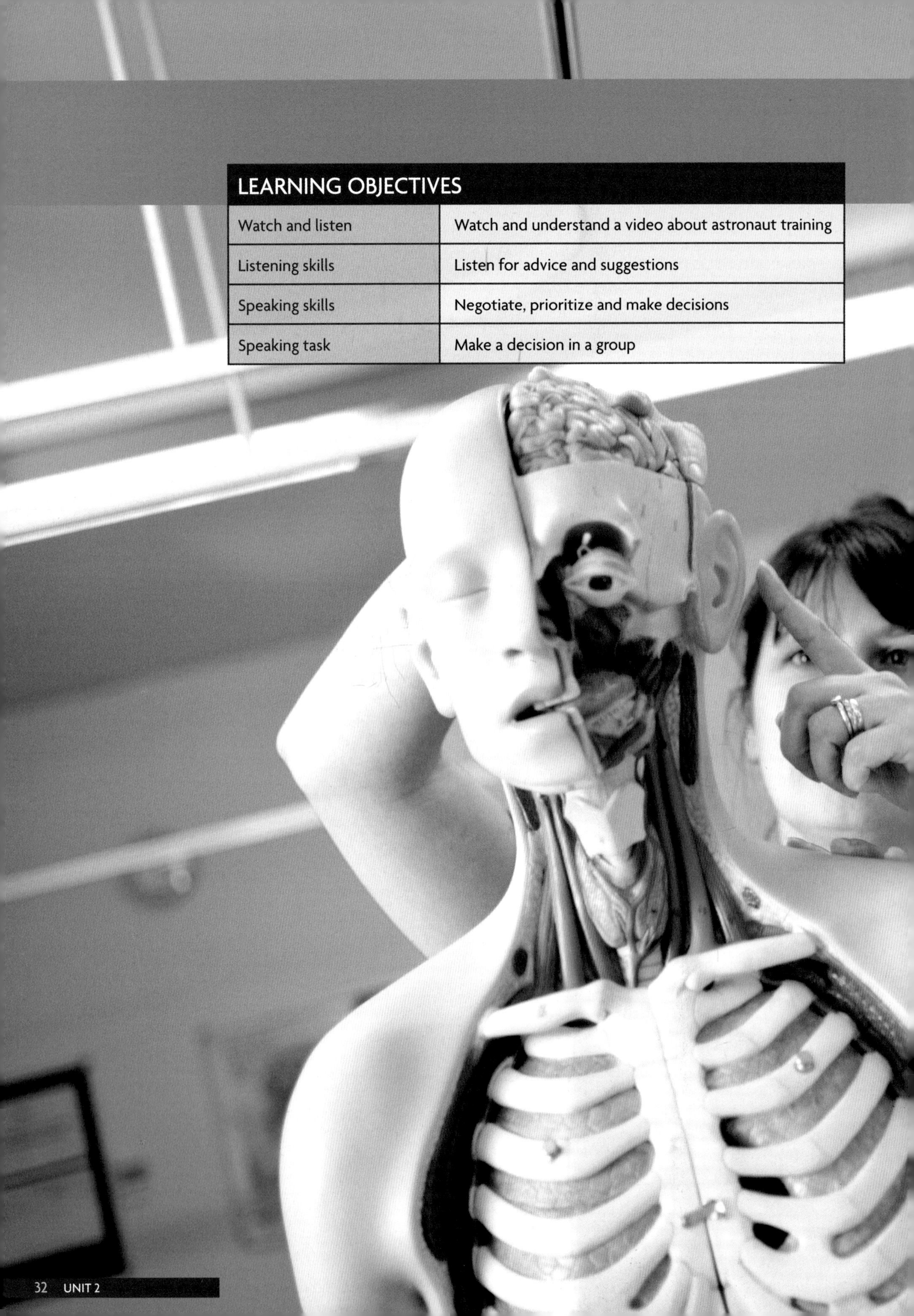

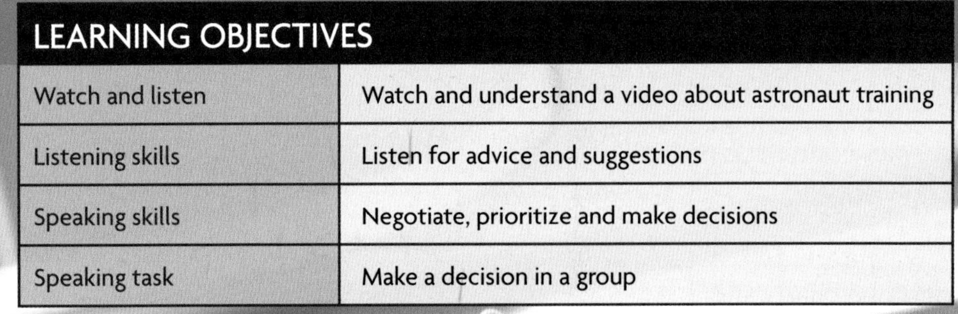

LEARNING OBJECTIVES	
Watch and listen	Watch and understand a video about astronaut training
Listening skills	Listen for advice and suggestions
Speaking skills	Negotiate, prioritize and make decisions
Speaking task	Make a decision in a group

EDUCATION UNIT 2

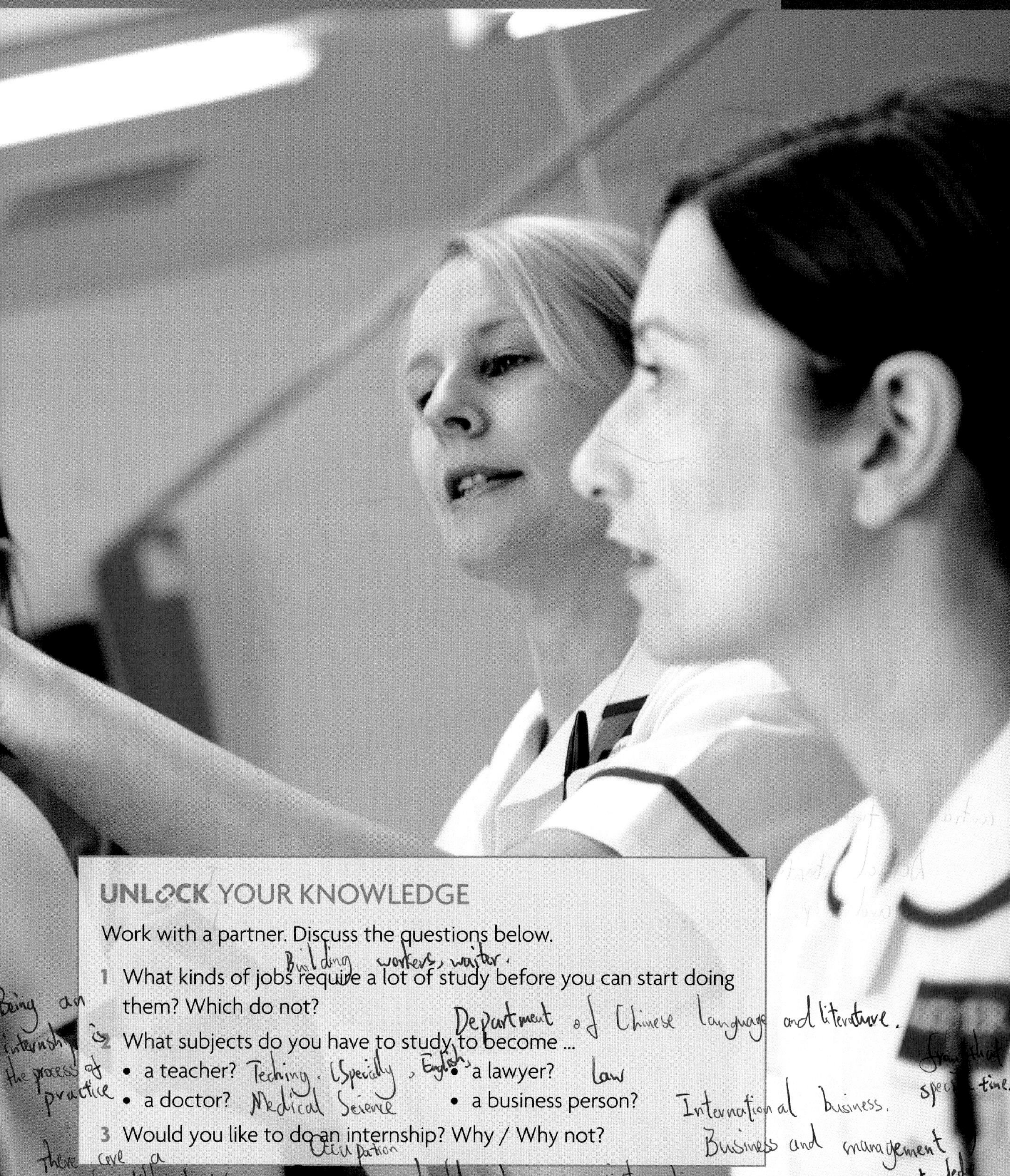

UNLOCK YOUR KNOWLEDGE

Work with a partner. Discuss the questions below.

1 What kinds of jobs require a lot of study before you can start doing them? Which do not?

2 What subjects do you have to study to become ...
- a teacher?
- a doctor?
- a lawyer?
- a business person?

3 Would you like to do an internship? Why / Why not?

WATCH AND LISTEN

PREPARING TO WATCH

UNDERSTANDING KEY VOCABULARY

1 You are going to watch a video about astronaut training. Before you watch, match the words below (1–8) to the definitions (a–h).

1 practical
2 theoretical
3 weightless
4 space station
5 arc
6 mission
7 partner
8 exhausted

a a vehicle in which people can travel in space, doing scientific tests
b very tired
c the shape of part of a circle
d based on ideas, rather than real experience
e an important job that someone is sent to do
f a person who does a job with someone else
g related to real experiences, rather than ideas
h having or appearing to have no weight

2 Look at the skills needed to become an astronaut. Write practical (P) or theoretical (T) next to the skills.

1 repairing broken machinery ____ ☐
2 using maths and physics to understand space travel ____ ☐
3 working while being weightless ____ ☐
4 being physically strong ____ ☐
5 understanding how electronic equipment works ____ ☐
6 be able to read and understand maps ____ ☐
7 be able to speak English well ____ ☐
8 understand the principles of engineering ____ ☐

WHILE WATCHING

UNDERSTANDING MAIN IDEAS

3 Watch the video. Tick the skills in Exercise 2 that are mentioned in the video.

UNDERSTANDING DETAIL

4 Watch again. Answer the questions below.

1 How long has Clay been training to work as an astronaut?
______
2 How long do the trainees experience weightlessness in the plane?
______
3 What are the dimensions of the pool? Length: ______ m.
Width: ______ m. Depth: ______ m.
4 How much water does the pool hold? ______
5 How many employees work at the pool? ______
6 How many hours does Clay train for each hour he will work in space?
______
7 How long has Clay spent in the training pool? ______
8 How long will Clay stay on the International Space Station?
______

DISCUSSION

5 Work with a partner. Discuss the questions.

1 Which parts of an astronaut's job do you think are the most difficult?
2 What subjects do you think astronauts need to be good at?
3 What other jobs do you think require a combination of strong theoretical knowledge and practical ability?
4 Which aspects of your studies or job are practical? Which are theoretical? Why?

LISTENING 1

PREPARING TO LISTEN

UNDERSTANDING KEY VOCABULARY

1 You are going to listen to a meeting between a student and a careers adviser. Before you listen, complete the definitions with the words from the box.

mechanical specialist acquire understanding academic vocational apprentice careers adviser

1 someone with a lot of skill or experience in a subject __________
2 related to a particular type of work __________
3 someone who works for a skilled person for a period of time, often for low pay, in order to gain work experience __________
4 to get or receive something __________
5 knowledge about a subject __________
6 related to subjects that require thinking and studying rather than being practical __________
7 related to machines __________
8 someone who gives information and advice about education and work opportunities __________

2 Complete the sentences with the words from Exercise 1.

1 The __________________ at my university recommended that I consider training to become a nurse.
2 I had a __________________ problem with my car, so I took it to the garage to be repaired.
3 I don't get paid much as an __________________ , but I'm learning valuable skills from my boss.
4 At university, you __________________ the knowledge you need to start a career.
5 Scientists are always increasing our __________________ of the natural world.
6 After high school, I took a course at a __________________ college and learnt to be a plumber.
7 I'm not that interested in studying in an __________________ environment like a university. I'd like to start work straight away.
8 I'd love to study engineering and become an aeronautical ______________ .

3 Work with a partner. Describe your studies and career using the words from Exercise 1.

WHILE LISTENING

LISTENING FOR MAIN IDEAS

4 2.1 Listen to the meeting. Answer the questions.

1 What is Bahar trying to make a decision about?

____

2 What field is she interested in working in?

____

3 What do Bahar and the careers adviser decide to do?

____

Listening for advice and suggestions

In situations like a careers advice meeting, advice and suggestions are key points to listen out for. Advice and suggestions are indicated with language such as *You should consider ... I think ...* and *Wouldn't you like / rather... ?*

LISTENING FOR DETAIL

5 2.1 Listen to the meeting again. What advice does the careers adviser give? Write true (T) or false (F) next to the statements below.

1 Choose a career that will use your maths and physics skills. ______
2 Consider a vocational course rather than university. ______
3 Think about a course in mechanical engineering. ______
4 Seriously consider becoming an industrial designer. ______
5 Specialize in electrical or architectural engineering and then consider astronaut training. ______
6 Visit some universities and find out more about engineering courses. ______
7 Borrow some engineering books from the library. ______
8 Visit an engineer at work and ask them what their job is like. ______

PRONUNCIATION FOR LISTENING

Certain and uncertain intonation

We can sometimes understand a speaker's attitude by listening to their intonation. A rising intonation can indicate uncertainty and a falling intonation can indicate certainty about what they are saying.

6 2.2 Listen and write certain (C) or uncertain (U) next to the statements below.

1 You're considering university, aren't you? U
2 I like Maths and Physics, and I'm doing well in those classes. C
3 You should make use of your Maths and Physics abilities. ______
4 I'm considering studying Engineering. ______
5 I've always been interested in the way things work. ______
6 I think I could do that. ______
7 I wouldn't mind the theoretical side of Engineering. ______
8 ... but I think I'd really enjoy the practical side of Engineering. ______

POST-LISTENING

7 The careers adviser and Bahar both use expressions that show they are certain or uncertain about what they are saying. Read the statements and write the word in bold in the correct category.

1 It would **definitely** be a way to use your talents.
2 So I'd like to study something technical, that's for **sure**.
3 I **wonder** if I should try something more vocational.
4 You're **considering** university, aren't you?
5 I'm **not sure** if Engineering is for me.

certain	uncertain

DISCUSSION

8 Work with a partner. Discuss the questions.

1 Do you think the adviser gave Bahar useful advice? Why / Why not?
2 Do many people go to university in your country? Why / Why not?
3 What sorts of job are popular with recent graduates in your country?
4 In your country, what jobs do people do if they don't go to university?

LANGUAGE DEVELOPMENT

STATING PREFERENCES

EXPLANATION

Stating preferences with *would*

We can use *would rather* to express or ask questions about preferences.

I'd rather take a vocational course.
Would you **rather** start straight after graduation?

We can also use *would* with verbs of preference, such as *like* or *prefer*.

I'd like to start working as soon as possible.
I'd prefer it if you studied a bit longer.
Would you **prefer** a short course to an academic degree?

1 Match the sentence halves.

1 Would you rather do
2 She'd rather do
3 Wouldn't you like to
4 I'd rather you tried visiting
5 He'd prefer not to go
6 Would you rather study

a mechanical engineering?
b a manual job.
c to university.
d an engineering company.
e a practical course?
f be a doctor?

2 Rewrite each sentence, using *would* + *rather* or a verb of preference.

1 Do you want to earn a lot of money?

____

2 I want to study a diploma course.

____

3 Do they want to apply for university in Riyadh?

____

4 He wants to consider studying medicine.

____

5 Does she want to do a theoretical course?

____

6 I don't want to start working right away.

____

ACADEMIC ADJECTIVES TO DESCRIBE PROFESSIONS

3 Match the words to the correct definitions.

1 manual	**a** involving a lot of different but related parts
2 medical	**b** connected with a job that needs special education or training
3 complex	**c** concerned with medicine and the treatment of disease
4 nuclear	**d** connected with practical knowledge, skills or methods
5 physical	**e** dependable, not likely to change
6 professional	**f** related to someone's body rather then their mind
7 secure	**g** using or connected with nuclear energy
8 technical	**h** involving the use of the hands

4 Complete the text below with the words from Exercise 3.

When I was younger, I wanted to be a doctor, but I don't think a (1) ________________ job is for me. I'm considering joining the army, because a military job would give me training in a (2) ________________ field such as telecommunications or information technology. I would also have to do a lot of (3) ________________ training. The exercise would help me keep fit. I enjoy (4) ________________ work occasionally, like repairing electronics or other jobs around the house, but I'd like to have a (5) ________________ career, doing something challenging and (6) ________________ that I'm trained to do. I also want to have a (7) ________________ job, so I'm not worried from one month to the next about having to find a new one. I'm very interested in physics, so if I don't join the army, I might consider studying (8) ________________ engineering. My country is planning to build several new power plants in the next few years and they'll need engineers.

LISTENING 2

PREPARING TO LISTEN

UNDERSTANDING KEY VOCABULARY

1 You are going to listen to a conversation between Adam, a student who is interested in a career in medicine, and a careers adviser. Before you listen, read his notes and discuss the questions in pairs.

Medical jobs

Emergency Medical Technician (EMT)
Works independently on an ambulance. Helps people in emergency situations, assessing a patient's condition and performing emergency medical procedures before they get to hospital. Must be self-confident. Requires excellent driving skills.

Emergency Room Nurse
Works in the emergency room of a hospital, dealing with patients as they arrive. Must have a high-level understanding of the human body and medicines and be able to assess patients quickly and correctly.

Which job do you think …

- requires closer work with hospital staff?
- requires making decisions on your own?
- requires you to be sure in yourself and your abilities?
- requires more training?
- provides more excitement and adventure?
- requires more academic study?

WHILE LISTENING

LISTENING FOR GIST

2 2.3 Listen to the conversation. What are Adam's answers to Exercise 1? Are they the same as yours?

LISTENING FOR OPINION

3 2.3 Listen to the conversation again and tick the statements in the table. Listen for the idea rather than the exact words.

	speaker		course/job	
	adviser	Adam	EMT	ERN
1 That is a tough job. Exciting, but tough.	✓		✓	
2 It seems like a great way to help people.				
3 You have to be very independent and self-confident.				
4 It would involve a lot more complex study.				
5 It would be great to actually work after so much study.				
6 It may not be the ideal course.				
7 I imagine the pay would be better.				
8 That would be a great idea.				

POST-LISTENING

Making inferences

When listening, you can find answers from clues rather than directly from what is being said. This can be tone, facial expressions and emotion in someone's voice.

4 Work with a partner. Discuss the questions below. Think about tone, expressions and emotion.

1 What does the adviser really think that Adam should do?
2 What are the most important factors in a job for Adam?
3 What information gave you the answers to questions 1 and 2?

DISCUSSION

5 Work with a partner. Discuss the questions.

1 What areas of study do you think you have the most natural ability in?
2 Can you think of an area you might like to become a specialist in?
3 Which seems more interesting to you: a practical, vocational diploma or a more theoretical university degree? Why?

CRITICAL THINKING

At the end of this unit you are going to do the speaking task below.

Decide as a group which candidate should receive the Mah scholarship.

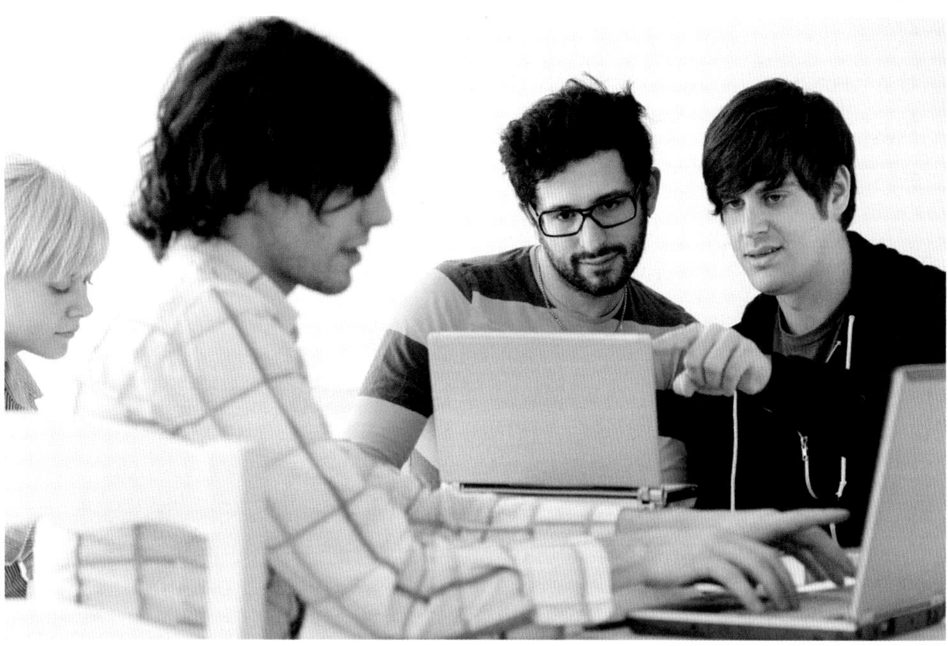

Prioritizing criteria

Making a choice from a number of options can be difficult. Sometimes understanding what is most and least important to us in a particular situation can help us make a better decision about what to do.

EVALUATE

1 Look at the list of job criteria. Number them 1–10 in terms of importance for you. (1 = most important, 10 = least important).

to make as much money as possible ______
to feel excited and challenged every day ______
to enjoy the social side of work and be friends with my colleagues ______
to work for a famous or important company ______
to travel for work ______
to speak more than one language in my role ______
to feel happy and secure ______
to work close to where I live now ______
to manage other people ______
to be creative in my work ______

2 Work with a partner. Compare your top five answers. Are they the same? Why did you put them in that order?

Using priorities to evaluate options

Groups of people (project teams, managers, or groups of students) often need to decide how to use money or other resources. This involves discussing priorities and evaluating different options.

3 Work with a partner. Read the text and prioritize the criteria for receiving the Mah Scholarship below from 1–5. (1 = the most important, 5 = the least important).

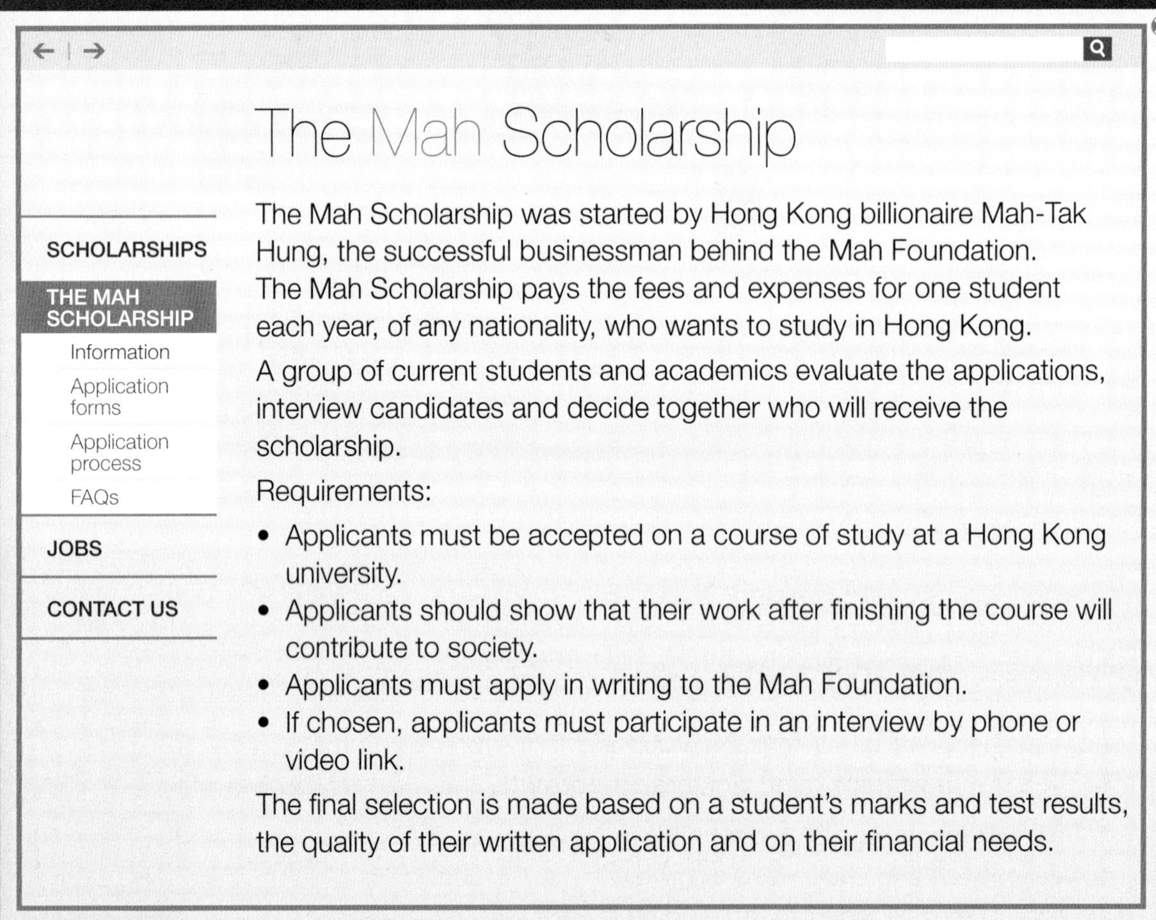

The Mah Scholarship

SCHOLARSHIPS
THE MAH SCHOLARSHIP
- Information
- Application forms
- Application process
- FAQs

JOBS
CONTACT US

The Mah Scholarship was started by Hong Kong billionaire Mah-Tak Hung, the successful businessman behind the Mah Foundation.

The Mah Scholarship pays the fees and expenses for one student each year, of any nationality, who wants to study in Hong Kong.

A group of current students and academics evaluate the applications, interview candidates and decide together who will receive the scholarship.

Requirements:

- Applicants must be accepted on a course of study at a Hong Kong university.
- Applicants should show that their work after finishing the course will contribute to society.
- Applicants must apply in writing to the Mah Foundation.
- If chosen, applicants must participate in an interview by phone or video link.

The final selection is made based on a student's marks and test results, the quality of their written application and on their financial needs.

Must be studying a course that contributes to society. _____
Must write a good written application. _____
Must have a good interview. _____
Must have good test scores. _____
Must be in financial need. _____

4 Compare your answers with another pair. Did you prioritize the same criteria as them? Why / Why not?

APPLY

5 Read the profiles of two students who have applied for the Mah Scholarship. Look at your prioritized criteria and answer the questions.

1 Which candidate has the best score for each of your criteria from Exercise 3?
2 Which candidate do you think should receive the scholarship? Why?

name	interview score	written application score	test score	financial need	proposed course of study
	All scores are out of 10 possible points				
Mark Walker	10	8	7	4	8 Teacher
Yasmin Saleh	8	9	9	1	10 Doctor

6 Work with another pair. Do you have the same answer for Exercise 5? Why / Why not?

SPEAKING

PREPARATION FOR SPEAKING

GIVING AN OPINION AND MAKING SUGGESTIONS

1 Match the sentence halves to make suggestions and opinions.

1 The most important
2 I think
3 Why don't we
4 What if we say that
5 Have you considered
6 I feel it's important

a rank the proposed courses of study according to their contribution to society?
b to really focus on the applicants' potential contribution to society.
c taking the applicants' family situations into account?
d the least important thing is the student's written application.
e factor is probably financial need.
f academic score is the most important factor?

2 2.4 Listen and check your answers.

Agreeing and disagreeing respectfully with a speaker

In a discussion where speakers have different opinions, it is important to use formal language to disagree respectfully with what someone has said, or even if you agree with another speaker's point. You can do this by using modal verbs before making a point, apologizing before disagreeing with someone's point, or saying you recognize someone's point and then following it with a *but* ... clause.

3 Write agree (A) or disagree (D) next to the statements below.

1 I can see what you're saying, but I have a different opinion. _____
2 I couldn't agree more. _____
3 I think that's right. _____
4 I'm not sure I share that viewpoint. _____
5 I'm sorry, but I have to disagree. _____
6 Yes, but have you considered the other factors involved? _____
7 I'm with you on that point. _____
8 That's a valid argument. _____

4 Work in pairs. Read your statements. Your partner should respond using language from Exercise 3 and their own ideas.

Student A

1 Chinese will be the most important world language in the future.
2 Engineering is one of the best subjects you can study at university.
3 Lawyers are some of the most important people in society.

Student B

4 Everyone should be given money to study at university.
5 Hotel management is an important university course.
6 It is more important to be able to speak English than to write it well.

COMPROMISING AND FINALIZING A DECISION

5 Complete the sentences with the words below.

agreement understandable point right that decision

1 I see. That's ____________________ .
2 OK, I see your ____________________ .
3 You might be ____________________ about that.
4 OK, I think we all can live with ____________________ .
5 Right. We've made a ____________________ .
6 I think we've come to an ____________________ .

6 2.5 Listen and check your answers.

PRONUNCIATION FOR SPEAKING

7 Listen again. Which of the sentences in Exercise 5 is said with certain intonation? Which is said with uncertain intonation?

8 Work in pairs. Take turns saying the sentences in Exercise 5 with either certain or uncertain intonation. Can your partner tell whether you're being certain or uncertain?

SPEAKING TASK

Decide as a group which candidate should receive the Mah scholarship.

The Mah Foundation committee has decided on five finalists for the scholarship. The table below summarizes their assessment of each applicant.

name	interview score	written application score	academic score	financial need	proposed course of study
	All scores are out of 10 possible points				
Lee Jin-Sil	9	7	4	6	______ Hotel management
Adam Al Zamil	6	9	7	3	______ EMT
Jack Evans	4	7	6	8	______ Chinese
Bahar Atil	6	5	9	4	______ Mechanical engineering
Thomas Nguyen	7	4	9	6	______ Law

PREPARE

1 Work in a group. Discuss the questions below.

1 Which course of study will make the greatest contribution to society? Which will make the smallest contribution? Why?
2 Give each course in the table on page 47 a mark out of 10 for contribution to society.

PRACTISE

2 Based on your discussion above and the Critical thinking section, decide who should receive the scholarship.

3 Looking at the criteria and the scores in the table on page 47, order the other four applicants. Use the language in the Preparation for speaking section to help you.

DISCUSS

4 Appoint one person from your group to present your first choice for the scholarship to the class. Did everyone pick the same candidate? What about the second and third placed candidates?

TASK CHECKLIST	✔
Did you give your opinion on criteria and priorities?	
Did you compromise?	
Did you agree?	
Did you respectfully disagree and make suggestions?	

OBJECTIVES REVIEW

I can …

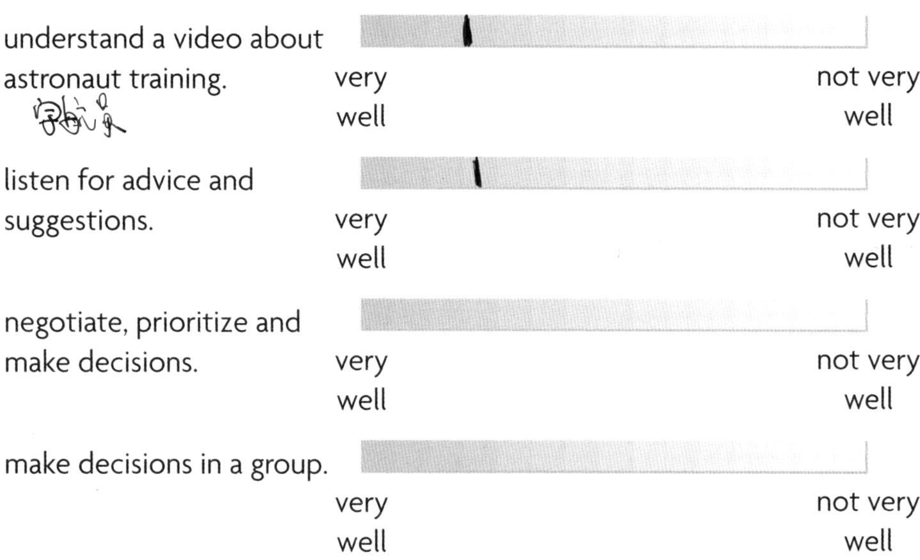

I can …		
understand a video about astronaut training.	very well	not very well
listen for advice and suggestions.	very well	not very well
negotiate, prioritize and make decisions.	very well	not very well
make decisions in a group.	very well	not very well

WORDLIST

UNIT VOCABULARY	ACADEMIC VOCABULARY
academic (adj)	acquire (v)
apprentice (n)	complex (adj)
arc (n)	manual (adj)
careers adviser (n)	nuclear (adj)
exhausted (adj)	partner (n)
mechanical (adj)	physical (adj)
mission (n)	practical (adj)
space station (n)	professional (adj)
specialist (n)	secure (adj)
theoretical (adj)	technical (adj)
understanding (n)	
vocational (adj)	
weightless (adj)	

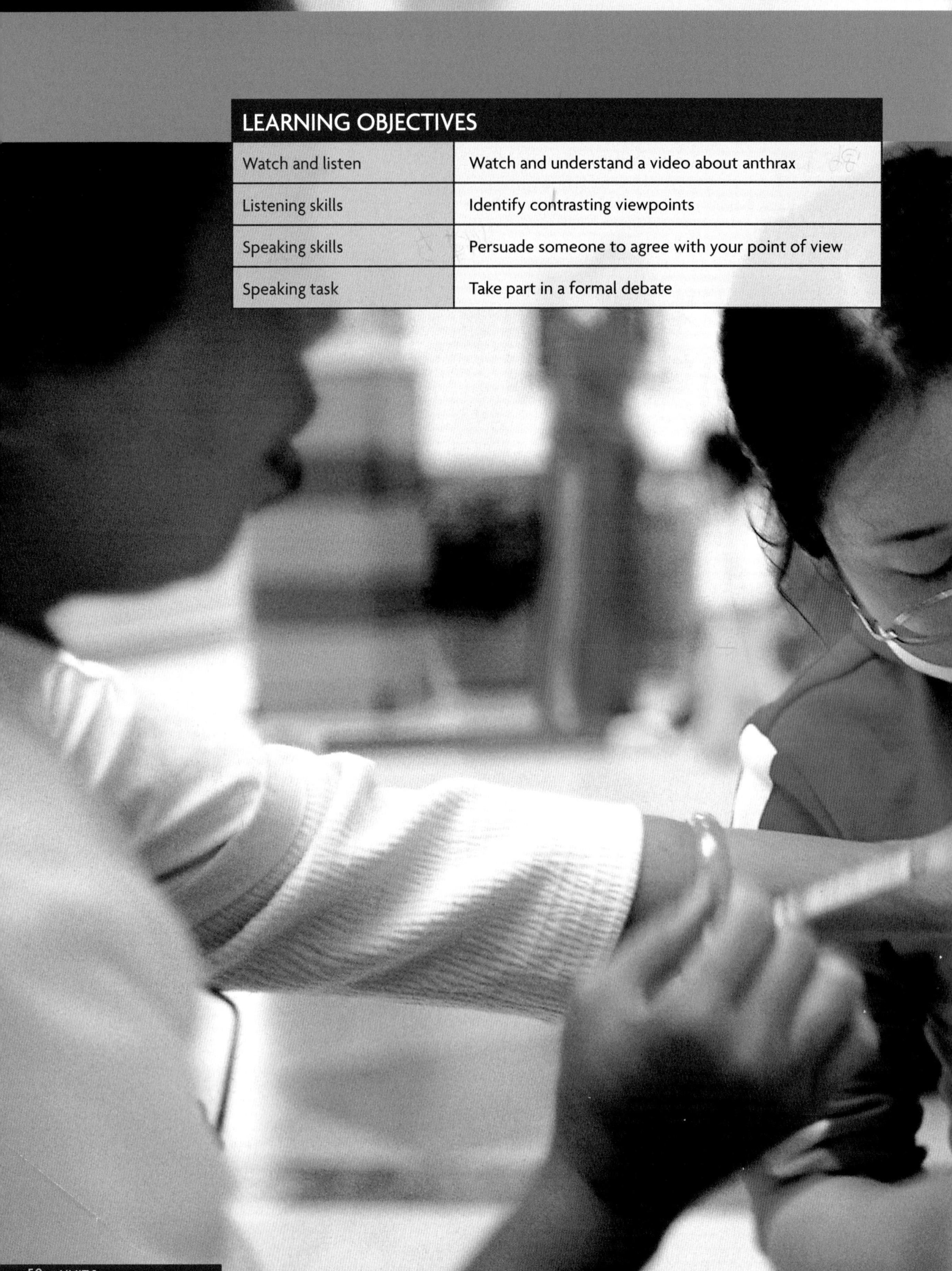

LEARNING OBJECTIVES

Watch and listen	Watch and understand a video about anthrax
Listening skills	Identify contrasting viewpoints
Speaking skills	Persuade someone to agree with your point of view
Speaking task	Take part in a formal debate

MEDICINE UNIT 3

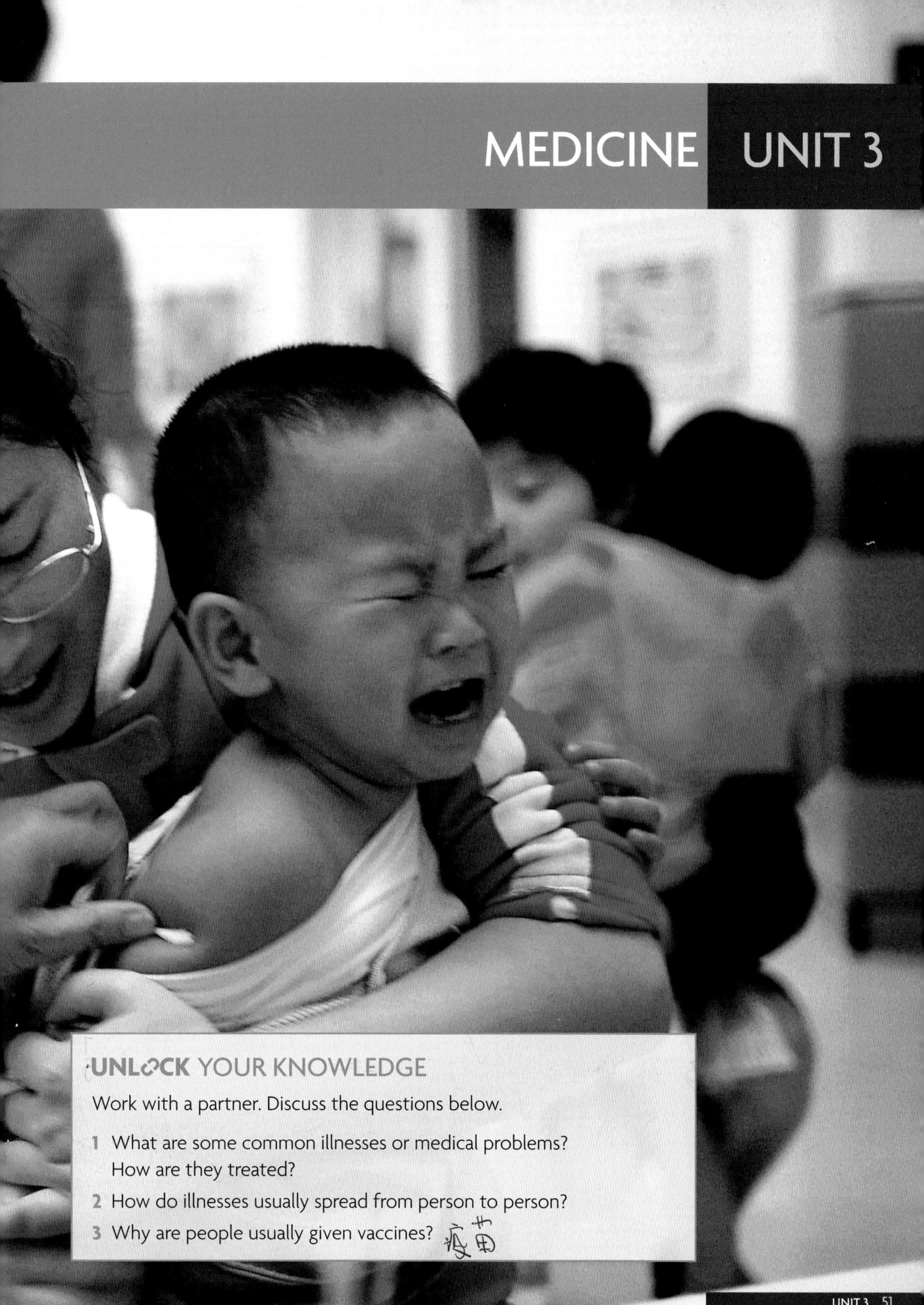

UNLOCK YOUR KNOWLEDGE

Work with a partner. Discuss the questions below.

1 What are some common illnesses or medical problems? How are they treated?
2 How do illnesses usually spread from person to person?
3 Why are people usually given vaccines? 

WATCH AND LISTEN

PREPARING TO WATCH

UNDERSTANDING KEY VOCABULARY

1 You are going to watch a video about anthrax. Before you watch, read the text. Match the words in bold (1–10) to the definitions (a–j) below.

> Anthrax is a very dangerous (1)**disease**, which (2)**occurs** naturally. Most people and animals that get it die within a few days. Fortunately, the disease doesn't spread very easily. You can only (3)**contract** it if tiny structures called (4)**spores** enter your body. They can be (5)**inhaled**, eaten, or enter the blood through a cut or other injury. An (6)**outbreak** of the disease can occur if a group of people or animals come into contact with anthrax spores. Doctors try to (7)**diagnose** people who have anthrax quickly. They usually give patients very strong (8)**antibiotics** to (9)**treat** the disease. Some patients make a full (10)**recovery**.

a cells that can carry illness ____
b an illness of people, animals or plants, caused by bad health ____
c drugs that destroy bacteria that cause illnesses ____
d the sudden appearance of an illness ____
e to use drugs and medical care to cure a person of an illness ____
f the process of becoming healthy again ____
g exists or is present in something ____
h to breathe something into your lungs ____
i to recognize illness or medical problem by examining it ____
j to catch an illness ____

USING YOUR KNOWLEDGE TO PREDICT CONTENT

2 Work with a partner and discuss the questions below.

1 What kind of diseases spread from person to person easily?
2 What can people do to stop the spread of diseases?
3 What can doctors do to stay safe when they treat patients who have a dangerous disease?

WHILE WATCHING

UNDERSTANDING MAIN IDEAS

3 Watch the video. Write true (T) or false (F) next to the statements below.

1 The doctors were very surprised when they discovered that Vado Diamande had anthrax. ____
2 Cases of anthrax are usually kept secret to avoid alarming the public. ____
3 Anthrax can be spread through human contact. ____
4 It's unlikely that anthrax would spread beyond a small area, such as a neighbourhood. ____
5 The experts had no idea where Vado had contracted anthrax. ____
6 Vado had caught the disease from animal skins that he used to make drums. ____

LISTENING FOR KEY INFORMATION

4 Watch again and complete the notes below.

1 Year Vado caught anthrax: ____
2 Vado's jobs: ____
3 People notified when Vado's anthrax was discovered: ____
4 Where anthrax is found naturally: ____
5 How anthrax is contracted: ____
6 Number of people anthrax could kill in a few days: ____
7 How anthrax is treated: ____
8 Source of Vado's anthrax: ____

DISCUSSION

5 Work with a partner. Discuss the questions.

1 What do you think governments could do to try to stop anthrax from entering a country?
2 If you heard that there was a case of anthrax where you lived, what would you do?

LISTENING 1

PREPARING TO LISTEN

USING YOUR KNOWLEDGE

1 You are going to listen to a student seminar about pandemics. Before you listen, read the text and look at the map. Then answer the questions below.

A pandemic is when a contagious disease spreads through the human population in a large region. This could be across multiple countries, or even the whole world. Throughout history there have been a number of pandemics of illnesses, such as flu and cholera. A disease must be infectious (passed directly from person to person) for it to be considered a pandemic.

Risk of pandemics across the globe

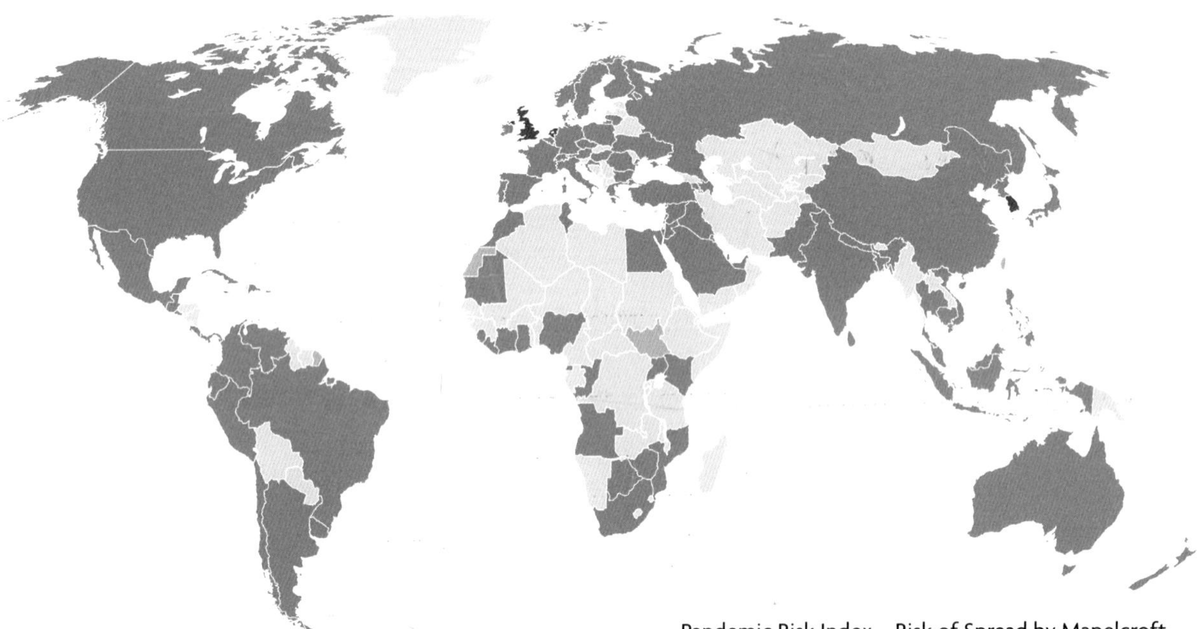

Pandemic Risk Index – Risk of Spread by Mapelcroft

1 How can a disease spread around the world? How can it be prevented from spreading?
2 What would make a country at high risk of a pandemic? Think about:
   - size of population
   - density of population
   - size of cities
   - number of international airports
   - borders with other countries
   - number of hospitals

2 Look at the map. Which colour do you think represents countries at high risk from pandemics? Which represents low-risk countries? What is the risk level in your country?

WHILE LISTENING

LISTENING FOR GIST

3 3.1 Listen to the seminar and check your answers to Exercise 1.

UNLOCK ONLINE

Identifying viewpoints

In a discussion, a group considers and explores different ideas. Key phrases such as *In my opinion* ... and *As far as I'm concerned* ... indicate viewpoints and can help you separate facts from what somebody thinks.

LISTENING FOR MAIN IDEAS

4 3.1 Listen to the seminar again. Complete the chart with the different viewpoints. T - T

idea for stopping the spread of disease	viewpoint 1	viewpoint 2
Governments must make sure populations are in good health and live in good conditions.	There's a limit to what governments can do in times of economic difficulty.	Governments don't always have the power to say exactly how everyone should live.
Everyone should be forced to have vaccines.	(1) ~~kind of medicine.~~ Encourage people to do.	(2) disease ~~vaccines~~ is change every year. Some people don't want
People with diseases shouldn't be allowed into the country.	(3) not sure I agree. They travel when they even know they have diseases.	(4) Travel for business. Borders. checking system.
All flights from countries with a pandemic should be stopped.	(5) have a flu should stay at home.	(6)

5 Compare your answers with a partner.

International travel. System for checking

POST-LISTENING

LISTENING FOR OPINION

6 Read the phrases with question tags from the listening. Work with a partner. Discuss what each phrase means.

1 A lot of people don't want to have a vaccine that might not work. They can't force people to take it, can they?
2 During a pandemic, we should stop all flights from countries that are affected, shouldn't we?
3 People travel all the time for business. It would have a terrible effect on the economy, wouldn't it?

PRONUNCIATION FOR LISTENING

Intonation in question tags

When a speaker uses a question tag with rising intonation it is usually a request for confirmation of their viewpoint from the listener. A question tag with falling intonation is usually a statement, and the speaker doesn't need or want the listener to agree with them. Listening for these differences in pronunciation can help you understand a speaker's meaning.

LISTENING FOR ATTITUDE

7 3.2 Listen to the sentences. Write question (Q) or statement (S) next to the sentences below. The first two have been done for you.

1 So this is a very serious disease, isn't it? Q
2 So this is a very serious disease, isn't it? S
3 It's a kind of medicine, isn't it? ____
4 Governments need to implement vaccination programmes for common diseases, don't they? ____
5 They can't force people to take a vaccine, can they? ____
6 People don't want to catch a disease, do they? ____
7 During a pandemic, we should stop all flights from countries that are affected, shouldn't we? ____
8 People who have flu should stay at home from school or from work, shouldn't they? ____

8 Work with a partner. Practise reading the sentences. Use rising or falling intonation. Can your partner tell whether you're asking a question or making a statement?

DISCUSSION

9 Work with a partner. Discuss the questions.

1 Do you think your country is prepared to deal with a pandemic? Why / Why not?
2 What measures do you think your government would take to stop a pandemic occurring?
3 What could you do in a pandemic to protect yourself from contracting a disease?

LANGUAGE DEVELOPMENT

CONNECTING ACTIONS

EXPLANATION

Connecting actions with time expressions

Time expressions, such as *before, after, until, between* and *throughout* show us the relationship between actions or events.

Before an an event

before is used to mean *at an earlier time*

At the start of an event

as from/of, from and *since* are used to show when something started

Since the vaccination was released, the number of sick people has decreased.

During an event

between, during, while and *through(out),* are used to talk about the duration of an event

During a pandemic, we should stop all flights from countries that are affected.

At the end of an event

until/till and *up to* are used to indicate the point when something stopped

Until a cure has been found, the young and elderly are still at risk.

After an event

after can be used to mean *later than*

1 Read the sentences. Underline the event that happened first in each statement. Underline the whole sentence if the two events happened at the same time.

1 During the pandemic, many people died because they didn't receive a vaccine.
2 Flu vaccines have improved a lot since their invention in 1914.
3 Before we make a vaccine, we have to try to guess how the flu is going to change.
4 After the 1918 pandemic, doctors got to work trying to develop a flu vaccine.
5 They need to be able to get a vaccine to everyone from the moment an outbreak occurs.
6 Throughout a pandemic, people should be reminded to take precautions.
7 International travel should be stopped until the pandemic has been contained.
8 People should be banned from visiting hospitals while there is a pandemic.

2 Complete the sentences below with a time expression. In some sentences, more than one option is possible.

1 ______ we started to vaccinate people, the number of cases have dropped.
2 We need to remind people to take precautions ______ the pandemic.
3 ______ now and when the vaccine is ready, there is a big risk of a pandemic.
4 We need to remind people to take care ______ they receive a vaccine.
5 ______ the pandemic is over, people still need to take care.
6 Scientists will continue to research the flu ______ they find a cure.
7 The flu season may last from now ______ next spring.
8 ______ next week, the vaccine will be available.

SCIENTIFIC RESEARCH VOCABULARY

3 Match the words below (1–8) to the definitions (a–h). Use the glossary on page 195 to help you.

1 researcher	a related to medical treatment and tests
2 controlled	b limited
3 scientific	c an action that is taken to stop something negative from happening
4 proven	d a test to find out how effective or safe something is
5 trial	e a person who studies a subject in detail to discover new information about it
6 clinical	f information or facts about something
7 data	g shown to be true
8 precaution	h related to science

4 Complete the text below with the correct form of the words from Exercise 3.

> Before a new vaccine can be released it must be (1) ______ to be safe for public use. First, (2) ______ (3) ______ conduct tests of the vaccine under carefully (4) ______ conditions in a laboratory environment. A lot of (5) ______ are taken to make sure the (6) ______ the scientists are collecting is accurate, so the vaccines are as safe as possible. Finally, (7) ______ (8) ______ are conducted with volunteers to test the vaccine before it is released for public use.

LISTENING 2

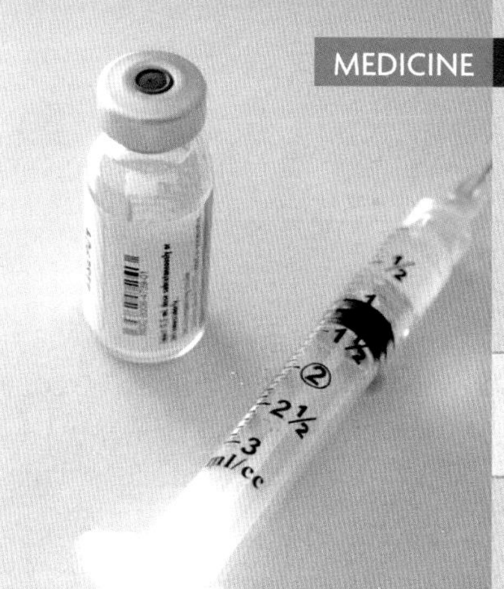

PREPARING TO LISTEN

USING YOUR KNOWLEDGE

1 You are going to listen to a formal debate about the flu vaccination. Before you listen, work with a partner and choose the answers that you think are correct.

1 Experts *agree* / *don't agree* about whether flu vaccinations are necessary.
2 Experts *believe* / *have proven* that the flu vaccination saves lives.
3 Experts *have* / *haven't* shown that the flu vaccination is unsafe.
4 *Some* / *Almost all* of the public want to get a flu vaccination.

2 3.3 Listen to a news report and check your answers.

WHILE LISTENING

LISTENING FOR GIST

3 3.4 Listen to the debate. Write Mark Li (M) or Sandra Smith (S) next to the opinions below.

1 Overall, flu vaccination is a good idea. ____
2 All medicines should be scientifically proven to be effective. ____
3 The flu vaccine isn't scientifically tested. ____
4 The flu vaccine can make you ill. ____
5 Certain people should definitely take the flu vaccine. ____

LISTENING FOR DETAIL

4 3.4 Listen to the debate again. Write true (T) or false (F) next to the statements below.

1 Millions of people get severely ill from the flu every year. ____
2 The majority of the population receive the flu vaccine. ____
3 Dr Smith has had the flu vaccine. ____
4 Mark Li is against all forms of vaccination. ____
5 There is scientific evidence that the flu vaccine might not work. ____
6 There is scientific evidence that the flu vaccine makes people ill. ____

POST-LISTENING

Strengthening your point in an argument

When you want to agree or disagree with someone and show that you are right in an argument, you can strengthen or support your point through techniques, such as offering a personal example or adding extra information.

5 Match the attempt to strengthen a point (1–6) to the correct explanation (a–f) below.

1 All of my colleagues have had the vaccination and none of us have got flu.
2 Dr Smith is absolutely right that many vaccines work very well and that millions of lives have been saved by vaccination.
3 I'd definitely like to challenge the idea that there's no scientific basis for our work. I disagree with Mr Li on that point. Let me tell you more about my work in that area.
4 If someone is vaccinated, and then they happen to become ill, that doesn't logically mean the vaccination caused the illness.
5 Well, I'm sure Dr Smith is a very good doctor, but I think the flu vaccination package I mentioned earlier is clear.

a disagreeing by offering additional information 3
b disagreeing by returning to an earlier reference 5
c agreeing by repeating the other person's point and saying it is correct 2
d disagreeing by giving a personal example 1
e disagreeing using logic 4

DISCUSSION

6 Work with a partner. Discuss the questions.

1 Are vaccinations routinely given in your country? Why / Why not?
2 When are they given? Who receives them?
3 Based on the debate, do you think you would have the flu vaccination or not?

CRITICAL THINKING

At the end of this unit you are going to do the speaking task below.

Debate whether healthcare should be free for everyone.

Understanding background and motivation

We can understand more about a speaker's point of view if we know something about their background, personal and professional motivations, role in society and other information about them.

ANALYZE

1 Work with a partner. Read the information about Dr Sandra Smith and Mark Li and discuss the questions.

Dr Sandra Smith is a medical doctor who researches the flu virus at a national university. Some of her research has been paid for by drug companies that manufacture flu vaccinations.

Mark Li is an alternative medicine practitioner of Chinese medicine. He's part of an organization that campaigns against drug companies that make flu vaccinations. They believe that the companies create the vaccinations to make money and that people don't need them.

1 How much money do you think each person earns?
2 What do you think their professional life is like?
3 What do you think they do in their free time?
4 What other beliefs do you think they have?

2 Compare your answers with another pair. Did you have the same ideas? Why / Why not?

3 Read the statements. Who probably said each one? Write Mark Li (M) or Sandra Smith (S).

1 People who eat the right foods don't need doctors or medicine. ______
2 Modern medicine is one of the greatest achievements of science. ______
3 One day, we'll have a vaccine for the common cold. ______
4 Illness is the body's way of telling you to change your lifestyle. ______
5 Drug companies make too much money from flu vaccines. ______
6 Not giving medication would be against everything I believe. ______

4 Compare your answers with a partner.

APPLY

5 Work with a partner. Discuss what Mark Li and Sandra Smith might think of the topics below. Would they have the same opinions on any of the topics? Why / Why not?

1 alternative medicine
2 treating diseases with food rather than medicine
3 drug companies advertising their products on television
4 doing exercise to promote health
5 giving a child medicine to reduce a fever or other symptoms of illness
6 free healthcare for everyone

SPEAKING

PREPARATION FOR SPEAKING

Using persuasive language

When we want to make listeners understand and agree with our point of view, we use persuasive language. This calls attention to our main opinions and invites listeners to think about and agree with our point of view. It also makes it more difficult for speakers to disagree with us.

1 Match the headings (1–5) to the examples (a–e).

1 give a personal example
2 ask challenging questions
3 use specific persuasive language
4 give information to support your position
5 address the other person's argument

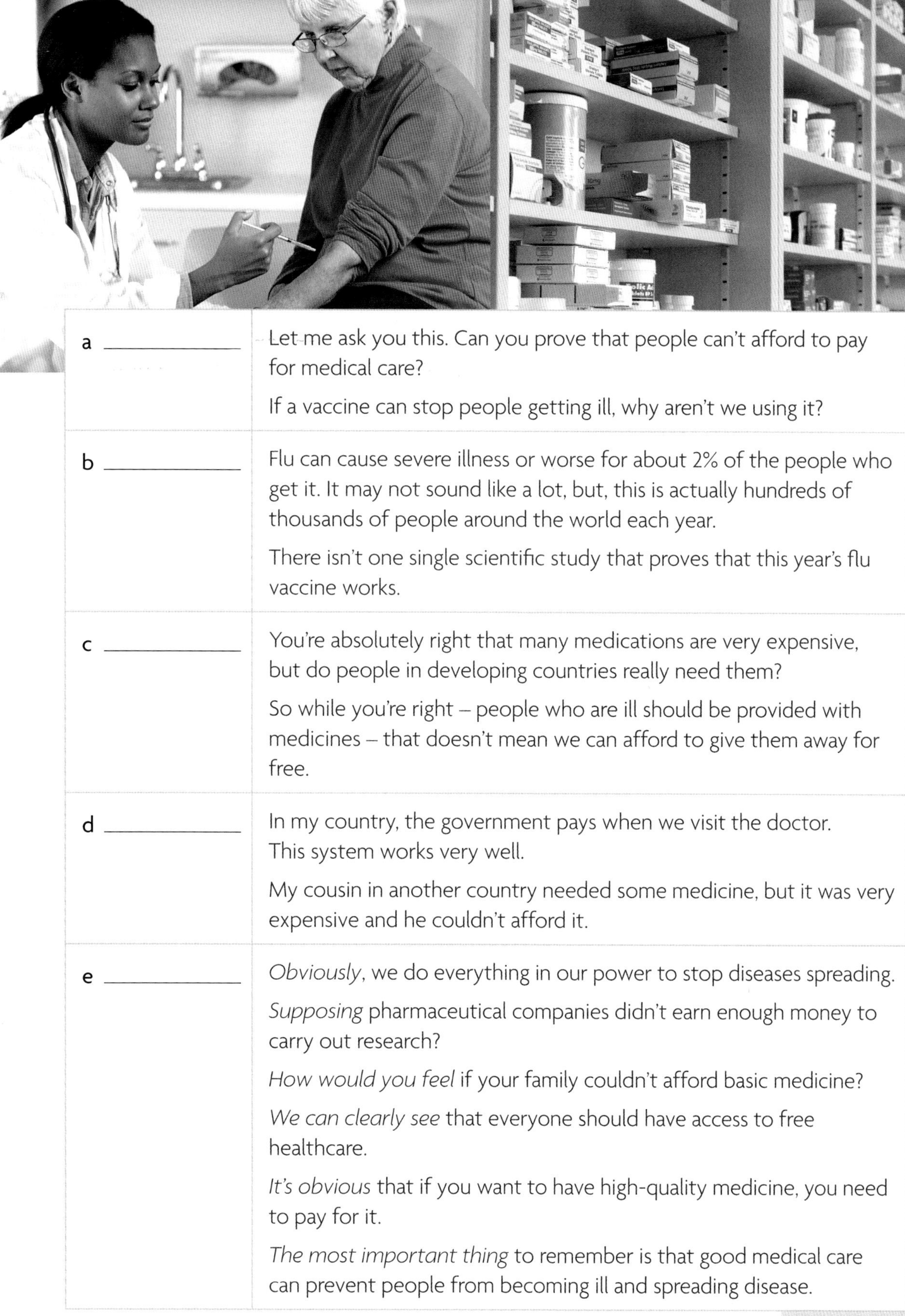

a __________	Let me ask you this. Can you prove that people can't afford to pay for medical care? If a vaccine can stop people getting ill, why aren't we using it?
b __________	Flu can cause severe illness or worse for about 2% of the people who get it. It may not sound like a lot, but, this is actually hundreds of thousands of people around the world each year. There isn't one single scientific study that proves that this year's flu vaccine works.
c __________	You're absolutely right that many medications are very expensive, but do people in developing countries really need them? So while you're right – people who are ill should be provided with medicines – that doesn't mean we can afford to give them away for free.
d __________	In my country, the government pays when we visit the doctor. This system works very well. My cousin in another country needed some medicine, but it was very expensive and he couldn't afford it.
e __________	*Obviously*, we do everything in our power to stop diseases spreading. *Supposing* pharmaceutical companies didn't earn enough money to carry out research? *How would you feel* if your family couldn't afford basic medicine? *We can clearly see* that everyone should have access to free healthcare. *It's obvious* that if you want to have high-quality medicine, you need to pay for it. *The most important thing* to remember is that good medical care can prevent people from becoming ill and spreading disease.

2 Work with a partner. Rewrite the facts below as persuasive statements. Use the language from Exercise 1 to help you.

1 Some big pharmaceutical companies spend more money on advertising than on research and development.

____

____

2 The cost of developing a new vaccine is $1.5 billion.

____

____

3 It takes years of study to become a doctor, which is why they are among the highest-paid professional workers.

____

____

4 The top five global drug companies are wealthier than many of the world's nations.

____

____

5 Malaria is an easily preventable disease, but people still contract it because they can't pay for a vaccine.

____

____

6 Only a small number of people in developing countries are able to afford basic, life-saving treatments for common illnesses.

____

____

3 Read your statements to another pair. Are their statements persuasive? Why / Why not?

SPEAKING TASK

Debate whether healthcare should be free for everyone.

PREPARE

1 Work in groups:
Group A: You work for an aid organization that sends doctors to help people in developing countries. You agree with the above statement.
Group B: You work for a large pharmaceutical company. You disagree with the above statement. In your groups, discuss what your side's background, motivation and viewpoints on this issue are. Use the following ideas to help you:

- people in cities versus rural populations
- different types of disease
- the fact that drug companies are businesses and have to make a profit
- issues of fairness for drug companies, individuals and nations

Discuss what you think the opposing group's background, motivation and views will be. How will they be similar? How will they be different?

PRACTISE

2 Prepare an opening statement for the debate. Practise your opening statement in your group. Make sure each person makes at least one comment.

3 Think about your opponent's views and make notes about what they might say in response to your opening statement. Make notes of persuasive language that you might use to counter their arguments. Remember to:

- give personal examples and opinions (if possible)
- ask challenging questions
- give information to support your viewpoint

4 Prepare for the debate.

- Be ready to make notes on what the other group says, as you will need to respond to their views in your counter-argument.
- Use your ideas from Exercise 3 to help you.
- Use the following format when you have the debate:

Group A: Announce the topic: Healthcare should be free for everyone.
Group A: Opening statement in favour
Group B: Opening statement against
Group A: Counter-argument in favour
Group B: Counter-argument against

5 Have the debate.

DISCUSS

6 Discuss the way the arguments were presented and try to agree which group won the debate.

TASK CHECKLIST	✔
Did you state your position in the debate clearly?	
Did you support your position with information?	
Did you ask challenging questions?	
Did you give personal examples?	
Did you address the other group's argument?	
Did you use persuasive language?	

OBJECTIVES REVIEW

I can ...

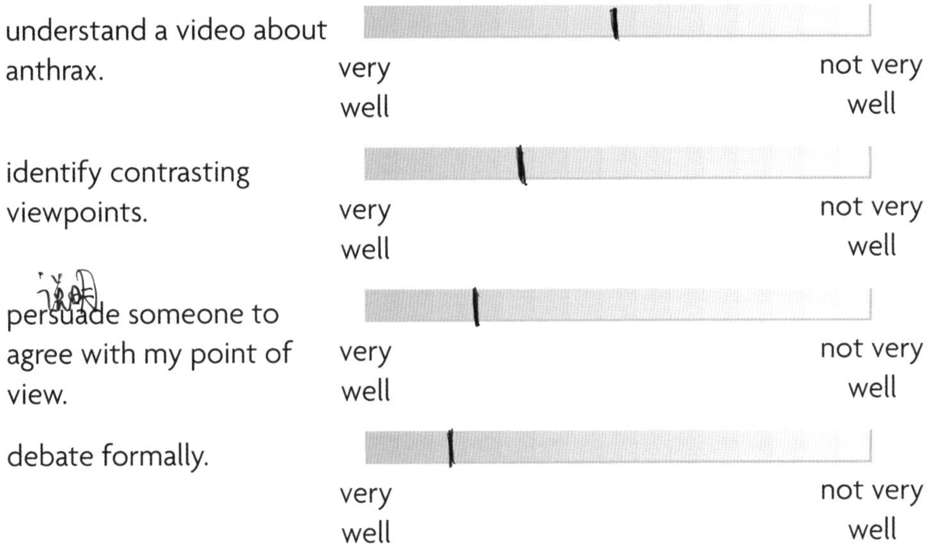

understand a video about anthrax.	very well	not very well
identify contrasting viewpoints.	very well	not very well
persuade someone to agree with my point of view.	very well	not very well
debate formally.	very well	not very well

WORDLIST

UNIT VOCABULARY	ACADEMIC VOCABULARY
antibiotic (n)	contract (v)
clinical (adj)	data (n)
controlled (adj)	disease (n)
diagnose (v)	occur (v)
inhale (v)	proven (adj)
outbreak (n)	recovery (n)
precaution (n)	scientific (adj)
researcher (n)	treat (v)
spore (n)	trial (n)

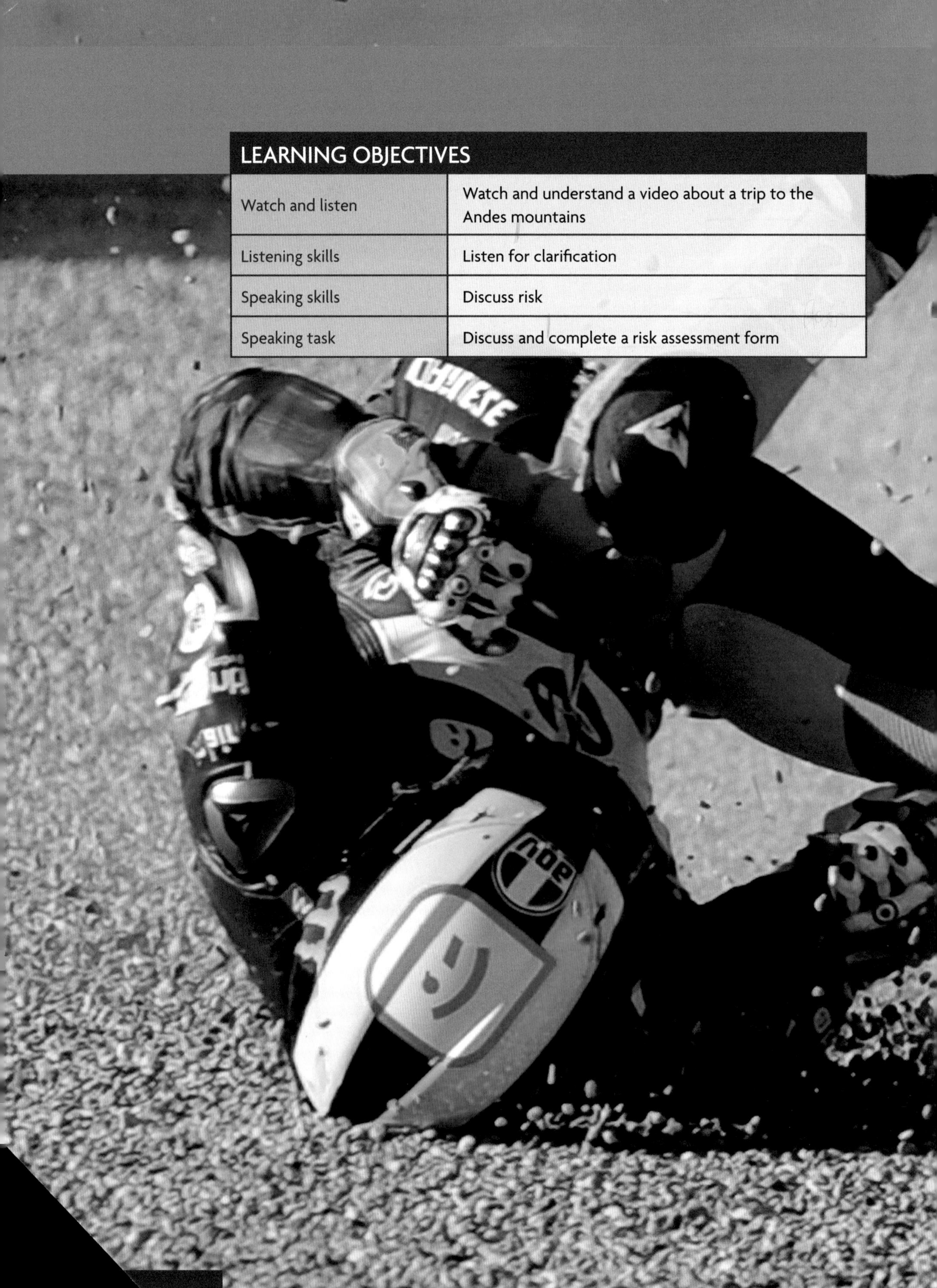

LEARNING OBJECTIVES	
Watch and listen	Watch and understand a video about a trip to the Andes mountains
Listening skills	Listen for clarification
Speaking skills	Discuss risk
Speaking task	Discuss and complete a risk assessment form

RISK UNIT 4

UNLOCK YOUR KNOWLEDGE

Work with a partner. Discuss the questions below.

1 Do you think it is important to take risks in life? Why / Why not?
2 What kind of risks do people often take in their personal or professional lives?
3 Do you think these risks normally pay off?

WATCH AND LISTEN

Discovery EDUCATION

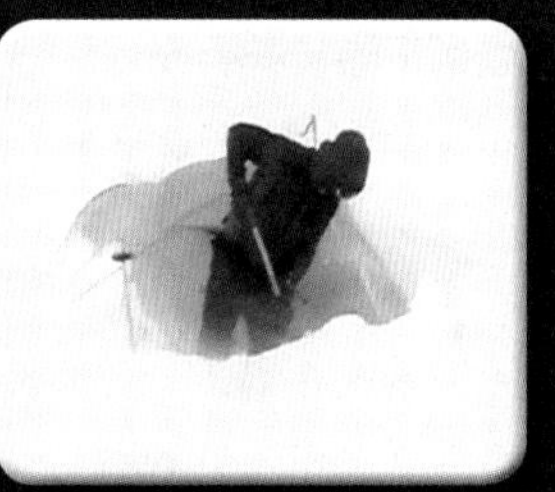

PREPARING TO WATCH

UNDERSTANDING KEY VOCABULARY

1 You are going to watch a video about a trip to the Andes Mountains. Before you watch, match the words (1–8) to the definitions (a–h).

1 protection
2 sea level
3 blizzard
4 fierce gusts
5 collapse
6 trek
7 trapped
8 buried

a sudden, strong movements of wind
b a severe snow storm
c be covered with a large quantity of something
d to fall down suddenly because of pressure and having no support
e something that protects someone or something from harm or injury
f the average height of the sea, used as a standard for measuring heights and depths
g to walk a long distance, usually over mountains, through forests, etc.
h unable to move or escape from a place or situation

USING VISUALS TO PREDICT CONTENT

2 Read the television listing and discuss the questions below in pairs.

Andes Mountain Adventure
9pm, Channel 1 ★★★★☆

The story of two trekkers who went missing for nearly two weeks in Patagonia, in the Andes mountains of South America. The pair spent ten days trapped in their tent by a severe snow storm. This programme relives an adventure that could have ended in tragedy, but instead was celebrated with their safe return home.

1 What risks do you think the two men took on their trip to the Andes?
2 Why do people usually participate in adventure sports?

WHILE WATCHING

LISTENING FOR GIST

3 Watch the video. Write true (T) or false (F) next to the statements below.

1 The men were skiing in a place nobody had ever been before. ____
2 The trip immediately went wrong. ____
3 The weather suddenly turned bad. ____
4 They got in their tent for protection. ____
5 An avalanche trapped them in their tent. ____
6 The trip was risky because this kind of weather isn't unusual. ____

UNDERSTANDING DETAIL

4 Watch again. Correct the notes below.

1 One of the biggest dangers when trekking in Patagonia is the wind.
____
2 At the start of the trip the weather was snowy and windy.
____
3 The two men faced winds of 200 kph in the mountains.
____
4 Avalanches buried the men's tent in snow.
____
5 After ten days, the men had to remove snow from the tent to stop it collapsing.
____
6 The total snowfall was five metres.
____
7 The storm lasted for ten days.
____
8 Ground blizzards are unusual in Patagonia.
____

DISCUSSION

5 Work with a partner. Discuss the questions.

1 What additional preparations could the men have made for their adventure?
2 Do you think people who do extreme sports in the mountains should expect to be rescued by emergency services if things go wrong? Why / Why not?
3 Do you think extreme sports in general are worth the risks people take to do them?

LISTENING 1

PREPARING TO LISTEN

PREDICTING CONTENT USING VISUALS

1 You are going to listen to a safety presentation for an extreme sport. Before you listen, look at the photograph. What do you think the risks of the sport are? How do you think they could be prevented?

UNDERSTANDING KEY VOCABULARY

2 Match the words (1–10) with the correct definitions (a–j).

risks	precautions
1 crash	6 helmet
2 injury	7 goggles
3 collision	8 harness
4 sunburn	9 sunscreen
5 heatstroke	10 sun-protective clothing

a eye protection made from glass or plastic ____
b an accident in which two or more people or vehicles hit each other with force ____
c a violent accident involving one or more vehicles ____
d clothing that covers your skin to protect you from the sun ____
e a piece of equipment used to control or hold someone in place ____
f physical damage caused to the body by an accident or an attack ____
g a condition in which your skin turns red and sore after too much time in the sun ____
h fever and weakness caused by being in the sun for too long ____
i a cream or oil rubbed into the skin to prevent it from being burned by the sun ____
j a strong, hard hat worn for protection ____

WHILE LISTENING

LISTENING FOR GIST

UNLOCK ONLINE

3 4.1 Listen to the safety presentation. Choose the correct answers (a–e).

1 Which of these hazards does the speaker mention?
- a hot sand
- b high wind
- c the sun
- d bad driving conditions off road
- e encounters with wild animals

2 What advice does the speaker give for dealing with a crash or collision?
- a don't panic
- b get out of the buggy
- c stop the buggy
- d check the buggy
- e take off your harness

POST-LISTENING

Listening for clarification

Speakers sometimes clarify what they have said to make sure the listener understands, often by repeating their point, summarizing the situation, or giving the opposite scenario to contrast with what they have said. Listening for clarification can help you if you don't understand something the first time it is said.

4 4.1 Listen to the safety presentation again. Tick the method of clarification used by the guide for each point below.

	summary of the situation	opposite scenario
1 Wear appropriate footwear.		
2 Use sun protection.		
3 Wear safety equipment.		
4 In a crash or collision stay in the vehicle.		

5 Rewrite the following sentences, using active and passive structures with *to be*.

1 You must wear adequate sun protection.
You are to wear adequate sun protection. / Adequate sun protection is to be worn.

2 You must not wear sandals.

3 You must wear goggles at all times.

4 You must not remove the harness.

PRONUNCIATION FOR LISTENING

Stress for emphasis

When clarifying something, a speaker may stress key or additional information, to help show what was previously said was important.

6 4.2 Listen and underline the stressed words. The first is done for you.

1 The sand is hot, and you always have to be prepared to walk.
2 You definitely need good foot protection. Does everyone else have suitable shoes?
3 I'm talking about using plenty of sunscreen and wearing sun-protective clothing; clothes that cover your skin.
4 If you don't wear a harness when we drive off the road, you bounce around in your seat and you could lose control, or you could fall out.

7 Work with a partner. Practise saying the sentences in Exercise 6 with the correct stress.

DISCUSSION

8 Work with a partner. Discuss the questions.

1 What types of jobs include facing risks?
2 Where do you face hazards in everyday life?
3 What can you do to avoid them?

LANGUAGE DEVELOPMENT

EXPLANATION

Expressing certainty about future events

You can use *will* and *won't* to express certainty about future events.

You **will** get sunstroke if you stay in the sun too long.

You use *be sure / bound / certain to* (*not*) + infinitive to talk about something that will definitely or definitely won't happen.

You're **sure to cut** yourself if you hold a knife that way.

We can use *likely to* (*not*) + infinitive to say that something will probably or probably won't happen.

You're **unlikely to fall** out if you wear a harness.

We can also use *can, could, may* and *might* to talk about future possibilities.

You **may** get sunburn if you don't wear sunscreen.

EXPRESSING CERTAINTY

1 Write certain (C), possible (Poss) or probable (Prob) next to the statements below.

1 You might get a head injury. ____
2 You could hurt your feet if you don't wear the right shoes. ____
3 You're sure to hurt yourself if you don't follow the rules. ____
4 You're bound to get sunburn if you wear short sleeves. ____
5 You're unlikely to fall out of the buggy if you are wearing the harness properly. ____
6 You'll get sunburn if you don't wear sunscreen. ____
7 You will get sand in your eyes if you don't wear goggles. ____
8 You're likely to fall out of the buggy if you don't wear a harness. ____

2 Put the words in order to make sentences.

1 head / so / could / wear / hurt / your / You / please / a helmet / .
____
2 you / crash / driving / like / to / into / You're / a rock / if / bound / keep / that / .
____
3 an eye injury / certain / goggles / not to / You're / if / you're / get / wearing / .
____
4 fall out / a harness / you're / to / if / unlikely / wearing / You're / .
____
5 sure / have / not / you're / concentrating / to / You're / a collision / if / .
____
6 you /may /Careful! /get / You / if / don't use / sunburn / sunscreen / .
____

ADJECTIVES TO DESCRIBE RISK

3 Match the words (1–8) to the definitions (a–h).

1 major
2 minor
3 potential
4 adequate
5 apparent
6 considerable
7 straightforward
8 appropriate

a possible when the necessary conditions exist
b obvious, or able to be seen or understood
c easy or simple to do or understand
d more important, bigger or more serious than something else
e suitable or right for a particular situation or occasion
f more serious than others of the same type
g enough, or satisfactory for a particular purpose
h not as serious as others of the same type

LISTENING 2

PREPARING TO LISTEN

USING YOUR KNOWLEDGE

1 You are going to listen to a risk assessment meeting. Before you listen, work with a partner and make a list of hazards that restaurant staff might face in a professional kitchen.

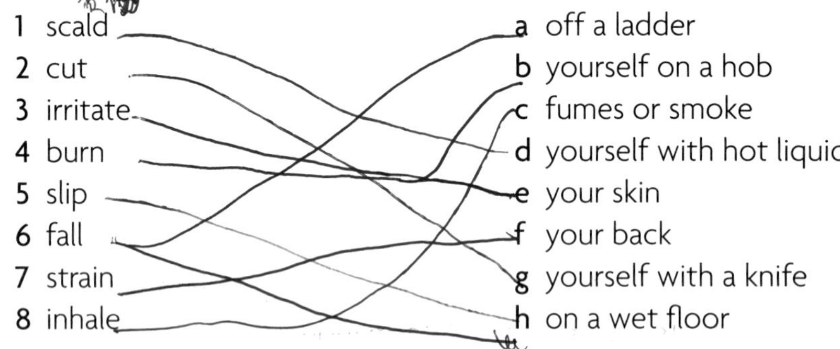

UNDERSTANDING KEY VOCABULARY

2 Match the verbs (1–8) to the hazards (a–h).

1 scald	a off a ladder
2 cut	b yourself on a hob
3 irritate	c fumes or smoke
4 burn	d yourself with hot liquid
5 slip	e your skin
6 fall	f your back
7 strain	g yourself with a knife
8 inhale	h on a wet floor

WHILE LISTENING

LISTENING FOR GIST

3 4.3 Listen to the risk assessment meeting. Choose the best answer (a–c) for each question.

1 What is the purpose of the meeting?
   a to make the kitchen safer
   b to inspect the hygiene of the kitchen
   c to officially warn the restaurant owner about safety problems

2 After discussing ladder safety, what do the men discuss?
   a fire hazards in the kitchen
   b potential risks related to food
   c appropriate precautions while cooking

3 What is the inspector's conclusion about the safety of the kitchen?
   a there are some major safety problems in the kitchen
   b the kitchen is generally safe and well-run
   c he needs to continue the inspection before he can comment

LISTENING FOR DETAIL

4 4.3 Listen to the risk assessment meeting again. Complete the table.

hazard	risk	risk level	risk reduction
falling from a height	major injury	very low	Two people should use the ladder, one climbing, the other holding it. Make sure the floor is dried.
stove: burns from the hob			
stove: scalds from hot liquids			
stove: smoke and fumes			

POST-LISTENING

5 Read the sentences from the listening. Underline the words in each sentence that indicate the important information.

1 First of all, we know that burns are highly probable.
2 So, in terms of risk assessment, the main thing is you need to make sure that the floor is dried after it has been cleaned.
3 The most important thing is we've never had a major injury.
4 First of all, you're generally running a really safe kitchen here, but there are some improvements to be made.
5 The main thing I'd like to see is that you get that risk down to low.
6 The most important thing is that the chefs shouldn't fill the pots too full.

DISCUSSION

6 Look at the photographs and discuss the questions.

1 What's the hazard?
2 What's the risk?
3 How serious would the problem be if it happened?
4 How could the risk be reduced or removed?

CRITICAL THINKING

At the end of this unit you are going to do the speaking task below.

Assess the table of statistics on accidents, illnesses and injuries at a theme park and complete a risk assessment form.

Understanding statistics

Statistics are collections of numbers which represent facts or measurements. When they are presented in an organized way, they can make information clearer and more useful.

UNDERSTAND

1 Work with a partner. Look at the title of the table. Which information would you expect to be included?

1 types of injury incurred at a theme park
2 the names of people injured at the theme park
3 the number of injuries in a given year
4 the most popular attractions in the park
5 detailed information about how injuries were treated
6 information about which injury is most common and least common

annual incidents report (accident, illness or injury): theme park		
incident	**total number of cases**	**% of total number of incidents**
1 minor injuries (cuts, scrapes, etc.)	1,253	30.5%
2 heatstroke	1,117	27.2%
3 slipping/tripping and falling	984	24.0%
4 falling off a ride	541	13.2%
5 choking on food	209	5.1%
6 burn from fireworks	3	0.1%
total number of incidents	4,107	100%
total theme park visitors last year: 2,290,010		

2 Look at the table. Discuss the questions below.

1 How many people had heatstroke at the theme park?
____

2 What percentage of the incidents were minor? ______________

3 How many people were burned by fireworks? ______________

4 What percentage of the incidents were caused by falling off a ride?
____

5 How many incidents were there in total? ______________

6 How many people visited the theme park in total? ______________

INTERPRETING STATISTICS

ANALYZE

3 Look at the table again. Answer the questions.

1 Based on the information, which incident is the most likely to occur?
____

2 Which incident is the least likely to occur?
____

4 Number the incident types in order of seriousness (1 = the most serious, 6 = the least serious).

minor injuries (cuts, scrapes, etc.) _____
heatstroke _____
slipping/tripping and falling _____
falling off a ride _____
choking on food _____
burn from fireworks _____

5 Work with a partner. Compare your answers for Exercise 4. Did you agree? Why / Why not?

Understanding anecdotal evidence

Anecdotal evidence is based on personal experience rather than statistics. Anecdotal evidence can agree with statistical evidence, but it may not. Together statistics and anecdotes can be used to give a wider picture of the risks in a particular situation.

APPLY

6 Write anecdotal (A) or statistical (S) next to the statements below.

1 I had really bad sunburn when I went on a dune buggy safari, so it must be a common problem. _____
2 Only one in ten injuries at the shopping centre required a visit to the doctor. _____
3 More than half of serious motorcycle injuries occur because the rider isn't wearing a helmet. _____
4 Abdullah has crashed his motorcycle several times, but he's never had a head injury, so that proves that wearing a helmet is effective. _____

7 Work in pairs. Number the restaurant kitchen injuries (a–c) in order of what you think is most common (1 = the most common, 3 = the least common).

a cut from knife _____
b slipping a falling on a wet floor _____
c burns from cooking _____

8 4.4 Listen to the conversation. Check your answers to Exercise 7.

9 4.4 Listen again. Answer the questions.

1 What anecdotal evidence is given in the conversation?

____

2 What statistical evidence is given?

____

3 Does the anecdotal evidence support the statistical evidence?

____

SPEAKING

PREPARATION FOR SPEAKING

TALKING ABOUT STATISTICAL EVIDENCE

1 4.5 Statistics in a table can be expressed as whole numbers or percentages and can be presented using comparative language. Listen and complete the sentences.

2,290,010 people visited the theme park last year and we **had** (1)______________ medical incidents. We **calculate only** (2)______________ of visitors had any kind of medical issue. Or **putting it another way**, (3)______________ visitors had a safe visit.

By far, **the most common incidents** were minor. (4)______________ of the medical issues were minor cuts and scrapes. **After that**, the next most common issue was heatstroke, with (5)______________ cases last year. **That's** (6)______________ visitors, or (7)______________ of all medical issues.

Fortunately, the three most serious problems – falling off a ride, choking on food, and getting burned by fireworks – were **the least common**. **Together** they made up (8)______________ of the issues we treated.

2 Work with a partner. Use the expressions in bold from Exercise 1 to explain the statistics below.

Burns from dune buggy engines were the least common incident last year.

annual incident report (accident, illness or injury): dune buggy tours		
incident	total number of cases	% of total number of incidents
1 minor injuries (cuts, scrapes, etc.)	25	31.3
2 heatstroke	19	23.75
3 slipping/tripping and falling	17	21.25
4 head injury	15	18.7
5 broken bone	3	3.75
6 burn from dune buggy engine	1	1.25
accident/injury total	80	
total dune buggy passengers last year: 1,200		

Language for clarification

Speakers often use certain expressions to indicate that they are going to clarify what they have just said.

3 Complete the statements and clarifications with the words from the box below.

say mean mean is in other talking about

1 Everyone needs appropriate shoes. What I ______________ shoes that won't fall off.
2 You need to take care when using knives. I'm ______________ using a good chopping technique and working carefully.
3 You may need to drink more than usual. ______________ words, you should carry a water bottle.
4 There's a problem with the weather today. By 'problem', I ______________ it's going to be very dry and dusty.
5 Be careful of the danger from stoves. When I ______________ 'danger', I'm thinking of the potential for burns and scalds.

USING MODALS TO TALK ABOUT HAZARDS AND RISKS

4 Work with a partner. Read the safety inspector's notes about hazards in the kitchen. Use *can, could, might* and *may* to say what risk each hazard may lead to.

NOTES:

High shelves in kitchen area can only be accessed by ladder.

A lot of boxes on shelves and poor lighting in storage area.

Broken tiles on main kitchen floor.

Pipe from one sink is leaking water on to tiled floor.

Pots full of hot soup noted on kitchen surfaces near to doorway.

Kitchen staff using a ladder to get to high shelves might fall and injure their backs.

EXPRESSIONS FOR TALKING ABOUT LIKELIHOOD AND PROBABILITY

5 Number the collocations in order of likelihood (1 = most likely, 5 = least likely).

definitely possible _____
one hundred percent certain _____
absolutely impossible _____
extremely unlikely _____
highly probable _____

SPEAKING TASK

Assess the table of statistics on accidents, illnesses and injuries at a theme park and complete a risk assessment form.

PREPARE

1 Work in groups. Look at the table of statistics from the Critical thinking section on page 79 on incidents at a theme park. Match the risks / incidents to the hazards in the risk assessment form below.

PRACTISE

2 Look at the statistics for each incident in the table. Discuss the risk level (*very low* to *very high*) for each risk in the risk assessment form.

RISK ASSESSMENT FORM

hazard	risk	risk level	risk reduction
rides			
paths			
firework display			
rubbish area			
queuing areas			
food areas			

3 Read the anecdotal evidence from theme park visitors. What types of risk reduction could be done for each hazard? Write them in the risk assessment form.

VISITOR COMMENTS

The seats on some of the rides were too big for young children to sit on safely.

There were broken bottles near the rubbish bins.

The seating for the fireworks display was in an area where fireworks could land on visitors.

A leak from the water system meant that one of the paths was wet all the time.

It was easy for us to buy expensive bottled water, but there weren't many drinking fountains, particularly in the areas of the park where there is no shade.

The food, particularly fried food, served in the restaurant was far too hot to eat.

DISCUSS

4 Compare answers with another group. Did you get the same answers for your risk assessment form? Why / Why not? Amend your form based on any answers that the other group had that you feel add to your own.

TASK CHECKLIST	✔
Did you use modals to talk about hazards and risks?	
Did you use clarification language?	
Did you use expressions for talking about likelihood and probability?	
Did you use stress for emphasis in clarification?	

OBJECTIVES REVIEW

I can ...

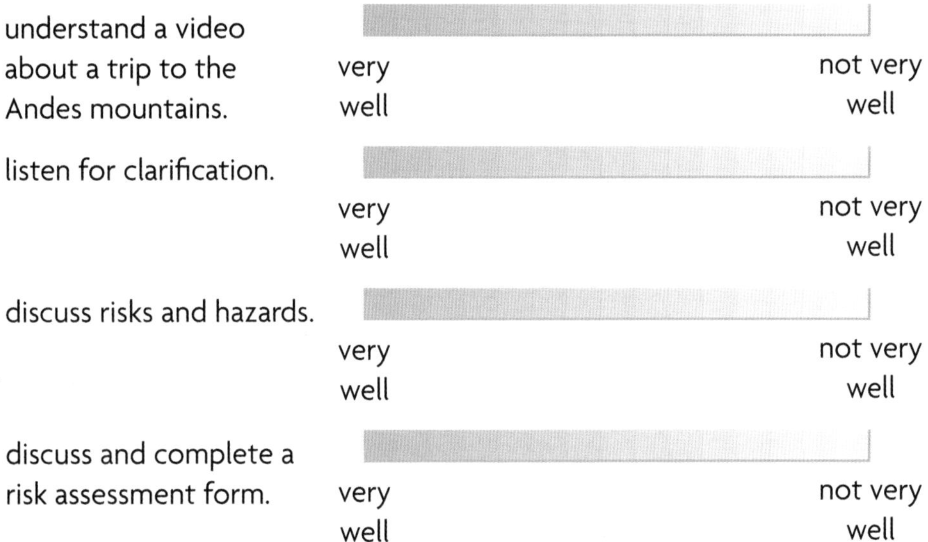

understand a video about a trip to the Andes mountains.	very well	not very well
listen for clarification.	very well	not very well
discuss risks and hazards.	very well	not very well
discuss and complete a risk assessment form.	very well	not very well

WORDLIST

UNIT VOCABULARY	ACADEMIC VOCABULARY
blizzard (n)	adequate (adj)
collision (n)	apparent (adj)
goggles (n)	appropriate (adj)
gust (n)	burn (v)
harness (n)	bury (v)
heatstroke (n)	collapse (v)
helmet (n)	considerable (adj)
injury (n)	crash (n)
irritate (v)	cut (v)
scald (v)	fall (v)
sea level (n)	fierce (adj)
strain (v)	major (adj)
sunburn (n)	minor (adj)
sunscreen (n)	potential (adj)
trek (v)	protection (n)
	slip (v)
	straightforward (adj)
	trap (v)

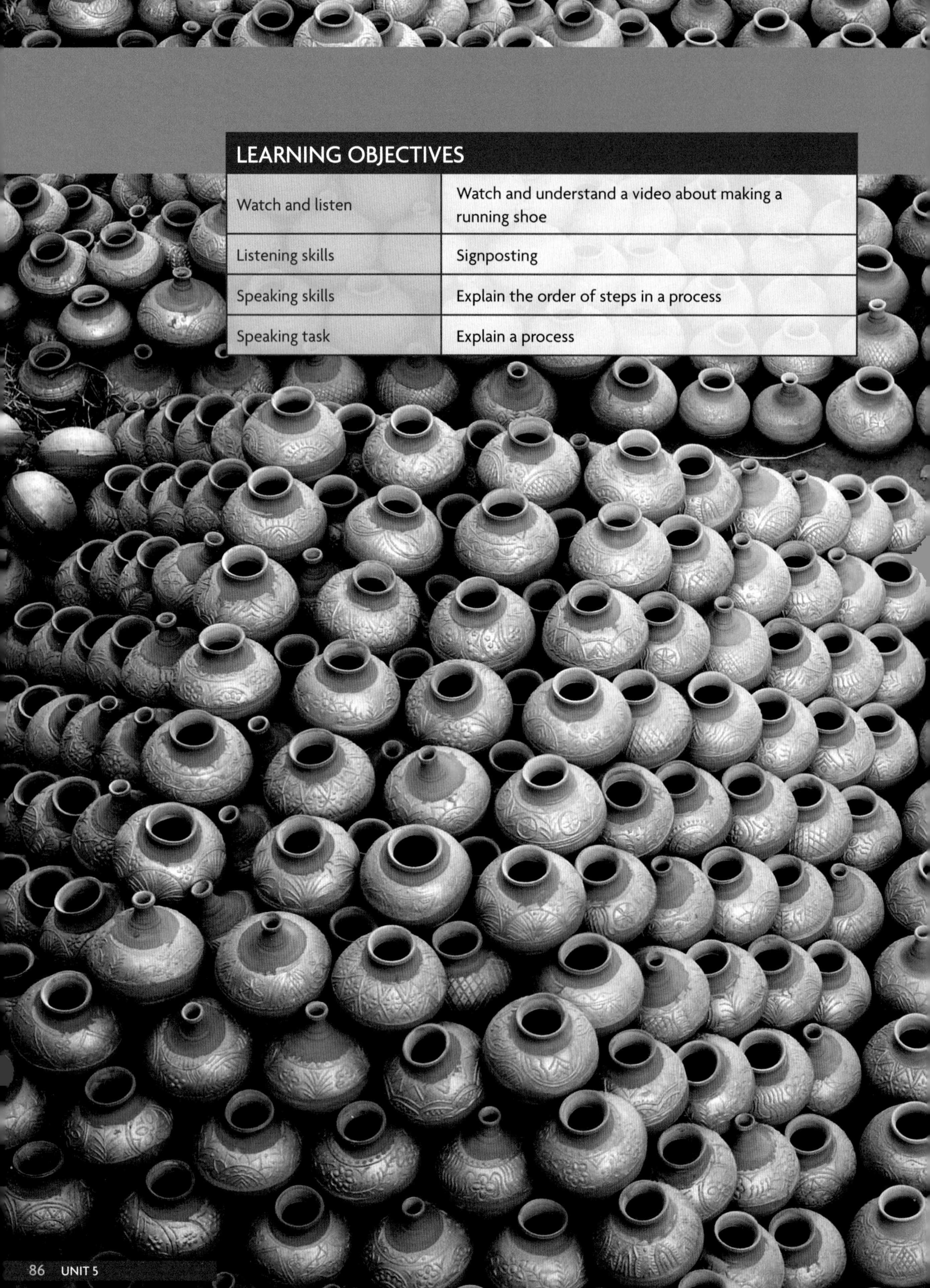

LEARNING OBJECTIVES

Watch and listen	Watch and understand a video about making a running shoe
Listening skills	Signposting
Speaking skills	Explain the order of steps in a process
Speaking task	Explain a process

MANUFACTURING UNIT 5

UNLOCK YOUR KNOWLEDGE

Work with a partner. Discuss the questions below.

1 What things is your country famous for manufacturing?
2 Do you own anything handmade? If so, what?
3 What items do you think are better when they are machine-made? What items do you think are better when they are handmade?

WATCH AND LISTEN

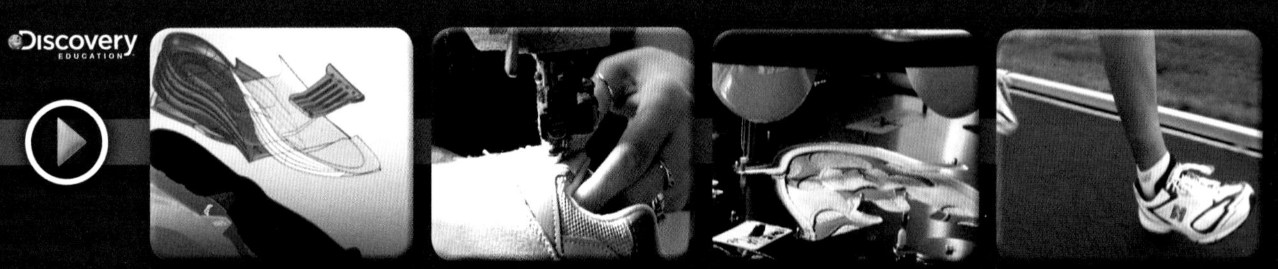

PREPARING TO WATCH

UNDERSTANDING KEY VOCABULARY

1 You are going to watch a video about making a running shoe. Before you watch, look at the photograph and match the words to the parts of the running shoe.

laces upper logo sole

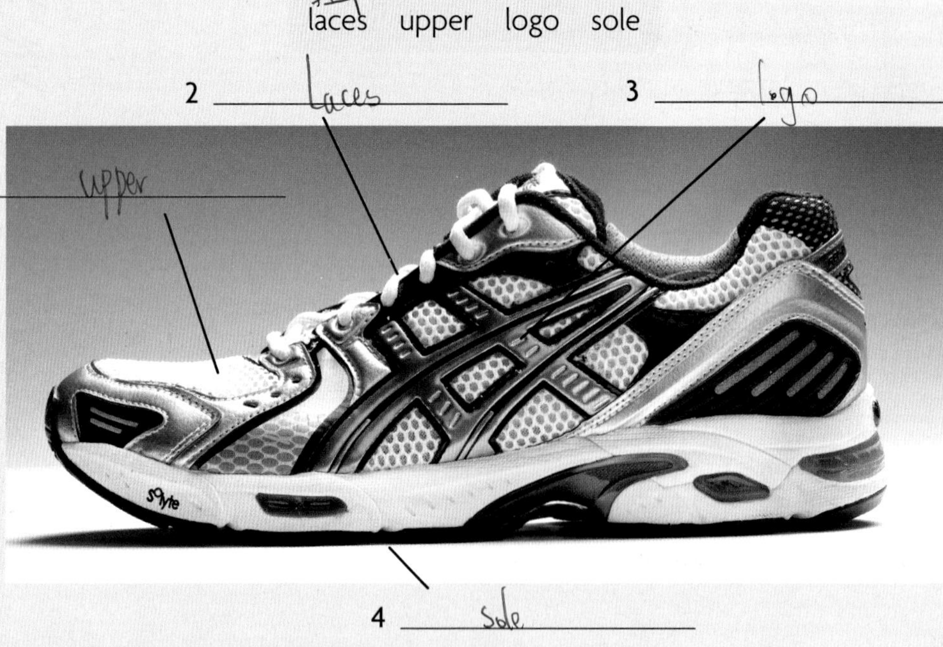

2 Match the words in bold (1–8) to the definitions (a–h).

1 Designing a running shoe is a very **skilled** job.
2 A good pair of shoes helps a runner's **performance**.
3 The technology is on the **cutting-edge** of shoe design.
4 **Stability** is important in any shoe, so you don't slip or fall easily.
5 Shoes should have a **balance** of stiffness for strength and softness for comfort.
6 The three pieces are sewn together into a **three-dimensional** shoe.
7 The **quality** of the shoe is high because it has been hand-sewn.
8 The shoes are tested using a **high-tech** computer process.

a a state where things are of equal weight or force
b how well a person, machine etc. does an activity
c the condition of being strong and steady
d the degree to which something is good or bad
e having length, width and height, something that is not flat
f having the ability to do a job well
g very modern with all the latest features
h using the most advanced machines and methods

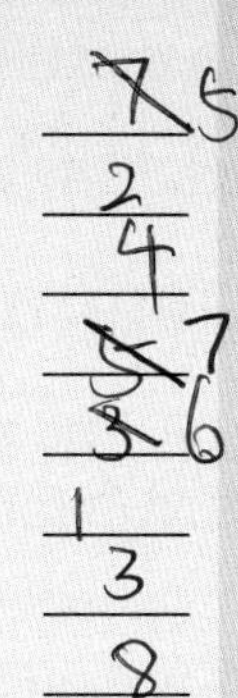

WHILE WATCHING

UNDERSTANDING MAIN IDEAS

3 Watch the video. Write true (T) or false (F) next to the statements below.

1 New Balance manufacture high-fashion shoes. ____
2 The shoes are designed by computer. ____
3 The factory makes 30,000 pairs of shoes a year. ____
4 The upper is sewn into three-dimensions by hand. ____
5 Each pair of shoes is checked by a robot. ____

LISTENING FOR KEY INFORMATION

4 Watch again. Match the sentence halves.

1 The shoes
2 The soles
3 The uppers
4 The sole and upper
5 The quality of the final shoes
6 The laces

a are glued together.
b are designed on a computer.
c are added and the shoes are put in a box.
d is carefully checked.
e are cut out of one piece of leather.
f are 'printed' in heated sand.

DISCUSSION

5 Work with a partner. Discuss the questions.

1 Are running shoes popular in your country? Why / Why not?
2 Do you think running shoes are worth the price it costs to buy them? Why / Why not?

LISTENING 1

PREPARING TO LISTEN

UNDERSTANDING KEY VOCABULARY

1 You are going to listen to a lecture on clothing manufacturing. Before you listen, match the words and phrases to the correct manufacturing process.

handmade individually produced industrial identical items high-quality factory-made mass-produced small-scale

2 Work with a partner. Write handmade (H) or factory-made (F) next to the statements below.

1 Before the 1800s most items of clothing were produced this way. ____
2 The process is slow and items are produced individually. ____
3 Groups of workers quickly produce identical items of clothing. ____
4 Large amounts of materials are bought at one time. ____
5 Items of clothing are individually produced for each customer. ____
6 The material is cut by machines. ____
7 Large numbers of identical items of clothing are produced quickly. ____
8 The customer chooses the correct size from a selection of similar items in a shop. ____

WHILE LISTENING

LISTENING FOR GIST

3 5.1 Listen to the lecture and check your answers.

LISTENING FOR DETAIL

4 5.1 Listen to the lecture again. Match the sentence halves.

1 Before the 1800s, almost everything was
2 Finer, more expensive clothing
3 Sewing machines made
4 Today, most clothing is made
5 Shirts made in factories are cheaper to make because
6 If workers are paid for each item they make,
7 Today's tailors hand-make clothes for people who
8 Tailors make a shirt individual

a by measuring the customer for an exact fit. 8
b want a perfect fit and don't mind paying more money. 7
c handmade using simple tools. 1
d fabric can be bought in large quantities. 5
e they will work as quickly as possible. 6
f by hand and by machine. 4
g clothing manufacturing much quicker. ~~5~~ 3
h was made by tailors. 2

Signposting

Signposting language is used in lectures and presentations to guide the listener through what the speaker is saying, and what they will say next. Listening for what is coming next can help you to understand a speaker better when you are not interacting with them.

POST-LISTENING

5 Read the sentences from the lecture (1–5) and match them to the signposting situations (a–e).

1 I'll divide the lecture into three parts.
2 The first part of the talk will look at the history of clothes manufacturing.
3 We've looked at mass-manufacturing, but are there any modern alternatives?
4 Let's turn now to the handmade process.
5 In short, mass-produced clothes will continue to dominate the marketplace, due to their low cost and high volume.

a finishing a section 3
b outlining the lecture 1
c starting a section 4
d summarizing 
e introducing a topic 2

PRONUNCIATION FOR LISTENING

Pauses in prepared speech

Prepared speech, such as in lectures and presentations, often has different intonation to natural speech. In a prepared speech, the speaker often pauses at clause boundaries, which are usually where punctuation marks are placed.

6 5.2 Listen to an extract from the lecture. Notice where the speaker pauses (//) when speaking.

Sewing machines were developed in the 1800s // which made clothing manufacture much quicker. // It was during this time // that industrial production of clothing began.

7 5.2 Listen and mark the pauses in the extract from the lecture.

Groups of factory workers started making identical items of clothing in high volumes using sewing machines. By the end of the 19th century lots of everyday items such as shirts, trousers and dresses were mass-produced.

8 Practise saying the paragraphs with a partner.

DISCUSSION

9 Work with a partner. Discuss the questions.

1 Why would someone want a tailor-made, rather than a factory-made suit?
2 Think of some mass-produced items you use every day. Would they ever be handmade? Why / Why not?
3 Think of some handmade items you own. Could they be mass-produced? Why / Why not?

LANGUAGE DEVELOPMENT

MODAL VERBS FOR NECESSITY AND OBLIGATION

EXPLANATION

Modal verbs for necessity and obligation

Obligation

We express obligation with *must* or *have to*. The meaning of these verbs is very similar, but *have to* is generally used when the obligation is outside of the speaker's control and *must* generally is used when the obligation is one the speaker has control over.

The factory workers **have to** arrive for work at eight o'clock.
With a tailor-made shirt, you **must** go to the shop to be measured and choose the fabric.

Necessity

We use *need to, must* and *have to* to talk about necessity.

You **need to** go to a tailor for an individually made shirt.

Prohibition

We use *must not* to say that something shouldn't be done.

You **mustn't** enter the factory without wearing ear protection.

No obligation or necessity

We use *don't have to* or *don't need to* to show that something isn't necessary.

You **don't have** to pick up your new suit; we can deliver it to you.

1 Read the sentences. Circle the negative modal verb in Sentence b that gives the same meaning as Sentence a.

1 a The design has to be made before the fabric can be cut.
  b The fabric *doesn't need to / mustn't* be cut out before the design is made.
2 a The sleeves don't need to be sewn on to the shirt in any order.
  b The left sleeve *doesn't have to / mustn't* be sewn on to the shirt before the right sleeve.
3 a The tailor needs to measure a client before he can make a suit.
  b The tailor *mustn't / doesn't have to* make a suit before he measures a client.
4 a With a tailor-made shirt, you must have a final fitting before the sewing is completely finished.
  b The sewing *mustn't / has to* be finished before the final fitting.
5 a The workers can sew the pockets on before or after the front and back of the shirt are joined together.
  b The workers *don't have to / must* sew the pockets on before the front and back of the shirt are joined together.

2 Complete the sentences with modal verbs. More than one answer may be possible.

1 You ______________ start a car's engine before you can drive it.
2 You ______________ switch off your computer before you select 'Shut Down' from the 'Start' menu, or you may damage it.
3 You ______________ charge your mobile phone every night, but it's probably a good idea.
4 You ______________ dial a country code first when you are telephoning someone abroad.
5 You ______________ plug your computer into a modem if you have a wireless internet connection.
6 You ______________ tell anyone your online banking password.

ACADEMIC VOCABULARY FOR PRODUCTION AND PROCESSES

3 Match the words (1–10) to the correct definitions (a–j).

1 method
2 manager
3 management
4 cost
5 volume
6 production
7 phase
8 process
9 approach
10 concept

a the amount of money that you pay for something
b a series of actions taken to achieve a result
c a principle or idea
d a stage in a series of events or a process
e a planned way of doing something
f the job of directing or controlling
g the process of making things
h the general number or amount of something
i someone whose job is to direct or control something
j a way of considering or doing something

4 Circle the incorrect collocation in the table.

1 traditional, scientific, assistant	method
2 general, reduced, assistant	manager
3 reduce, average, innovative	cost
4 high, new, reduced	volume
5 industrial, small-scale, scientific	production
6 initial, assistant, second	phase
7 new, innovative, reduce	approach
8 basic, office, fundamental	concept

LISTENING 2

PREPARING TO LISTEN

UNDERSTANDING KEY VOCABULARY

1 You are going to listen to a tour of a car factory. Before you listen, match the verbs (1–6) to the definitions (a–f).

1 apply
2 assemble / put together
3 dip
4 scratch
5 seal
6 ensure

a to put something into a liquid and quickly lift it out again
b to cover the surface of something with a substance to protect it
c to make something by joining the different parts together
d to make certain that something happens
e to rub something sharp on a hard surface so that it makes a mark
f to put or spread something such as paint onto a surface

PREDICTING CONTENT USING VISUALS

2 Look at the diagram of the layers of paint on a car manufactured in a factory. Write the order in which you think the layers are applied.

rust-protection coat clear coat colour coat sealant base coat

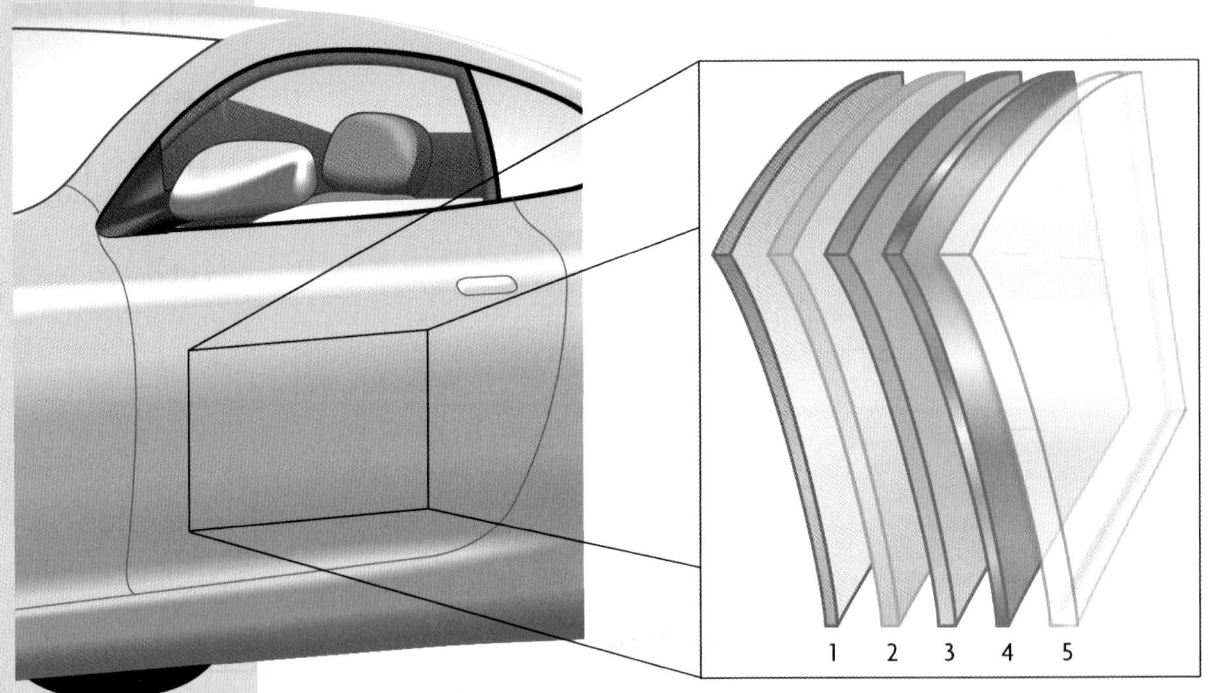

1 base coat
2 ~~sealant~~ rust-protection coat
3 ~~clear coat~~ sealant
4 colour coat
5 ~~rust-protection coat~~ clear coat

WHILE LISTENING

LISTENING FOR GIST

3 5.3 Listen to the car factory tour and check your answers to Exercise 2.

4 5.3 Listen to the car factory tour again. Write notes on the purpose of each layer of paint.

LISTENING FOR DETAIL

paint layer	purpose
1	
2	
3	
4	
5	

POST-LISTENING

5 Work in pairs. Read the text and answer the questions below.

> Cars have to be painted after the body has been assembled, but before the engine, windows, wheels, seats or any other parts that aren't painted are attached. This is done so that we can cover the metal parts of the car completely with paint.

1 Which underlined words above signal the order of steps in a process?
2 Which signal the *reason* for the order of steps?

6 Underline the words below that signal the order of steps in a process. Circle the words that signal the reason for the order.

1 The rust-protection coat wouldn't stick to bare metal, but it sticks to the base layer very well, which is why the base layer goes on first.
2 This sealant is the final layer to be applied before the colour goes on. We do this so that the colour layer will cover the sealant.
3 After this, the coloured paint is applied. Obviously the colour coat has to go on after the base coat, the rust protection coat and the sealant, because otherwise you wouldn't see it.

DISCUSSION

7 Work with a partner. Discuss the questions.

1 What do you think is the most important part of the car-painting process? Why?
2 What are the advantages of mass-produced cars?
3 Can you think of any reasons why somebody would want an individually produced car?

CRITICAL THINKING

At the end of this unit you are going to do the speaking task below.

Choose a process to explain to a partner. This could be describing how to make something by hand, or something that is manufactured.

Dependency diagrams

A dependency diagram shows the steps in the process of making something. It is useful for showing which tasks in a sequence have to be completed before other tasks can be performed.

ANALYZE

1 Work with a partner. Number the steps of manufacturing a T-shirt in the order that you think is correct. More than one answer is possible.

a assembling the front and back of the body ______
b finishing the neck ______
c designing the shirt ______
d adding the label with size, washing instructions ______
e cutting out the fabric ______
f attaching the sleeves to the body ______
g assembling the sleeves ______
h adding the pocket ______

2 Look at the dependency diagram showing the first part of the process of manufacturing a T-shirt. Answer the questions.

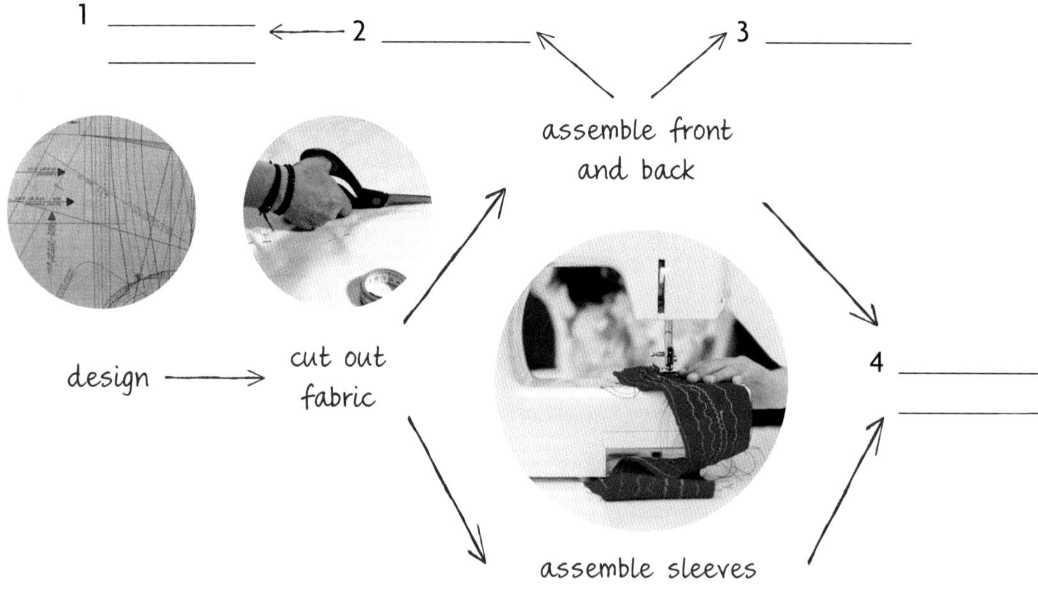

1 Which steps in the diagram must be completed before other steps can be done?
2 Are there any steps that you think could be done in a different order? Why / Why not?

APPLY

3 Complete the gaps in the dependency diagram in Exercise 2. Use the phrases below to help you.

add pocket finish neck attach sleeves to body add label

UNDERSTAND

4 Work with a partner. Answer the questions.

1 What are the most important steps of the process?
2 Are there any steps that could be left out?
3 Are there any additional steps that could be added to the dependency diagram?
4 Would they come before, during or after the process above?

SPEAKING

PREPARATION FOR SPEAKING

EXPLANATION

Explaining processes

When explaining a process, the passive voice is often used. We use the passive when explaining a process as we want to focus directly on the action and where it comes in a series of further steps, rather than who did the action.

*After the base coat **is applied**, the car body **is dipped** in a rust coat.*

1 Rewrite the sentences, putting the verbs in the passive.

1 Firstly, the tailor measures the client.

____

2 Then the customer chooses the style and fabric of the suit.

____

3 Next, the tailor cuts out and sews the pieces together to make the suit.

____

4 When the suit is ready, the tailor checks the fit and alters it as necessary.

____

5 Finally, the customer wears the suit.

____

2 5.4 Listen and check your answers. Practise saying the sentences with a partner.

EXPLAINING DEPENDENCY IN A PROCESS

3 Look at the language for describing dependency in a process and write the words/phrases into the correct place in the table.

simultaneously firstly meanwhile last of all
the process starts with consequently after so
first of all at the same time to begin with then
next subsequently the next step initially after that
as a result afterwards finally later

first steps	next steps	things that happen at the same time	results and consequences	final steps

PRONUNCIATION FOR SPEAKING

Stress on words that indicate order

When you explain a process, the words that indicate the order of the steps are stressed to make the explanation clear.

4 5.5 Listen to the sentences. Underline the stressed words. The first one is done for you.

1 The process of making coffee starts with boiling the water.
2 When making a cup of coffee, you have to measure the coffee carefully before you add it to the coffee maker.
3 If you are adding milk, or sugar, this must be added after the coffee is brewed.
4 Coffee can be put in the coffee maker at the same time as boiling the water.
5 Cups of coffee can be allowed to cool. Meanwhile, you can prepare a snack to eat with your coffee.

5 Listen and check your answers. Practise saying the sentences with a partner.

6 Work with a partner. Look at the diagram and use the language from Exercise 3 to describe the process of making coffee.

PREPARATION	COMBINING INGREDIENTS				DRINKING	
Boil water. →	Pour hot water into coffee maker. →	Leave the coffee to brew for a few minutes. →	Pour the coffee into a cup. →	Put milk in cup (optional). →	Allow the coffee to cool (optional).	Drink the coffee.
Put coffee in coffee maker. →				Put sugar in cup (optional). →		

SPEAKING TASK

Choose a process to explain to a partner. This could be describing how to make something by hand, or something that is manufactured.

PREPARE

1 Think of all of the steps in the process (there should be a minimum of six steps). Answer the questions.

   1 What are the main steps of the process?
   2 Are there any more steps before or after the main process you could include?
   3 Which steps have to be completed one after the other? Which can be done at any stage in the process? Can any steps be done at the same time?

2 Draw a dependency diagram for your process. Remember to show all of the steps of the process and the order in which they have to be done, as you will have to describe the process to your partner. Use language from the speaking preparation section to help you.

PRACTISE

3 Describe your processes to each other. While you are listening you should make notes on the process your partner is describing.

DISCUSS

4 Describe your processes back to each other. Did you get your partner's process right? If not, what was different?

TASK CHECKLIST	✔
Did you use language to indicate the order of steps?	
Did you use modals to talk about the order of the process?	
Did you use the passive to explain the process?	
Did you stress the words that indicate the order of the process?	

OBJECTIVES REVIEW

I can ...

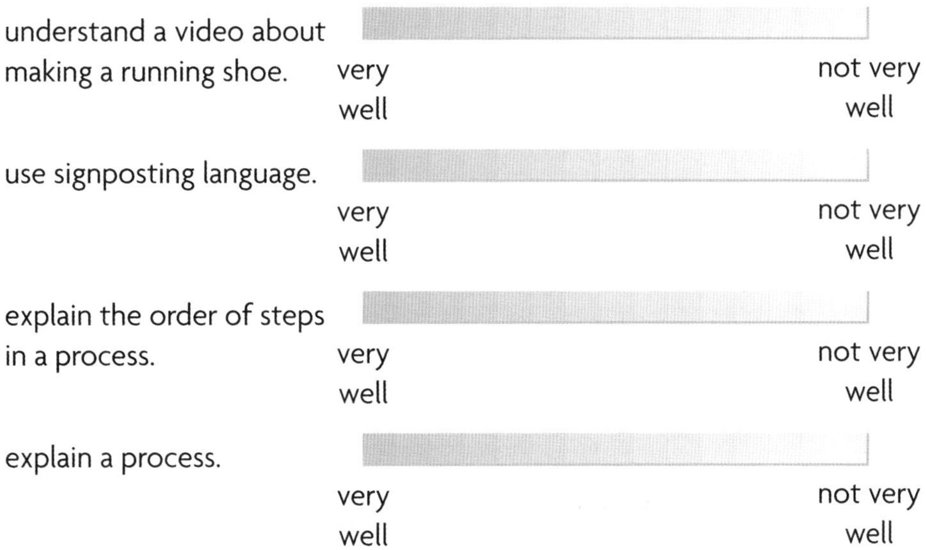

I can ...		
understand a video about making a running shoe.	very well	not very well
use signposting language.	very well	not very well
explain the order of steps in a process.	very well	not very well
explain a process.	very well	not very well

WORDLIST

UNIT VOCABULARY	ACADEMIC VOCABULARY
handmade (adj)	apply (v)
high-quality (adj)	approach (n)
individually-produced (adj)	assemble (v)
industrial (adj)	concept (n)
mass-produced (adj)	cost (n)
seal (v)	dip (v)
small-scale (adj)	ensure (v)
	identical (adj)
	management (n)
	manager (n)
	method (n)
	phase (n)
	process (n)
	production (n)
	scratch (v)
	volume (n)

LEARNING OBJECTIVES

Watch and listen	Watch and understand a video about rescuing orangutans
Listening skills	Distinguish main ideas from details
Speaking skills	Explain a problem and offer a solution
Speaking task	Give a problem and solution presentation

ENVIRONMENT UNIT 6

UNLOCK YOUR KNOWLEDGE

Work with a partner. Discuss the questions below.

1 What is deforestation?
2 What are the causes and consequences of it?
3 What other things do people do that affect the environment?
4 How can people use natural resources without destroying the environment?

WATCH AND LISTEN

PREPARING TO WATCH

USING YOUR KNOWLEDGE TO PREDICT CONTENT

1 You are going to watch a video about rescuing animals. Before you watch, work with a partner and answer the questions.

1 Can you think of any human activities that destroy animal habitats?
2 Why do they happen?
3 What can people do to stop these activities?

UNDERSTANDING KEY VOCABULARY

2 Match the words (1–8) to the definitions (a–h).

1 logging
2 habitat
3 orangutan
4 endangered species
5 conservationist
6 rainforest
7 rescue centre
8 capture

a a large ape with red hair and long arms
b a tropical forest that receives a lot of rain
c to take something or someone into your possession, often by force
d the act of cutting down trees for their wood
e someone who works to protect animals or plants from the effects of human activity
f a place or building which has been set up to help animals in danger
g a type of animal or plant that may soon no longer exist
h the natural surroundings in which an animal or plant lives

WHILE WATCHING

UNDERSTANDING MAIN IDEAS

3 Watch the video. Which sentence best gives the main idea of the video?

1 Conservationists don't agree on the reasons for problems facing orangutan populations.
2 Conservationists are trying to rescue orangutans from areas facing deforestation.
3 Conservationists are encouraging orangutan populations to return to deforested areas.

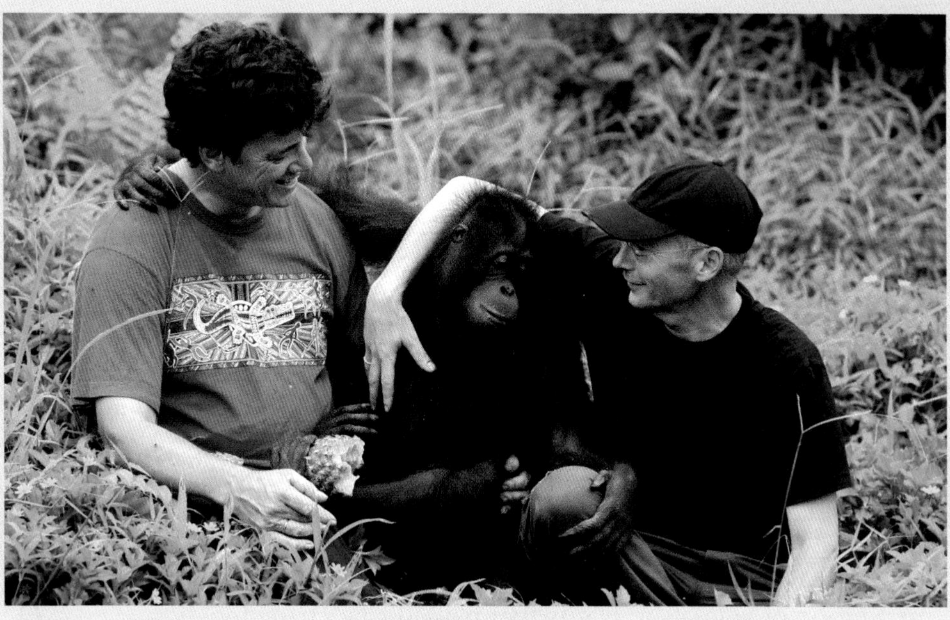

LISTENING FOR KEY INFORMATION

4 Watch again. Answer the questions below.

1 How many orangutans still live in their natural habitat?

2 How has much of the orangutans' natural habitat been destroyed?

3 What other reason is given for the destruction of the orangutans' habitat?

4 What are conservationists at the rescue centre doing to help orangutans?

5 Why do many orphaned baby orangutans arrive at the centre?

6 What do the orangutans need to learn before they leave the rescue centre?

DISCUSSION

5 Work with a partner. Discuss the questions.

1 What other animals can you think of that are endangered by human activities?
2 Do you think using natural products benefits the environment? Why / Why not?
3 What natural products or items do you own? Where do they come from?
4 Of the things you thought of above, which could be made from different materials?

LISTENING 1

PREPARING TO LISTEN

UNDERSTANDING KEY VOCABULARY

1 You are going to listen to a lecture about habitat destruction. Before you listen, read the text and match the words in bold (1–6) to the definitions (a–f).

> (1)**Conservation** of our (2)**coastal** regions is now vital as habitat (3)**destruction** is causing the extinction of many plant and animal (4)**species**. This has been caused by (5)**waste** and pollution from our constant exploitation of the habitat for its (6)**resources**.

a the protection of plants, animals and natural areas ____
b a group of animals or plants that have similar characteristics ____
c unwanted matter or material ____
d on or related to land by the sea or ocean ____
e the action of destroying something ____
f things that can be used to help you ____

Distinguishing main ideas from details

Speakers often support their main ideas with details. Listening for main ideas and details can help us understand a speaker's meaning.

2 Look at sentences (1–6) and (a–f). Which set expresses main ideas? Which set expresses details?

1 Planet Earth is dynamic and always changing.
2 Sometimes natural forces can destroy the environment.
3 However, humans are also responsible for a lot of habitat destruction.
4 Humans haven't only affected the land and its animals, they have also affected the sea.
5 One other animal that is as at home in the city and in the countryside is the squirrel.
6 Not everyone feels that ecotourism is actually helping the environment.

a Pollution from coastal cities has damaged the ocean. ____
b In Europe, only about 15% of land hasn't been modified by humans. ____
c 10,000 years ago, about half of the planet was covered in ice. ____
d In 1991, a volcano in the Philippines erupted and killed many people and animals. ____
e Tourists who travel long distances by aeroplane create pollution. ____
f The number of city squirrels has increased. ____

3 Match the main ideas in Exercise 2 to the details that support them.

WHILE LISTENING

LISTENING FOR MAIN IDEAS

4 6.1 Listen to the lecture and check your answers.

LISTENING FOR DETAIL

5 6.1 Listen to the lecture again and complete the notes.

The Earth always changes: (1) ______________ years ago, half of it was covered in ice.

Humans have changed the Earth: originally there were 16 million square kilometres of (2) ______________, today there are (3) ______________. Each year, (4) ______________ square metres are destroyed.

In (5) ______________, monkeys exploit the city environment by (6) ______________ from humans.

Ecotourism example: La Selva Amazon Eco Lodge. Visitors learn about local (7) ______________, visit (8) ______________ in the forest; when they leave, they're (9) ______________.

Criticism of eco-tourism: air travel and waste from the hotel causes (10) ______________.

POST-LISTENING

LISTENING FOR OPINION

6 Choose the statement (a–c) that best matches the lecturer's opinion.

'Part of this environmental change is due to natural, rather than human causes.'
   - a Natural causes result in some environmental change.
   - b Natural causes result in most environmental change.
   - c Human causes result in most environmental change.

2 'Habitat destruction hasn't been bad news for all animals.'
   - a The destruction of animal habitats is always a bad thing.
   - b The destruction of animal habitats is not necessarily negative.
   - c The destruction of animal habitats is inevitable.

3 'We tend to think of human activity as always having a negative impact on the environment.'
   - a It's common to think that humans only negatively affect the environment.
   - b It's wrong to think that humans only negatively affect the environment.
   - c It's correct to think that humans only negatively affect the environment.

PRONUNCIATION FOR LISTENING

SENTENCE STRESS

7 6.2 In English, stressing different words can change the meaning or the focus of a sentence. Listen to the sentences and underline the word with the main stress. The first two are done for you.

1 Sometimes, natural forces destroy animal habitats ...
2 Sometimes, natural forces destroy animal habitats ...
3 Humans have changed the Earth ...
4 Humans have changed the Earth ...
5 Humans have changed the Earth ...
6 Humans have changed the Earth ...

8 Based on the stress in Exercise 7, match the sentence halves.

a ... but animals haven't changed it too much. ______
b ... but most of the time they don't. ______
c ... but they haven't changed the Moon. ______
d ... and you can't say that we haven't. ______
e ... rather than humans. ______
f ... and in some cases we've improved it. ______

9 Work with a partner. Practise saying the sentences.

DISCUSSION

10 Work with a partner. Discuss the questions.

1 How have people changed the habitats of the country you live in?
2 Think of an environment you know. Which animals live there naturally? Do any animals live there that are originally from somewhere else?
3 Have humans had an impact on the environment where you live? If so, how?

LANGUAGE DEVELOPMENT

PREPOSITIONS

EXPLANATION

Complex prepositions

Complex prepositions are two or three-word phrases used before nouns to show connections between words or ideas.

1 Match the headings (1–5) to the complex prepositions (a–e).

UNLOCK ONLINE

1 making an exception
2 giving a source
3 giving another option
4 including
5 giving a reason

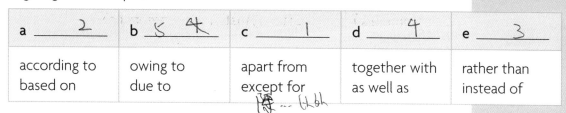

a ______	b ______	c ______	d ______	e ______
according to based on	owing to due to	apart from except for	together with as well as	rather than instead of

2 Circle the correct preposition to complete the sentence.

1 *Based on* / *Apart from* research that I carried out in Ethiopia, I can conclude that the destruction of deserts can be reversed.
2 Visitors rarely go to the research station *according to* / *due to* its extremely remote location.
3 *According to* / *Rather than* the Economist magazine, share prices fell sharply last month.
4 The engineers decided to use solar power *owing to* / *instead of* a conventional battery.
5 The doctors used strong medication *as well as* / *except for* lots of liquid to cure the patients.
6 The phone is assembled almost entirely by machines, *instead of* / *except for* the outer case.

VERBS TO DESCRIBE ENVIRONMENTAL CHANGE

3 Match words (1–8) to the correct definitions (a–h).

1 adapt	a to strongly affect something
2 affect	b to remove or take out something
3 decline	c to happen
4 exploit	d to gradually become less, worse or lower
5 extract	e to continue to live or exist
6 impact	f to change something to suit different conditions or uses
7 occur	g to have an influence on something
8 survive	h to use something for an advantage

4 Complete the sentences with the words in the box.

adapted occurred affected declined
impacted exploited extracted survived

1 Foxes have ______________ to living in cities.
2 Extinct species could have ______________ if more care was taken to protect them.
3 The number of wild squirrels in the UK has ______________ over many years.
4 Resources have been ______________ from endangered habitats without destroying them.
5 Humans have ______________ negatively on the environment by destroying forests.
6 Animals are ______________ by changes in their habitat.
7 Once squirrel populations ______________ naturally in the forests of the UK, but now they live mainly in urban areas.
8 Urban foxes have ______________ the new habitat that they find themselves in.

LISTENING 2

PREPARING TO LISTEN

UNDERSTANDING KEY VOCABULARY

1 You are going to listen to a talk about desert habitats. Before you listen, read the sentences and match the words in bold (1–8) to the definitions (a–h).

1 70% of the Earth's **surface** is covered in water.
2 The annual number of **dust storms** in dry regions has increased.
3 **Minerals** occur naturally in the Earth's surface.
4 **Diamonds** are the hardest naturally occurring substance on Earth.
5 **Copper** is important because it is used in electricity wires.
6 It is difficult to find a good **source** of oil.
7 The price of coal, oil and **natural gas** is increasing.
8 The **mining** industry is reliant on the existence of desert environments.

a the industry or activity of removing substances from the ground by digging ______
b fuel in a form like air used for heating or cooking ______
c a valuable or useful substance naturally found in the earth ______
d very hard, valuable stones ______
e strong winds carrying lots of fine sand ______
f the outer layer or top part of something ______
g a reddish-brown metal, used for making wires and coins ______
h the place something comes from or starts at ______

WHILE LISTENING

LISTENING FOR MAIN IDEAS

2 6.3 Listen to the talk and choose the correct answers (a–d).

1 Which two environments does the speaker talk about?
   a the desert **b** the ocean **c** cities **d** the countryside
2 Which two living things does the speaker talk about the survival of?
   a insects **b** humans **c** plants **d** animals
3 Which two things will happen if the desert is destroyed?
   a The soil will become saltier and plants will die.
   b The whole world will get hotter.
   c There will be more dirt and dust in the air.
   d We will lose the acacia tree as a food source.

LISTENING FOR DETAIL

3 6.3 Listen to the talk again. Number the facts in the order you hear them.

a Water for agriculture can make desert soil too salty. ____
b Computer technology can forecast how climate change will affect deserts. ____
c The Earth's deserts cover 33.7 million square kilometres. ____
d Solar energy can be used to produce water in deserts. ____
e The Topnaar people have deep understanding of the natural world. ____
f Deserts provide many of the world's minerals and metals. ____
g There are 2,200 desert plant species in Saudi Arabia. ____
h Desert surface temperatures in summer can reach 80 degrees. ____

POST-LISTENING

LISTEN FOR TEXT ORGANIZATION FEATURES

4 Match the parts of a presentation (1–3) to the sentences from the talk (a–c).

1 giving background information
2 explaining a problem
3 offering a solution

a The United Nations reports in their online publication 'Global Deserts Outlook', that the Earth's deserts take up about 33.7 million square kilometres, or 25% of the Earth's surface. ____
b The problem is that human activity is affecting deserts all over the world. According to the United Nations, traditional ways of life are changing as human activities such as cattle ranching, farming and large-scale tourism grow. ____
c The UN gives the example of using the latest computer technology to forecast how climate change will affect deserts and to use that information to prepare for changes. ____

5 Read the three details below. Which part of the talk in Exercise 4 (1–3) do they come from?

a According to a blog called 'A Smarter Planet', scientists in Saudi Arabia are using solar energy to produce fresh water in the desert. ___

b Data from the United Nations shows that every year, nearly 2% of healthy desert disappears. ___

c 'Global Deserts Outlook' says that tribes such as the Topnaar, in Southwestern Africa, are known for their ability to survive in the desert because of their deep understanding of the natural world. ___

DISCUSSION

6 Work with a partner. Discuss the questions.

1 What natural habitats exist in your country?
2 What human activities take place in those habitats?
3 Do you use any products or foods that come from those habitats?

CRITICAL THINKING

At the end of this unit you are going to do the speaking task below.

Give a presentation on the destruction of the Saharan desert habitat.

Organizing information in a presentation

Understanding the organization of information in a presentation can help you understand the development of the speaker's ideas. Outlines are useful ways to show the connection between main points, specific examples and details.

ANALYZE

1 Look at the outline on the next page of the first part of the talk from Listening 2. Label the columns with the words in the box.

background main idea detail example introduction solution

______	______	______	______	______	______
The decline and destruction of deserts	The desert environment	I Human survival	a People in deserts	1 Topnaar	Responsible mining, adopting animals, crop rotation
				2 Bedouins	
			b People in cities	1 minerals	
				2 agriculture	
		II Plant and animal survival	a Desert plants	1 Acacia tree	
			b Desert animals	1 Arabian oryx	

2 Look at the table again and write true (T) or false (F) next to the statements below.

The outline ...

1 ... shows clear connections between the presentation topic, main ideas, examples and supporting details. ______
2 ... shows the order of the parts of the presentation. ______
3 ... tells the speaker exactly what to say in the presentation. ______
4 ... includes irrelevant details that do not belong in the talk. ______
5 ... shows where the speaker got the information for the talk. ______
6 ... shows the name of the person giving the presentation. ______

CREATE

3 Work with a partner. Look at the notes and create an outline for a talk on page 116.

Habitat destruction:

- *Habitat destruction caused by humans*
- *Habitat destruction that occurs naturally*
- *Natural disasters*
- *Agriculture*
- *Building*
- *Pollution*
- *Natural climate change*
- *40% of Iraq's agricultural land now too salty to grow crops*
- *About 70% of Amazon rainforest now used for cattle ranching*
- *Average size of living space per person has doubled since 1950*
- *City growth in the Alps destroys plant and animal habitats*
- *Even very wild places such as the Arctic are now polluted*
- *Huge storms damage forests*
- *Many animals have become extinct naturally*
- *Past 10,000 years, Earth slowly warming*
- *Volcanic eruption in Indonesia in 2012 destroyed four square kilometres of forest*
- *Whales and dolphins often become ill from chemical pollution*

introduction	background	main idea	example	detail	solution

4 Compare your answers with a partner. Did you have the same answers?

SPEAKING

PREPARATION FOR SPEAKING

Signpositing language in a presentation

Signposting explains the structure of your presentation to your audience. You can use signposting throughout your talk to help the audience understand the talk's structure.

1 Look at the signposting language below. Match the phrases in bold (1–8) to the purpose they serve in the presentation (a–h).

1 But, **what does this mean** for the rest of the world?
2 **To put it another way**, we will all be affected.
3 **Moving on now to** the typical desert environment.
4 **A good example of this** is Egyptian cotton, famous all over the world.
5 **That's all I have to say** on that point.
6 **Let's begin by** looking at information from the United Nations Environment Programme.
7 **To summarize**, deserts are not only important to the people who live in them.
8 **The subject of my talk today** is the decline and destruction of the world's deserts.

a introducing the topic ______
b overview ______
c finishing a section ______
d starting a new section ______
e querying and analyzing ______
f giving examples ______
g paraphrasing and clarifying ______
h summarizing and concluding ______

2 Match the phrases below to the purpose that they serve in a presentation in Exercise 1 (a–h).

1 That concludes this part of the talk ... ______
2 To give you an example ... ______
3 Let's turn now to ... ______
4 I'd like to now recap ... ______
5 Today I'm going to talk about ... ______
6 Let's consider this in more detail ... ______
7 So what I'm saying is ... ______
8 I have three main points to make in this talk ... ______

Giving background information and explaining a problem

Background information is usually necessary to put a problem in context, i.e. say *why* it is a problem. One way of structuring this background information is to give main ideas, examples of those ideas and details to clarify the examples.

3 Read the phrases. Match the items (1–6) with the purposes they serve in a presentation (a–f).

1 According to the Food and Agriculture Organization of the United Nations, millions of people around the world survive by eating fish.
2 Data shows that the amount of man-made chemicals in the oceans is increasing. 80% of ocean pollution comes from human activity on land.
3 If we continue to pollute the world's oceans, marine plants and animals will not survive.
4 Oceans are essential for life on Earth. People rely on them for survival.
5 All of us who rely on the oceans for food will then have to find different food sources.
6 Human activity is destroying oceans all over the world. The two main problems are pollution and over-fishing.

a introduces the background information
b gives a specific detail that illustrates the background information
c says what the main problem is
d gives details that explain the problem
e explains the consequences of the problem
f says how the problem might personally affect the audience

SPEAKING TASK

Give a presentation on the destruction of the Saharan desert habitat.

PREPARE

1 Work in groups to plan your presentation. Look at the information in the fact file on page 119 and brainstorm three main points to include in the presentation. Try to include interesting information that will attract your listeners' attention.

SAHARA DESERT FACT FILE

- Largest desert in the world – 9 million square kilometres
- Aswan Dam on River Nile provides electricity and water storage
- In recent years has been spreading to the south
- About 90 major, inhabited oases in Sahara
- River Nile provides fresh water
- Thousands of years ago – Sahara was greener and not so dry
- Damage to Sahara: overgrazing, poor irrigation, removal of plants that hold soil in place – leads to desertification
- New technology: a glue-like substance can be put on desert sands to stop it blowing away in dust storms
- Trees have been planted along southern edge of Sahara to form windbreaks and to stop sand entering populated areas
- Scientists predict that rainfall in the Sahara will decline in the future
- Rapid population growth can lead to resource overuse and killing of plant life
- 2.5 million people live in the Sahara desert
- 50 degrees centigrade temperatures are not unusual
- Camels are used for transport, meat, and milk

2 Think of solutions to each point you chose. Use the information (main points, detail on each main point and examples) from the fact file to use to give background to your presentation. Write your final ideas in the chart below.

main idea	detail	example	solution

3 Your presentation will need a short introduction and conclusion. Make notes based on the fact file about what you could include in these sections of your presentation. Use language from the Preparation for speaking section to help you.

PRACTISE

4 Practise your presentation in your group.

DISCUSS

5 Form a new group and give your presentation. Were the other students' presentations similar to your own? Why / Why not?

TASK CHECKLIST	✔
Did you use signposting?	
Did you give background information?	
Did you explain the problem?	
Did you stress words for emphasis?	
Did you explain solutions?	

OBJECTIVES REVIEW

I can ...

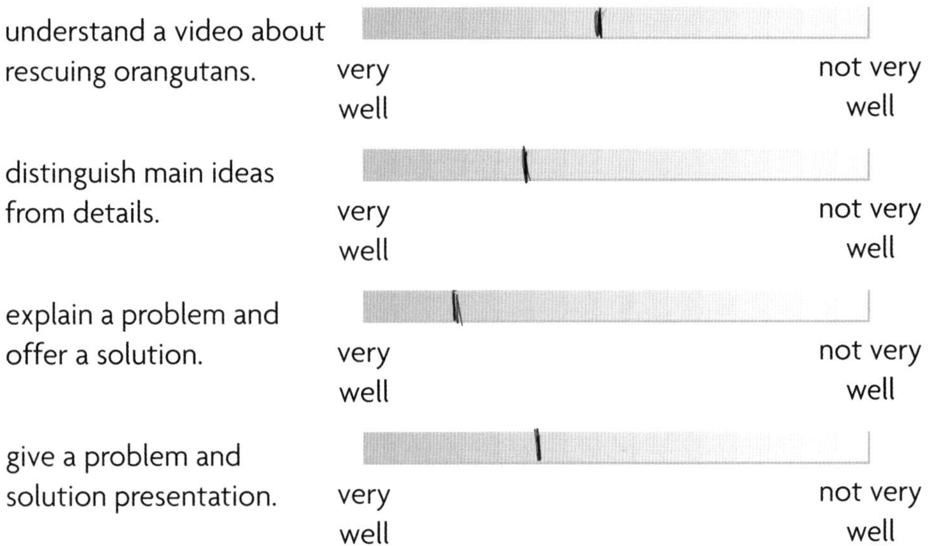

understand a video about rescuing orangutans. very well — not very well

distinguish main ideas from details. very well — not very well

explain a problem and offer a solution. very well — not very well

give a problem and solution presentation. very well — not very well

WORDLIST

UNIT VOCABULARY	ACADEMIC VOCABULARY
capture (v)	adapt (v)
coastal (adj)	affect (v)
conservation (n)	decline (v)
conservationist (n)	destruction (n)
copper (n)	diamond (n)
dust storm (n)	exploit (v)
endangered species (n)	extract (v)
habitat (n)	impact (v)
logging (n)	mineral (n)
mining (n)	resource (n)
natural gas (n)	source (n)
orangutan (n)	surface (n)
rainforest (n)	survive (v)
rescue centre (n)	waste (n)
species (n)	

LEARNING OBJECTIVES

Watch and listen	Watch and understand a video about architecture in China
Listening skills	Understand analogies
Speaking skills	Identify problems and suggest solutions
Speaking task	Discuss a problem and possible solutions

ARCHITECTURE UNIT 7

UNLOCK YOUR KNOWLEDGE

Work with a partner. Discuss the questions below.

1 Where do you think this building is?
2 Who do you think might use the building? What it is used for?
3 What do you think the advantages and disadvantages of the building are?

WATCH AND LISTEN

PREPARING TO WATCH

UNDERSTANDING KEY VOCABULARY

1 You are going to watch a video about architecture in China. Before you watch, match the words (1–8) to the definitions (a–h).

1 brick
2 construction
3 preserve
4 complex
5 landmark
6 development
7 heritage
8 structure

a a large building that has been made from different parts
b a building that can be easily recognized, that helps you to locate where you are
c a large building with connected rooms, or a related group of buildings
d a hard, rectangular block used to build walls and houses
e traditional buildings, art, etc which have existed in a culture for a long time
f the act of building something, especially houses, offices, etc.
g to keep something as it is and stop it becoming damaged
h an area on which new buildings are built to make a profit

2 Complete the sentences below with the words from Exercise 1.

1 To build the new building, the developer first had to destroy a ______________ wall.
2 They expected the new shopping ______________ to cost $1 billion.
3 They wanted it to be a ______________ building, like the Eiffel Tower.
4 The building design was traditional to keep in with the ______________ of the area.
5 It was important that the developers ______________ the old buildings in the area.
6 Care was taken to make sure that the ______________ of the building was as quiet as possible.

7 The new housing ______________ consisted of over 200 houses.
8 The new office block is a steel and glass ______________ .

WHILE WATCHING

UNDERSTANDING MAIN IDEAS

3 Watch the video. Circle the correct expression to complete the sentences.

1 The Forbidden City is an example of *traditional / high-rise* Chinese architecture.
2 The Great Wall stretches from Shanhaiguan to *Beijing / Lop Lake*.
3 There is increasing pressure on Chinese architects to build new *housing developments / architectural landmarks*.
4 Traditional housing in Beijing is being *preserved / constructed* for future generations to enjoy.

UNDERSTANDING DETAIL

4 Watch again. Write true (T) or false (F) next to the statements below.

1 Beijing is home to over 12 million people. _____
2 The city boasts internationally famous architectural sites such as the Forbidden City. _____
3 The Forbidden City is the largest single wooden structure in the world. _____
4 The Great Wall of China is over 8000 kilometres long. _____
5 There is a ship on the top of each watchtower on the Great Wall. _____
6 High-rise buildings in Beijing are quick and cheap to put up. _____
7 All of the housing in Beijing is modern. _____

DISCUSSION

5 Work with a partner. Discuss the questions.

1 What are the advantages and disadvantages of high and low-rise buildings?
2 What are the differences between traditional and modern buildings in your country?
3 Are there any architectural wonders in your country? When were they built? How were or are they used?

LISTENING 1

PREPARING TO LISTEN

UNDERSTANDING KEY VOCABULARY

1 You are going to listen to a conversation between two property developers. Before you listen, label the diagram with the words in the box below. Some of them have been done for you.

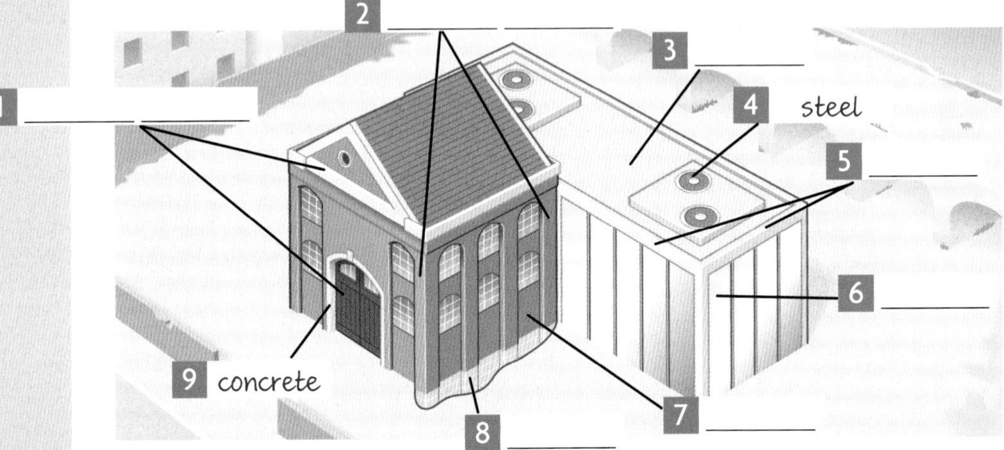

beams original features glass foundations steel supporting walls concrete stone extension

2 Write the words from the box above in the correct column below.

building materials	architectural features

USING YOUR KNOWLEDGE

3 Work with a partner. Discuss the questions.

1 What materials are old buildings usually made of?
2 What materials are modern buildings usually made of?
3 Would you like to live in an apartment like the one in Exercise 1? Why / Why not?

WHILE LISTENING

LISTENING FOR MAIN IDEAS

4 7.1 Listen to the conversation. What do the developers decide to do?

1 Contact a local neighbourhood association for their views on plans for the warehouse.
2 Restore the warehouse and put offices and flats in the building.
3 Knock down the warehouse and build a restaurant on the site.

LISTENING FOR DETAIL

5 7.1 Listen to the conversation again. Correct the notes below.

1 Both developers think a building development in Westside is a good idea.

2 There isn't any regeneration going on in Westside.

3 There has been a lot of investment in the area in the past 20 years.

4 The developers think the best idea would be to knock down the warehouse.

5 The developers need to choose between a contemporary building style and a traditional one.

6 The building can't offer floor space for any shops.

7 Shop units would have to be on the second floor.

8 Refurbishment would mean removing all the original features of the building.

POST-LISTENING

Understanding analogies

An analogy describes something by comparing it to another thing with similar qualities. Understanding the qualities of something can help you understand the meaning of an analogy. If we say *The room was as cold as ice* we usually mean that the room was very cold, though probably not literally freezing.

LISTENING FOR OPINION

6 Match the analogies (1–4) to the meanings below (a–d).

1 I'm afraid we might be **biting off more than we can chew**.
2 I think it's a **potential goldmine**.
3 That building is more **like a prison** than a potential shopping centre.
4 We could give the old building **a new lease of life**.

a a fresh beginning ______
b trying to do a bigger job than we can realistically do ______
c a building that no one wants to visit ______
d an opportunity to make a lot of money ______

7 Which analogies support knocking the old building down? Which support converting and modernizing it? Why?

8 Work with a partner. Use the four analogies from Exercise 6 to describe a building in your local area.

PRONUNCIATION FOR LISTENING

Emphasis in contrasting opinions

When you state an opinion that is different from somebody else's, you can emphasize your opinion by stressing the information that is different from theirs.

9 7.2 Listen to the sentences. Underline the words that are emphasized in Sentence B in each case. The first one has been done for you.

1 A: I think the original building has a lot of potential.
  B: I think we really want to transform the area with something modern.
2 A: It has some beautiful original features.
  B: It looks as though it's about to collapse!
3 A: Acquiring such an old building could be a mistake.
  B: Really? I think the project could be a great success.
4 A: It would be more of a transformation if we built a modern building made of materials like steel and glass.
  B: We'll maintain more of a connection to the past if we include the old building as part of the new one.

10 Work with a partner. Practise saying the sentences.

DISCUSSION

11 Work with a partner. Discuss the questions.

1 Think of an old building in your area. What materials is it made of? What architectural features does it have?
2 Think of a building you would like to change. How would you do it? What materials would you use?
3 Do you think it is a good idea to add modern features to historical buildings? Why / Why not?

LANGUAGE DEVELOPMENT

VERBS WITH FUTURE MEANING

EXPLANATION

Verbs with future meaning

We usually use *will*, *be going to* and present tense forms to talk about the future. However, some verbs imply that something will happen without having to use a future tense.

We **hope** to finish the job on time.
We **envisage** building something modern.

1 Complete the sentences below with the words from the box.

to begin   to consult   to call   keeping   to visit
constructing   to meet   to have

1 We **hope** ______________________ work on the development next week.
2 We **anticipate** ______________________ a glass and steel extension.
3 They **intend** ______________________ the local business association on the project.
4 They **envisage** ______________________ the building's original features.
5 He **promises** ______________________ you if we have any questions.
6 I **expect** ______________________ more customers next year.
7 She **plans** ______________________ Riyadh next month.
8 I **can arrange** ______________________ the architect next week.

2 Use the prompts to write sentences about the future.

1 He / hope / study law / at university
____
2 She / plan / live / in the UK
____
3 She / promise / send / you an email
____
4 They /anticipate / take / university entrance exams next year
____
5 I / expect / see Fawaz in the library
____
6 We / intend / start / construction on the project / next weekend
____

ACADEMIC VOCABULARY FOR ARCHITECTURE AND TRANSFORMATION

3 Read the newspaper article. Match the words in bold (1–8) to the definitions (a–h).

ARCHITECTURE AND TRANSFORMATION

Architecture can (1)**transform** the way people interact with the world, and architects must (2) **anticipate** how a building will impact on the local area. If the design of a building includes a lot of large windows, the people working inside (3)**maintain** a connection with nature, because they can see the sky. When people (4)**abandon** old warehouses, which are left to collapse, this creates an opportunity for developers, who (5)**acquire** such properties to (6)**convert** into shops, flats and offices. Developing an old building can (7)**contribute** to the improvement of a whole neighbourhood, but suitable sites can be difficult to identify as cities (8)**expand**.

a to give something, especially money, to achieve something ______
b to completely change the appearance, form or character of something ______
c to continue to have, or keep in existence ______
d to increase in size, number or importance ______
e to imagine or expect that something will happen ______
f the act of leaving something forever ______
g the act of changing something from one thing to another ______
h to buy or get something ______

4 Complete the table below with the words from Exercise 3.

verb	noun	verb	noun
______	anticipation	______	abandonment
______	contribution	______	conversion
______	maintenence	______	acquisition
______	transformation	______	expansion

5 Complete the sentences with words from the table.

1 We need to ________________ the amount of retail space available.
2 We could ________________ the local area with a new retail complex.
3 A new business district would make a vital ________________ to the local economy.
4 We ________________ that the shopping area will bring $30 million in profit over the year.
5 The ________________ from warehouse to apartment block was a major success.
6 It may be difficult to ________________ a piece of land within the city.
7 We can't ________________ this project just because of a few set backs.
8 We will ________________ the number of houses in the new development, not increase it.

LISTENING 2

PREPARING TO LISTEN

USING YOUR KNOWLEDGE

1 You are going to listen to a housing development meeting. Before you listen, work with a partner and think of solutions to the potential problems in the housing development plan below.

1 There isn't enough parking for people visiting the development.

2 There is a tall building blocking the light into another apartment block in the development.

3 There are no green spaces or parks around the development.

4 The modern design of the development doesn't fit with the traditional buildings in the area.

2 Compare your answers with another pair. Did you have the same ideas?

UNDERSTANDING KEY VOCABULARY

3 Match the words in bold in the sentences (1–8) to the meanings (a–h).

1 We're **concerned** about the size of the building.
2 The old building is **adequate**.
3 The **current** building doesn't need to change.
4 The **existing** decoration needs to be changed completely.
5 We need something that is **appropriate** for the local area.
6 The plan is very **sympathetic** to the existing buildings.
7 A building of that size could be **controversial**.
8 The plan is very **ambitious**.

a The decoration at the moment is terrible.
b The plan will be difficult to achieve.
c We need a building that fits in with the local environment.
d The building we have now is fine.
e People will disagree about whether the size of the building is acceptable.
f Even though the building could be better, it's good enough.
g The plan fits in with the style of the buildings in the area.
h We're worried it's just too big.

4 Work with a partner. Use the adjectives in bold from Exercise 3 to describe the pictures in Exercise 5.

WHILE LISTENING

LISTENING FOR GIST

5 7.3 Listen to the housing development meeting. Match the descriptions to the correct pictures.

1 The proposed building site ______
2 The developers' proposal ______
3 The clients' preferred proposal ______
4 A proposal not discussed in the meeting ______

6 7.3 Listen to the meeting again. Write developers (D) or clients (C) next to the statements.

LISTENING FOR DETAIL

1 One of the biggest benefits of this plan is that it will create accommodation for up to 80 households. _____
2 We could consider using reflective glass. _____
3 You've described the natural area you'd like to build on as wasteland, but actually, that's a woodland. _____
4 As it stands, this plan would be very controversial. _____
5 Have you thought about more, smaller, lower buildings? _____
6 Lots of glass is a great idea, but in my view the only viable option is to use brick. _____
7 How about if we position the new buildings near the edge of the site? _____
8 I feel confident we can come up with a suitable plan if you give us a couple of weeks. _____

POST-LISTENING

Making Suggestions

When making suggestions speakers use different language to emphasize their point, depending on how strongly they feel about it. To make a strong suggestion adverbs like *highly* and *strongly* are used. To make a tentative suggestion, polite expressions like *Could I suggest* and *Wouldn't it be better if ...* are used.

7 Write strong (S) or tentative (T) next to the sentences below.

LISTENING FOR ATTITUDE

1 What about more, smaller, lower buildings? _____
2 In my view the only viable option is to use brick. _____
3 This would probably be better with the existing houses. _____
4 I strongly recommend that we reconsider the size. _____
5 Can I suggest we use this first design you've supplied to identify a few priorities? _____
6 I like your thinking. I agree completely. _____

DISCUSSION

8 Work with a partner. Discuss the questions.

1 In your country, what makes a house or apartment attractive?
2 Do you think it is better to live in an apartment or a house? Why?
3 Where do you think it is best to build new houses or developments on old sites or in new green areas? Why?

CRITICAL THINKING

At the end of this unit you are going to do the speaking task below.

> Discuss the problem and possible solutions: A petroleum company owns an apartment block where 200 single workers and 50 families live. The apartments are cramped, uncomfortable and too far away from international schools and the workers' main offices. The company needs the workers to move out of the current block one year from now. They have $3.8 million to spend on new accommodation projects.

REMEMBER

1 Work with a partner to make a list of requirements for the new accommodation.

- Must have more space

ANALYZE

2 Look at the three accommodation solutions below (a–c). Compare your list of project requirements to each solution and answer the questions.

1 Which project requirements does the solution meet?
2 Which project requirements does the solution not meet?
3 What would you need to change to make each solution fit the project requirements better?

Option A: Al Qasim Tower

- Available in six months
- Eight-storey office block made of glass and steel
- Offices could be converted to bedrooms
- Toilets would be shared
- Shower rooms could be added on each floor
- Could accommodate up to 180 single workers and 40 families
- Located 3 kilometres from offices/factory
- Near subway line for 8 kilometre journey to international school
- No facilities (parks, green spaces) for children nearby
- Price: $3.2 million
- Conversion cost: $600,000

Option B: Iqbal House Hotel

- Available now
- 1920s hotel made of brick
- Could accommodate up to 210 single workers and 30 families
- Lots of traditional architectural features
- Hotel was abandoned 10 years ago
- Located 4 kilometres from offices/factory
- Located 10 kilometres from international school by road
- Plenty of open space for children to play and for adults to walk, cycle, etc.
- Price: $1.6 million
- Conversion cost: $2.4 million

Option C: Land purchase

- Land available now
- Would need to complete government planning process before building (about 3 months, building would take another 3 months)
- Could accommodate up to 250 single people and 60 families in up to 6 apartment blocks, option to build more accommodation in future
- Located 6 kilometres from offices/factory
- Located 12 kilometres from international school by road, bus and train
- Plans could include full recreational facilities for adults and children
- Land price: $1.1 million
- Estimated building costs: $3 million

3 Work with another pair. Compare your answers to Exercise 2 and answer the questions below.

EVALUATE

1 Which solution do you think best meets the project requirements?
2 What points does each scheme have that might impact on your decision?
3 Can you come to a group decision? Why / Why not?

SPEAKING

PREPARATION FOR SPEAKING

PRONUNCIATION FOR SPEAKING

Emphasizing a word or idea to signal a problem

Emphasizing or stressing a word in a sentence can help listeners understand its importance. Changing the emphasized or stressed word also changes the important piece of information in that sentence, and can be used to signal a problem.

1 7.4 Listen. Underline the word emphasized in each sentence. The first one is done for you.

1 The <u>main</u> issue is that most retailers don't want to do business here.
2 The main issue is that most retailers don't want to do business here.
3 The main issue is that most retailers don't want to do business here.
4 The main issue is that most retailers don't want to do business here.

2 Match the explanations below (a–d) with a sentence from Exercise 1.

a There are other types of business that will be happy to do business here, but retailers don't want to. ______
b There are other issues, but this is the most important one. ______
c Retailers are happy to put up advertising here, but they don't want to open shops in this area. ______
d There are aspects of the project that aren't issues, but this particular fact is a problem. ______

Presenting a problem

When presenting a problem, we often use phrases that signal there is an issue, such as: *The problem is … , The main issue is … ,* and *We need to find a way around …*

3 Put the words in order to make sentences.

1 of / prices / We / a / high / need / problem / to / the / find/ around / way / .
2 time / The / is / problem / enough / we / that / have / don't / .
3 issue / main / The / is / people / that / our / don't / design / like / .
4 a / around / way / find / need / We / to / problem / the / attracting / business / of / .
5 the / is / building / The / issue / main / that / is / collapsing / .
6 problem / that / The / is / no-one / to / wants / area / in / live / the / .

Making polite suggestions

Making a suggestion in the form of a question can be more polite than using a direct statement such as *I think …* or *We have to …* This approach to making suggestions is more common when people are brainstorming and exploring a variety of ideas. Using it means the speaker is less likely to offend anyone. It is also a more formal way of speaking.

4 Write six suggestions using the structures in the box.

<table>
<tr><td rowspan="2">1 Could we …
2 Can I suggest we …
3 Should we consider …
4 How about …
5 Have you thought about …
6 Why don't we …</td><td>increase</td><td rowspan="2">the budget?</td></tr>
<tr><td>increasing</td></tr>
</table>

5 Work with a partner. Take turns to make suggestions for each of the problems below. Use the structures from Exercise 4 to help you.

1 We have no facilities for car parking in the local area. (build car park)
We could build a car park.
2 The planned building is too high. (reduce height)
3 There isn't enough outdoor space in the area. (turn wasteland into a park)
4 There isn't any space for a garden around the apartment block. (build a roof garden)
5 The shop units are too small to attract large retailers. (have more, larger units)
6 We won't be able to attract businesses to this area. (offer lower rents)

RESPONDING TO SUGGESTED SOLUTIONS

6 Read the suggested solutions and tick the correct box.

	accepting	rejecting
1 That's a great idea, but I'm not sure it addresses the problem.		
2 I like your thinking. I agree completely.		
3 I think that's a great idea.		
4 We thought that might be an option at first, but now we realize it won't work.		
5 That seems an obvious solution, but it doesn't address the issue of cost.		
6 Let's do it.		

7 Work with a partner. Practise saying the sentences below. Take turns to make the suggestion and to accept or reject it, using phrases from Exercises 4 and 6.

1 How about building four smaller apartment blocks rather than one large one?
2 Should we include a community garden in the new development?
3 Can I suggest we reduce the size and scale of this development?

SPEAKING TASK

Discuss the problem and possible solutions: A petroleum company owns an apartment block where 200 single workers and 50 families live. The apartments are cramped, uncomfortable and too far away from international schools and the workers' main offices. The company needs the workers to move out of the current block one year from now. They have $3.8 million to spend on new accommodation projects.

PREPARE

1 Work in groups of four. Look at the list of project requirements that you wrote in the Critical thinking section. Choose one solution to the problem to look at.

2 Work in two pairs. One pair are the project developers. The other pair are the project clients.

3 In your pairs, look at the project requirements and the solution. Answer the questions.

1 Which of the requirements does the solution meet?
2 Which of the requirements does the solution not meet?
3 What would have to change to make each solution fit the requirements?

Project developers: You will present your solution to your clients. You need to highlight the positive aspects of your solution. Think about the negative aspects to your solution. What problems might the client identify? How could you respond?
Project clients: You will listen to a presentation from the project developers. You need to ask questions about any information that they don't mention in their solution, or anything you aren't sure about. What problems might you need to identify?

PRACTISE

4 Practise your presentation/questions with your partner.

DISCUSS

5 Discuss the problem and solution as a group.

TASK CHECKLIST	✔
Did you identify problems and suggest solutions?	
Did you emphasize words and ideas to signal problems?	
Did you make polite suggestions?	
Did you respond to suggested solutions?	

OBJECTIVES REVIEW

I can ...

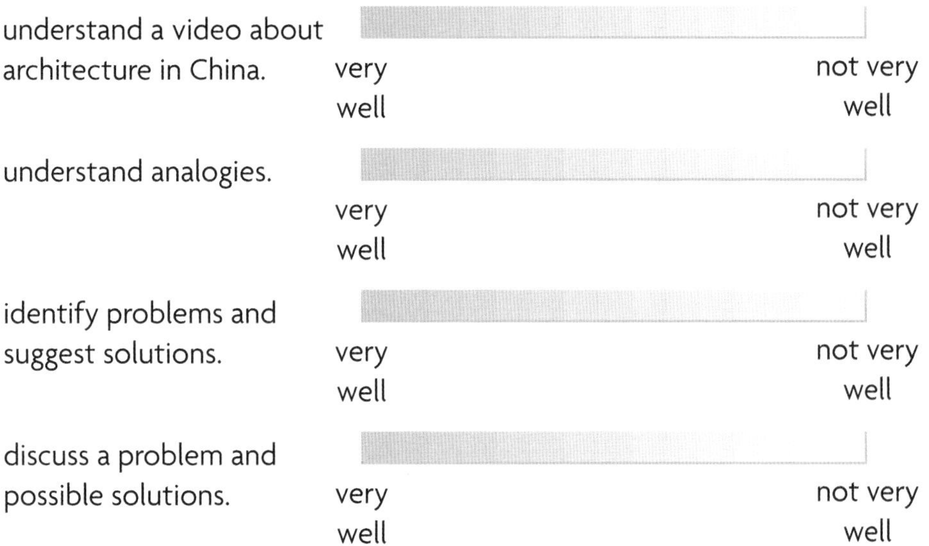

understand a video about architecture in China.	very well	not very well
understand analogies.	very well	not very well
identify problems and suggest solutions.	very well	not very well
discuss a problem and possible solutions.	very well	not very well

WORDLIST

UNIT VOCABULARY	ACADEMIC VOCABULARY
beam (n)	abandon (v)
concerned (adj)	ambitious (adj)
concrete (n)	brick (n)
convert (v)	contribute (v)
development (n)	controversial (adj)
existing (adj)	current (adj)
extension (n)	expand (v)
foundation (n)	feature (n)
heritage (n)	maintain (v)
landmark (n)	preserve (v)
supporting wall (n)	steel (n)
	stone (n)
	structure (n)
	sympathetic (adj)
	transform (v)

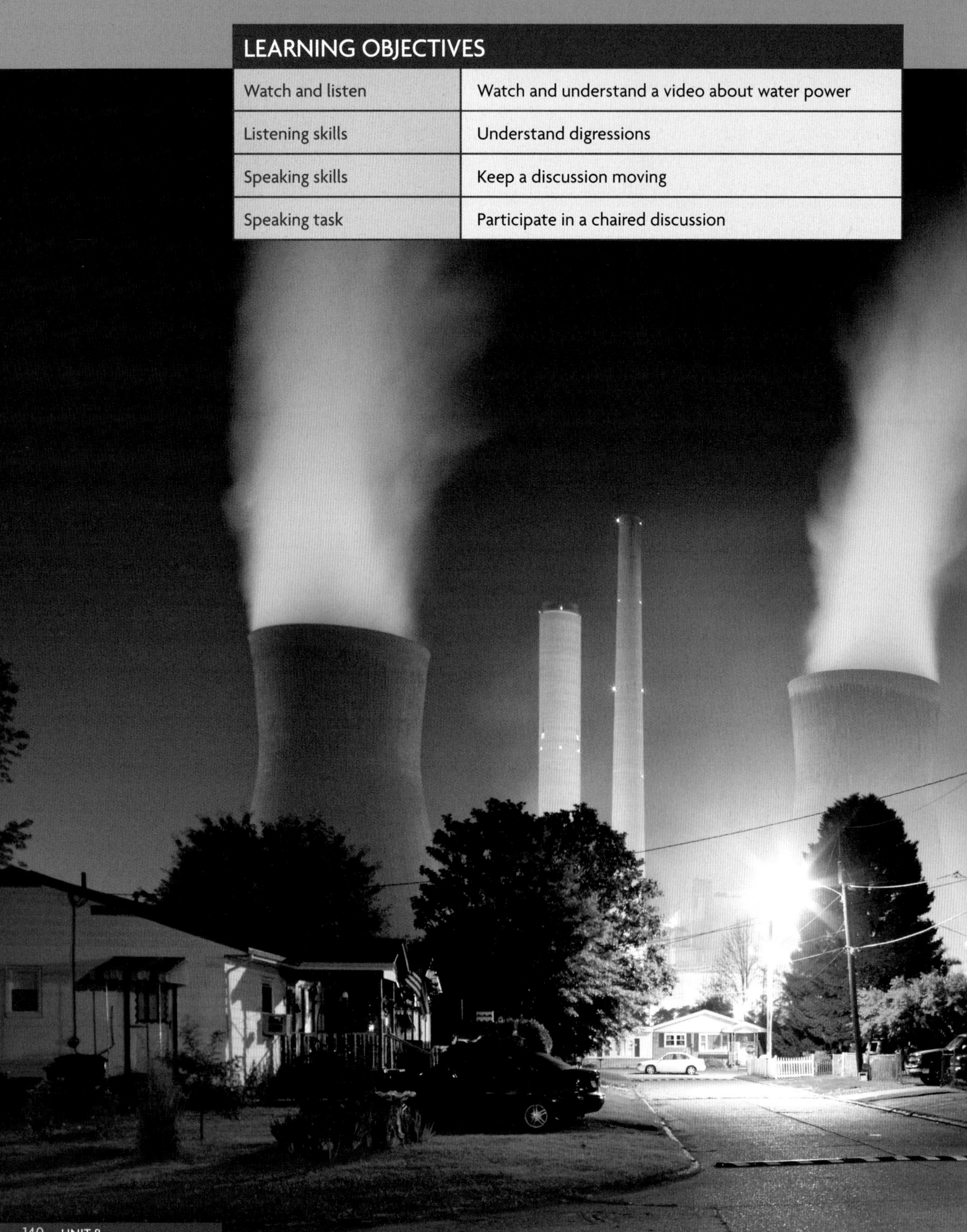

LEARNING OBJECTIVES

Watch and listen	Watch and understand a video about water power
Listening skills	Understand digressions
Speaking skills	Keep a discussion moving
Speaking task	Participate in a chaired discussion

ENERGY UNIT 8

UNLOCK YOUR KNOWLEDGE

Work with a partner. Discuss the questions below.

1 What did people use to generate light and heat before electricity was discovered?
2 How did people travel before cars were invented?
3 What fuel sources do we use for heat, light and transport today?
4 What fuel sources do you think we will be using in 100 years' time?

WATCH AND LISTEN

PREPARING TO WATCH

UNDERSTANDING KEY VOCABULARY

1 You are going to watch a video about water power. Before you watch, match the words (1–7) to the definitions (a–g).

1 dam
2 reservoir
3 generator
4 turbine
5 pipe
6 shaft
7 tower

a an artificial lake where water is stored
b a machine which uses the pressure of a liquid or gas to produce power
c a wall built across a river to stop the river's flow and collect water
d a machine that produces electricity
e a tall, narrow structure
f a tube through which a liquid or gas flows
g a rod in an engine or machine that turns to pass power on to another part of the machine

2 Complete the diagram using words from Exercise 1.

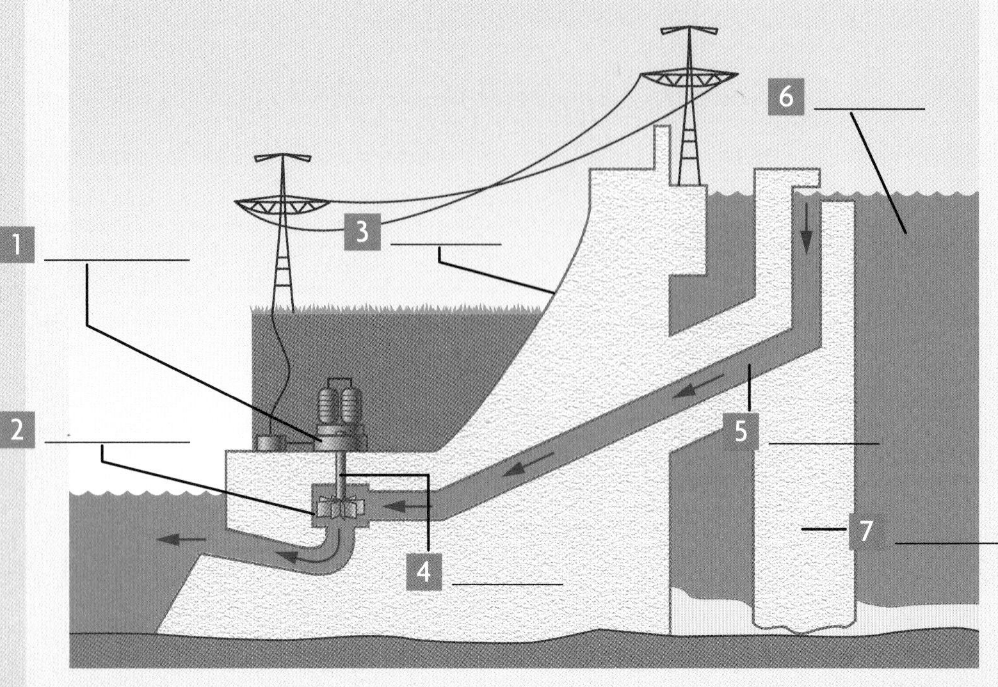

WHILE WATCHING

UNDERSTANDING MAIN IDEAS

3 Watch the video. Write true (T) or false (F) next to the statements about hydroelectric power.

1 Hydroelectric power provides the majority of the world's energy. ____
2 Building dams makes rivers flow faster. ____
3 Building dams often destroys animal habitats. ____
4 Water in reservoirs is colder than in rivers. ____

LISTENING FOR KEY INFORMATION

4 Watch again. Number the information (a–h) in the order you hear it.

a Lake Mead is 180 kilometres long. ____
b California has perfect weather and soil for agriculture. ____
c Rainfall in California can be a little as 18 centimetres per year. ____
d Water enters the dam through the towers. ____
e About 24 % of the world's electricity is generated hydroelectrically. ____
f The turbines turn 180 times per minute. ____
g Water from a reservoir may be the wrong temperature for some plants and animals. ____
h When the water reaches the turbines, it's moving at about 100 kilometres per hour. ____

DISCUSSION

5 Work with a partner. Discuss the questions.

1 Does your country use hydroelectric power? If so, where?
2 What other ways is electricity generated in your country?
3 What are the benefits of hydroelectric power compared with other sources of energy?

LISTENING 1

PREPARING TO LISTEN

USING YOUR KNOWLEDGE

1 You are going to listen to a radio interview about the island of El Hierro. Before you listen, complete the fact file with the words in the box.

area government mainland population

FACT FILE: *The Island of* **EL HIERRO**

(1)____________________ : part of Spain
(2)____________________ : 11,000
(3)____________________ : 278 km^2
Distance to the nearest
(4)________________ : 400 km
Claim to fame: energy independent

2 Work in pairs. Answer the questions.

1 What do you think life is like on El Hierro?
2 What would probably need to be imported from the mainland?
3 What sort of energy supply do you think is available there?
4 What do you think *energy independent* means?

3 Compare answers with another pair.

WHILE LISTENING

LISTENING FOR GIST

4 8.1 Listen to the radio interview about El Hierro. Choose the best option (a–c) to complete the sentence.

1 The people of El Hierro ...
   a need to buy all of their oil.
   b need to buy 30% of their oil.
   c don't need to buy any oil.
2 El Hierro's energy is provided by ...
   a wind and hydroelectric power.
   b solar and wind power and imported oil.
   c solar and hydroelectric power.
3 The system also provides water for ...
   a a small lake filled with fish.
   b a water park.
   c drinking and agriculture.

LISTENING FOR DETAIL

5 8.1 Listen to the radio interview again. Complete the sentences.

1 El Hierro is ____________ from Madrid, off the coast of ____________ .
2 The island used to ship ____________ barrels of oil from the mainland every year.
3 The wind now generates power for about ____________ of the year.
4 This is enough electricity to power about ____________ homes.
5 El Hierro has a reservoir in a ____________ , 700 metres above sea level.
6 ____________ are used to pump water uphill into the reservoir.
7 Wind turbines power ____________ so hydroelectric power can be used.
8 Water from the desalination plant is used as ____________ and in ____________ .

POST-LISTENING

Understanding digressions

Speakers sometimes move away from the main topic in a conversation, often because they haven't prepared answers to questions, or simply because they aren't thinking about the question they have been asked. Recognising when someone is digressing can help you move the focus back to the main topic of a conversation.

LISTEN FOR TEXT ORGANIZATION FEATURES

6 Look at the topics Pedro talks about during the interview. Write relevant (R) or digression (D).

1 Peace and quiet	_____	4 The sound of the sea	_____
2 Traffic in Madrid	_____	5 The banking profession	_____
3 The fast pace of city life	_____	6 Freedom on the island	_____

7 Match the questions (1–3) to the relevant answers (a–c) and a digression related to the same topic (i–iii).

1 What is the most important power source on El Hierro?
2 Can life be hard on El Hierro?
3 What do you miss about living on the mainland?

a Having easy access to facilities, like cinemas and a variety or restaurants.
b Probably the wind turbines. Without them we wouldn't be able to power the pump system for the water.
c It can be difficult in the winter, when the sea is rough. Basic supplies often take several days longer to arrive.

i My children think it's boring here, but I wanted them to grow up with the freedom to explore outside.
ii I didn't like living in my old city. It was too noisy and the buildings were too tall.
iii We've thought about installing solar panels to generate extra electricity on the island.

PRONUNCIATION FOR LISTENING

Intonation related to emotion

Intonation can tell us a lot about a person's feelings when they are talking.

8 8.2 Listen to the same sentence spoken with four different emotions.

Max has gone to Spain.

1 annoyance
2 sadness
3 surprise
4 excitement

9 8.3 Listen. Circle the emotion expressed in the sentences.

1 Don't you like it here? *sadness / excitement*
2 El Hierro is completely energy-independent. *excitement / sadness*
3 Well, if you've spent a day or two here, you may have noticed we have a lot of wind on El Hierro. *excitement / annoyance*
4 But doesn't hydroelectric power require a river and a dam? *surprise / excitement*
5 In fact, I've just come from the desalination plant. *annoyance / sadness*

10 Work with a partner. Take turns saying the sentences with different emotions. Can your partner guess which emotion you're expressing?

DISCUSSION

11 Work with a partner. Discuss the questions.

1 Would you like to live on El Hierro? Why / Why not?
2 Are there any products or services that are difficult to get where you live? Why / Why not?
3 Does the weather in your country have any advantages or disadvantages for energy production?

LANGUAGE DEVELOPMENT

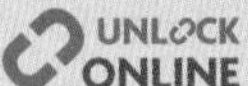

CONNECTING IDEAS BETWEEN SENTENCES

1 Read the sentences. Match the phrases in bold (1–3) to their function (a–c).

1 We're a long way from the mainland, **so** deliveries always take a few days.
2 You never feel like you can really relax. **What's more**, my career was in banking, which is an especially stressful job.
3 It's a real challenge living here. **On the other hand**, we all love it.

a giving extra information
b comparing and contrasting
c explaining a result

2 Complete the tables below with the titles (a–c) from Exercise 1, and the words and expressions from the box.

as a result   Moreover   Furthermore   In addition,
Even so   Nevertheless   therefore

______________________		
You never feel like you can really relax.	What's more, ______________ ______________ ______________	my career was in banking, which is an especially stressful job.

______________________		
It's a real challenge living here.	On the other hand, ______________ ______________	we all love it.

______________________		
We're a long way from the mainland,	so ______________ ______________	deliveries always take a few days.

3 Work in pairs. Use the expressions above to connect the sentences.

1 City life is stressful. Island life is relaxing. (compare and contrast)

____

2 The houses use solar energy. They have water recycling systems. (extra information)

____

3 Dams can damage habitats. They have to be planned carefully. (result)

____

4 The wind blows for 30% of the year. That isn't enough to provide all of the island's electricity. (compare and contrast)

____

5 This electric car can go 100 kilometres per hour. The battery can be charged using solar power. (extra information)

____

6 The system requires that water moves from a high place to a lower place. We've placed a water tank on a hill. (result)

____

ACADEMIC VOCABULARY FOR NETWORKS AND SYSTEMS

4 Read the article. Match the words in bold (1–10) to the correct definitions (a–j).

With the steady (1)**decline** in supplies of coal and oil, exploring the (2)**potential** of alternative energy sources has increased in recent decades. Installing an alternative energy (3)**generation** system to power an entire town is a huge (4)**challenge**. A single energy (5)**source**, such as solar or wind power, rarely has the (6)**capacity** to do this. Engineers and designers therefore need to come up with a (7)**network** of technologies to provide a consistent power supply from a variety of sources. Each (8)**element** of the system must take advantage of a natural resource when it is available. Wind turbines need a certain (9)**volume** of wind to produce electricity, so when the wind slows or stops, another part of the system needs to be able to perform the same (10)**function**.

a the production of energy in a particular form ______
b part of something ______
c the total amount of something ______
d the total amount of something that can be produced ______
e the origin or place something comes from ______
f something that requires great effort to be done successfully ______
g the natural purpose of something ______
h a system of parts that work together ______
i ability for something to develop, achieve or succeed ______
j a gradual decrease in something ______

5 Complete the collocations table with the words from Exercise 4.

biggest, face a, meet a, greatest, present a	1 ______________	faced, ahead
renewable alternative, main, primary, reliable	2 ______________	of energy/power
spare, storage, increase	3 ______________	of *X* litres
national, extensive	4 ______________	systems
key, essential, important, crucial, basic, critical	5 ______________	of *X*
sheer, sales, large, total, increase	6 ______________	of transactions, increased
perform a, normal, primary, specific	7 ______________	performed
fulfil, growth, enormous, full, realize	8 ______________	for appreciation, growth, harm
sharp, steep, steady, rapid, gradual, dramatic	9 ______________	in sales/prices/ manufacturing/revenue
electricity, power, renewable, energy	10 ______________	of (nuclear, biofuels), plant, network

6 Choose five collocations from the table and write sentences about your country using them. Read your sentences to a partner.

LISTENING 2

PREPARING TO LISTEN

USING YOUR KNOWLEDGE

1 You are going to listen to a meeting about saving energy in an office. Before you listen, look at the photograph and discuss the questions with a partner.

1 What things in an office environment use energy?
2 How could energy be saved in an office environment?

2 Read the text. Match the words in bold (1–8) to the definitions (a–h).

Simple measures to reduce energy (1)**consumption** can cut office energy bills by up to 20%. Some businesses, however, are going further to be (2)**environmentally-friendly**. Large energy saving schemes can save a lot of money as well as the environment, but there are (3)**limitations**. One (4)**drawback** of making an office (5)**energy-efficient** is that it is expensive in the beginning, although money is saved over time. Large, (6)**complex**, energy saving projects can also have a (7)**maintenance** cost that isn't often factored in, which can be costly, especially when the new technology is still (8)**experimental**.

a the amount of something used ______
b the work needed to keep something in good condition ______
c new and not tested ______
d using little energy ______
e something that is not as good as it could be ______
f involving a lot of different but related parts ______
g not harmful to the environment ______
h a disadvantage or negative part of a situation ______

WHILE LISTENING

LISTENING FOR GIST

3 8.4 Listen to the meeting. Write true (T) or false (F) next to the statements below.

1 The group are considering options for improving the office's energy efficiency. ______
2 The office currently uses a solar energy system. ______
3 Everyone agrees only large-scale systems offer effective ways to save energy in the office. ______
4 The group decides to implement small-scale changes at the end of the discussion. ______

LISTENING FOR DETAIL

4 8.4 Listen to the meeting again. Correct the sentences below.

1 The office wants to find one main solution to office energy consumption.

____

2 Energy efficient light bulbs take a long time to make cost savings.

____

3 The windows in the office are too small to let in enough daylight.

____

4 The office is going to install a low-energy photocopier.

____

5 It wouldn't be a good idea to market the business as 'green'.

____

6 The office will install a solar energy system on the roof of the building.

____

POST-LISTENING

Persuasive techniques

When giving an opinion or a suggestion in a discussion, speakers often use persuasive language to try to convince listeners that they are right, that their suggestion is a good idea, or that there is a problem with someone else's idea.

LISTENING FOR OPINION

5 Match the sentences (1–5) to the persuasive techniques (a–e).

1 Why don't we consider an alternative energy source?
2 There are other considerations. We'd have to look at the generating capacity of the systems.
3 The fact is, both systems Zara mentioned are technically complex and expensive to install.
4 I can't help but feel that a solar energy project would be too ambitious.
5 I can assure you that the company wouldn't do anything unsafe or illegal.

a challenging a point
b asking a question
c reassuring
d adding information
e expressing reservations

6 Work with a partner. Match the statements (1–5) to the persuasive techniques (a–e) in Exercise 5.

1 On that point, we could employ a window cleaner at a relatively low cost. ______
2 I don't think we need to worry about the cost of installing a system until we find one that would work for us. ______
3 I'm not convinced that we get enough sunshine here to make a solar power system effective. ______
4 Have you thought more about my idea of getting rid of a photocopier? ______
5 I see what you mean, but have you considered the fact that sometimes we do need to leave our computer screens on? ______

DISCUSSION

7 Work with a partner. Discuss the questions.

1 What other reasons can you think of for using alternative energy sources at home or in the workplace?
2 Can you think of ways to reduce energy consumption at home?
3 Would it be possible to install an energy generation system at your home? If so, what type of system would be suitable? If not, why not?

CRITICAL THINKING

At the end of this unit you are going to do the speaking task below.

> Discuss the question: How can we save energy in our college / university?

EXPLANATION

Identifying pros and cons when making a decision

A *pro* is a positive fact or feature of something. A *con* is a negative fact or feature of something. It is important to identify these points when assessing whether something is a good idea or not.

ANALYZE

1 In pairs, read the statements about removing one of two photocopiers from an office. Write pro (P) or con (C) for each statement.

1 Office energy consumption would be reduced. ______
2 Machine maintenance costs would be lower. ______
3 People might have to wait longer to make copies. ______
4 If the machine broke, there would be no way to make copies. ______
5 It might reduce the number of unnecessary copies made. ______

EVALUATE

2 Considering pros and cons is part of making a decision. Work with a partner and answer the questions.

1 When making a decision about an action to take, why is it useful to consider pros and cons?
2 How could a list of pros and cons help you make a decision about something?

APPLY

3 Work with a partner. Think of one way you could save energy at your university or college. Write your idea below. Then, in each box, write the pros and cons of the idea.

Idea ______________________________

The pros:	The cons:
______________	______________
______________	______________
______________	______________

4 In each box below, now write the pros and cons of NOT using your idea.

The pros of *not*:	The cons of *not*:
______________	______________
______________	______________
______________	______________

5 Look at the boxes above and answer the questions.

1 Which section has the most pros? Which section has the most cons?
2 Based on the chart, which decision do you think is the best: To implement the change or to not implement the change?

6 Work with another pair. Explain the pros and cons of your idea to them. Do they agree with your conclusion? Why / Why not?

SPEAKING

PREPARATION FOR SPEAKING

Asking for input, summarizing and keeping a discussion moving

A chaired meeting is a meeting or discussion with a leader (referred to as the *chair* or the *chairperson*). The chair usually asks participants to input on the discussion, summarizes main points and keeps the discussion moving.

1 Match the sentences (1–6) to the functions of a chairperson (a–c).

1 Sorry, but that's not really what we're discussing right now. ______
2 Does anyone have anything to say about this idea? ______
3 What are your views on the proposal? ______
4 I'd just like to recap the key points so far. ______
5 So, to sum up so far ... ______
6 Sorry, but could you hold that thought until I've finished, please? ______

a asking for input
b keeping the discussion moving / on topic
c summarizing

2 Complete the dialogue using expressions from Exercise 1.

A: ______________________ the key points so far: We agree that we want to reduce energy consumption and we want to consider an alternative energy source. ______________________ about a solar energy system?
B: I'm more concerned about the rubbish problem.
A: ______________________ discussing right now.

3 8.5 Listen and check your answers.

PRONUNCIATION FOR SPEAKING

Using a neutral tone of voice

When we feel excited, upset or angry, our tone of voice can become challenging. Maintaining a neutral, relaxed tone of voice can help stop a request for clarification on a point from sounding like a challenge or argument.

UNLOCK ONLINE

4 8.6 Listen. Write challenging (C) or neutral (N) next to the sentences below.

1 Sorry, but could you hold that thought until Abdul has finished, please? C
2 Sorry, but could you hold that thought until Abdul has finished, please? N
3 So are you saying you're against using solar power? ______
4 Could I just clarify something here? Are we talking about solar power or wind power? ______
5 Do you mean this is completely new technology? ______
6 Could I just clarify something here? Could we use a solar system on the roof of the building? ______
7 So are you saying we shouldn't get rid of one photocopier? ______
8 Do you mean that traditional light bulbs are much more expensive to run than the low-energy ones? ______

5 Work with a partner. Take turns saying the sentences in Exercise 4. Use either a neutral or a challenging tone. Can your partner tell which tone you're using?

Being firm but polite

The chair of a meeting sometimes needs to keep a discussion focused, deal with interruptions or ask people to stop talking. When speaking firmly to someone, you can still be polite by beginning phrases with *Sorry, but* ... and using expressions such as *Could you possibly* ... and *Would you mind* ... .

6 Read the examples. Work with a partner and practise making the sentences below (1–6) more polite.

direct	polite
Wait until Adil finishes.	Sorry, but would you mind waiting until Adil finishes, please?
That isn't what we're talking about.	Thank you for pointing that out, but it isn't really what we're talking about.
Save that for later in the discussion.	Please could you save that for later in the discussion?

1 Wait. I haven't finished speaking.
2 I don't understand. Explain.
3 That's off the topic.
4 Stop talking. We can't hear what Tom is saying.
5 Repeat that.
6 We need to move on to the next point.

SPEAKING TASK

Discuss the question: How can we save energy in our college/university?

Work in groups of three or four. Have a chaired meeting using the agenda below. Each student should be chair for one numbered item on the agenda.

AGENDA

1 Current problems with energy consumption
2 Possible alternative sources of energy (large scale ideas)
3 Other ways of reducing consumption (small scale ideas)
4 Summary and conclusions

PREPARE

1 Discuss the main problems with energy consumption in your college/ university. Write down a list of as many ideas as you can of ways to save energy.

2 Look at each idea and analyze the pros and cons.

3 Each member of the group picks two or three ideas to raise for each agenda point in the discussion. Work on your own and make notes on the language you might use to raise your point.

4 Think of digressions that might happen during the agenda point that you will chair and make notes on the language that you might use to keep the discussion on topic.

PRACTISE

5 Have the discussion. Did you come to any conclusions at the end of the discussion? Why / Why not?

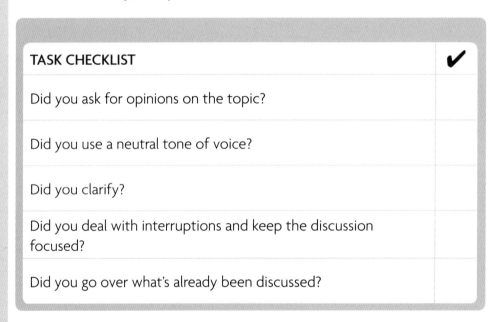

TASK CHECKLIST	✔
Did you ask for opinions on the topic?	
Did you use a neutral tone of voice?	
Did you clarify?	
Did you deal with interruptions and keep the discussion focused?	
Did you go over what's already been discussed?	

OBJECTIVES REVIEW

I can ...

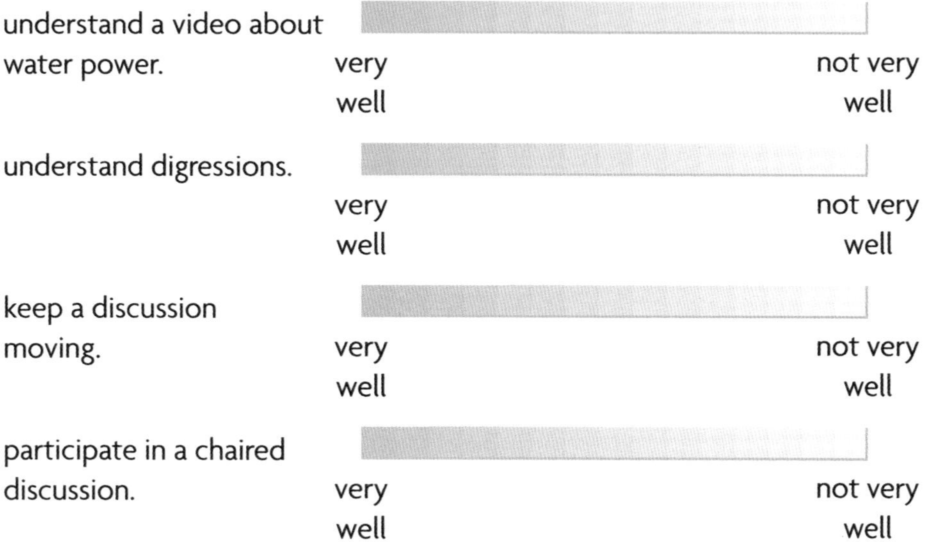

understand a video about water power.	very well	not very well
understand digressions.	very well	not very well
keep a discussion moving.	very well	not very well
participate in a chaired discussion.	very well	not very well

WORDLIST

UNIT VOCABULARY	ACADEMIC VOCABULARY
consumption (n)	capacity (n)
dam (n)	challenge(n)
energy-efficient (adj)	complex (adj)
environmentally friendly (adj)	element (n)
experimental (adj)	function (n)
generator (n)	generation (n)
limitation (n)	network (n)
maintenance (n)	pipe (n)
reservoir (n)	tower (n)
shaft (n)	
turbine (n)	

LEARNING OBJECTIVES

Watch and listen	Watch and understand a video about a sculptor in Mexico
Listening skills	Infer opinions
Speaking skills	Express opinions in a debate
Speaking task	Participate in an informal debate

ART AND DESIGN UNIT 9

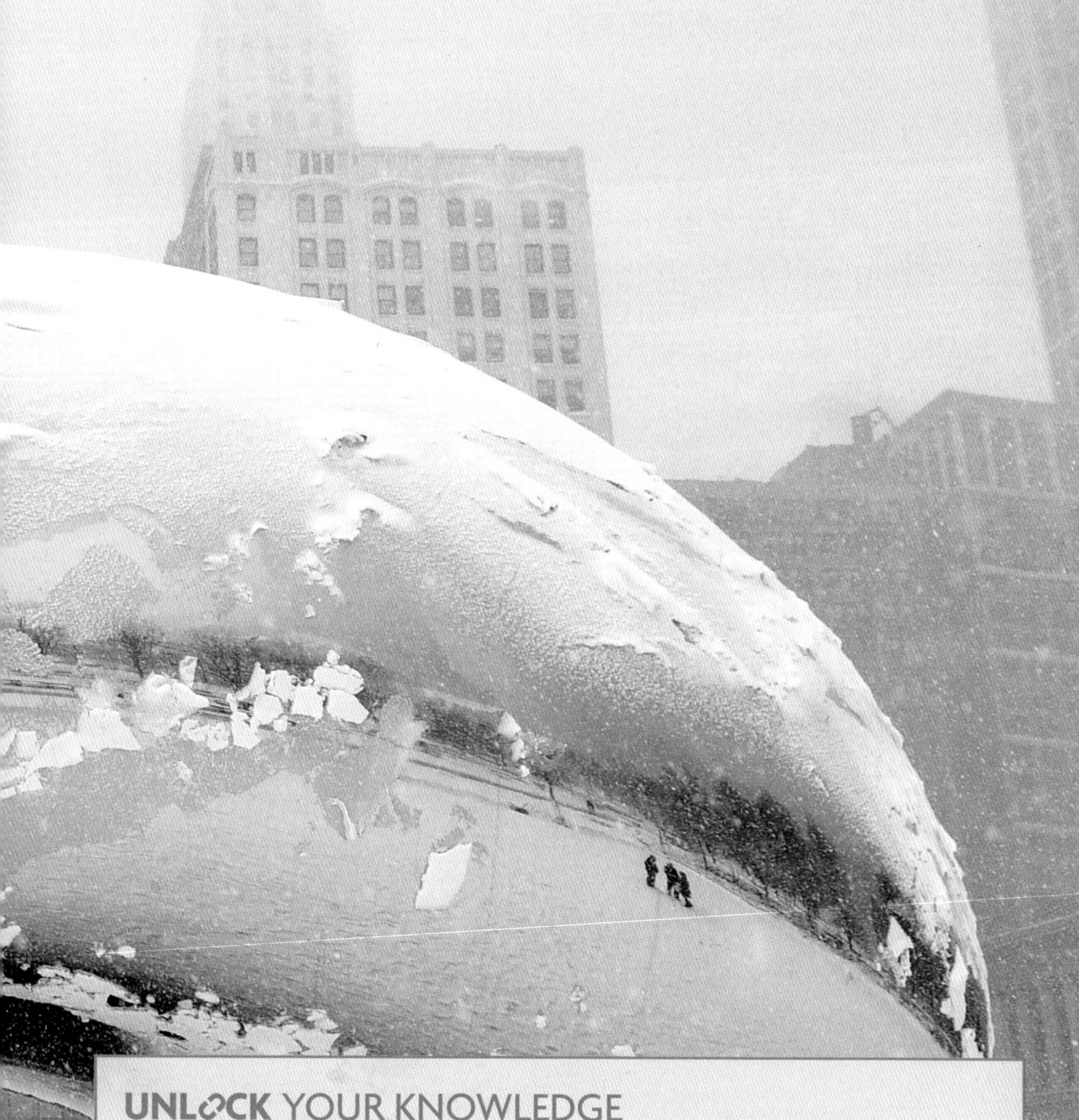

UNLOCK YOUR KNOWLEDGE

Work with a partner. Discuss the questions below.

1 Do you think the sculpture in this photograph is art? Why / Why not?
2 What do you think makes something art?
3 What kind of art is popular in your country? What kind of art do you like?

WATCH AND LISTEN

PREPARING TO WATCH

USING YOUR KNOWLEDGE TO PREDICT CONTENT

1 You are going to watch a video about a sculptor in Mexico. Before you watch, discuss the questions below in a group.

1 Can you think of any famous artists?
2 Where do they come from?
3 What are their most famous works of art?

UNDERSTANDING KEY VOCABULARY

2 Look at the vocabulary in bold (1–6) and match the sentence halves (a–f).

1 A **geometric** pattern is made up of
2 A **crystal** is a transparent rock
3 A **mine** is a deep hole in the ground
4 An **inspiration** is someone or something
5 An **intense** or **bold** colour is
6 A **junction** is a place

a where things, especially roads or railways, come together. ______
b that gives you the ideas for doing something else. ______
c very strong or extreme. ______
d used to make jewellery. ______
e where substances such as gold, coal, tin, etc. are removed. ______
f other shapes such as squares, triangles and rectangles. ______

3 Work with a partner. Use the words from Exercise 2 to describe the photographs at the top of the page.

WHILE WATCHING

UNDERSTANDING MAIN IDEAS

4 Watch the video. Choose the best option (a–c) to complete each sentence.

1 Sebastián's work is inspired by ...
 a mathematics. b the natural world. c his dreams.
2 In the video, Sebastián goes underground to see ...
 a works of art. b miners working. c rock formations.
3 The crystals were formed thousands of years ago when the cave was filled with ...
 a air. b water. c miners.
4 Sebastián's next work of art will be ...
 a secret. b inside a building. c huge and highly visible.

LISTENING FOR KEY INFORMATION

5 Watch again. Complete the fact file about Sebastián and his work.

Sebastián: **Fact File**

1 What inspired Sebastián as a child:
____

2 What Sebastián tries to communicate through his artwork:
____

3 Where Sebastián's sculptures are displayed:
____

4 How the visit to the cave affects Sebastián:
____

5 Where Sebastián's new sculpture will stand:
____

6 How Sebastián will make his sculpture noticeable:
____

DISCUSSION

6 Work with a partner. Discuss the questions.

1 Why do cities often display large pieces of art in public spaces?
2 Do you think it is a good idea to spend money on public art? Why / Why not?
3 Do you think Sebastián's artwork would look good in a public space in your town or city? Why / Why not?

LISTENING 1

PREPARING TO LISTEN

UNDERSTANDING KEY VOCABULARY

1 You are going to listen to a radio report about graffiti. Before you listen, match the words (1–8) to the definitions (a–h).

1 street art
2 graffiti
3 vandalism
4 self-expression
5 colour scheme
6 composition
7 creativity
8 criticism

a the crime of deliberately damaging property belonging to other people
b a type of art usually displayed in public places without official permission
c sharing your ideas with the world, often through art, music or acting
d words or drawings on the walls of buildings or other public places
e the way in which things are arranged in a picture
f saying that something or someone is bad
g the ability to produce new, interesting ideas
h the combination of colours chosen for a particular area or painting

PREDICTING CONTENT USING VISUALS

2 Look at the photograph. Discuss the questions in pairs.

1 Describe the image. Where do you think it might be found?
2 Who do you think might have painted it, and why?

3 Match the people (1–5) to the opinions about the painting (a–e).

1 A neighbour
2 A local office worker
3 A police officer
4 An art critic
5 A teenage graffiti artist

a It's vandalism, not artwork. ______
b The painter could be a commercially successful artist. ______
c It's an interesting feature to have in the area. ______
d The painting communicates a message to young people. ______
e It's illegal and therefore we're going to have to paint over it. ______

WHILE LISTENING

LISTENING FOR GIST

4 9.1 Listen to the radio report and check your answers to Exercise 3.

LISTENING FOR OPINION

5 Listen to the radio report again. Match the speakers (1–5) to the statements (a–j).

a All graffiti should be completely removed by law. 3
b I don't really like it. It's just graffiti, isn't it? ______
c I just think it's cool – it has a distinctive style. ______
d The people who own this building didn't ask for this. ______
e I think he or she could make a lot of money. ______
f It's something interesting to look at, and it's well done, isn't it? ______
g I think this type of art is a really good way of expressing your ideas. ______
h I think it's really cool. ______
i The colour scheme and the composition work very well together. ______
j I actually quite like it, despite the fact that it's illegal. ______

UNLOCK ONLINE

POST-LISTENING

Inferring opinions

Sometimes when people speak, they try to sound neutral or conceal their opinion about a topic, usually to appear fair and professional. However, thinking about the words and phrases used can often reveal different, more personal viewpoints.

MAKING INFERENCES

6 Look at the words used to describe the graffiti. Answer the questions.

	words used to describe the person who did the graffiti and the work itself
police officer	the artist, very creative, a piece of art, artistic, expressive, artwork, vandalism
host	the (mystery) graffiti painter, our illegal painter, this piece of vandalism

1 Which words and phrases in the table have positive connotations?
2 Which words and phrases have neutral or more negative connotations?
3 Based on this, which person do you think likes the painting more? Is this what you would expect?

PRONUNCIATION FOR LISTENING

Stress in word families

Changing the form of a word sometimes changes the stress too.

7 9.2 Listen and underline the stressed syllable in each word. The first two are done for you.

verb – noun

1 decorate – decoration
2 compose – composition
3 communicate – communication
4 create – creation
5 exhibit – exhibition
6 recommend – recommendation

noun – adjective

7 permit – permitted
8 artist – artistic

8 Work with a partner. Practise reading your word pairs with the correct stress.

DISCUSSION

9 Work with a partner. Discuss the questions.

1 Is there street art in your town or city? If so, what do you think of it?
2 How would you feel if a piece of street art appeared near your home?
3 Do you think street art and graffiti should be illegal? Why / Why not?

LANGUAGE DEVELOPMENT

EXPRESSING CONTRASTING OPINIONS

EXPLANATION

Expressing contrasting opinions

In a debate or discussion, people may state opinions or facts that you disagree with. If you want to persuade people that your opinion is correct or that what the other person said is untrue, you can restate that opinion or fact and then introduce your own point using a contrasting expression.

*This **looks like** spray painting, **but in fact**, it's a very artistic piece of work.*

1 Read the example sentence and answer the questions below.

1 What does the speaker think of the work?
2 Which expression in bold signals the opinion that the speaker disagrees with?
3 Which expression in bold signals the speaker's opinion?

2 Look at the words and phrases in the box and put them in the correct place in the table.

Many people think that In reality, The fact of the matter is
It looks like However, We take it for granted that It seems as if
but actually, Some people say It may seem but in fact
The truth of the matter is

introducing a statement	expressing a contrasting opinion

3 Rewrite the sentences below using the prompts in brackets.

1 Statement 1: A lot of money is spent on public art.
Statement 2: Only 0.5% of public money is spent on art. (It may seem, but in fact)

____

____

2 Statement 1: Public art has no long-term cost.
Statement 2: Cleaning and maintenance need to be considered (Many people think, however)

____

____

3 Statement 1: The new sculpture is very popular.
Statement 2: A thousand people signed a petition to have it removed. (It seems, but actually)

____

____

4 Statement 1: The government wasted a lot of money on the sculpture.
Statement 2: It was donated to the city. (It looks like, The fact of the matter is)

____

____

ACADEMIC VOCABULARY RELATED TO ART

4 Match the words (1–10) to the definitions (a–j).

1 appreciate	**a** to show something in a public place
2 display	**b** to show something that was previously hidden, or secret
3 interpret	**c** to refuse to accept, or believe something
4 reject	**d** to give your opinion on something
5 remove	**e** to recognize how good or useful something is
6 analyze	**f** to give a lot of attention to something
7 comment on	**g** to take something or someone away from somewhere
8 focus on	**h** to study or examine something in detail
9 restore	**i** to decide on, or explain the meaning of something
10 reveal	**j** to return something to an earlier good condition

5 Circle the correct verb to complete the sentence.

1 I don't think you fully *appreciate / restore* the talent of the artist.
2 We should critically *reject / analyze* the piece before removing it.
3 I hope that the artist will publicly *comment / focus* on their work.
4 I would proudly *appreciate / display* the artwork in my gallery.
5 We should primarily *focus / comment* on finding the vandal.
6 It would be difficult to correctly *interpret / reveal* the artwork.
7 I firmly *analyze / reject* the idea that the artist is a criminal.
8 By law, we must completely *display / remove* the graffiti.

LISTENING 2

PREPARING TO LISTEN

USING YOUR KNOWLEDGE

1 You are going to listen to an informal debate about public art. Before you listen, work with a partner and discuss the questions below.

1 A local city government is considering selling a public sculpture to help pay for some new sports facilities. Which do you think is more important for a community? Why?
2 What arguments can you think of for selling the sculpture?
3 What arguments can you think of for keeping the sculpture?

WHILE LISTENING

LISTENING FOR MAIN IDEAS

UNLOCK ONLINE

2 9.3 Listen to the informal debate and choose the points mentioned in the discussion.

1 Maintaining the sculpture costs too much money. ☐
2 Public buildings could be sold instead of the sculpture. ☐
3 Art is an important part of any culture. ☐
4 Removing the sculpture could cause big disruptions in the city. ☐
5 The sculpture is dangerous. ☐
6 The sculpture could become a tourist attraction. ☐
7 A private collector has offered to buy the sculpture. ☐
8 The government's right to sell the sculpture. ☐

LISTENING FOR DETAIL

3 9.3 Listen to the debate again. Complete the notes below about the talk.

Statement 1: Public art is a waste of money.
Response 1.1: Art is an important part of any culture.
Response 1.2: We don't know if we can sell the sculpture.
Decision 1: (1) ____________

Statement 2: If we remove the sculpture, we need to put something in its place.
Response 2.1: We won't be able to find other public art everyone likes.
Response 2.2: (2) ____________
Decision 2: (3) ____________

Statement 3: The sculpture is a danger to the public.
Response 3.1: (4) ____________
Response 3.2: We should move the sculpture.
Decision 3: (5) ____________

Statement 4: The government may not have the right to sell the sculpture.
Response 4.1: (6) ____________
Response 4.2: We need to balance art and sport in the lives of our children.
Decision 4: (7) ____________

4 Compare answers in pairs.

POST-LISTENING

Thinking about fact and opinion

A fact is a piece of information that is known to be true. An opinion is an individual's ideas or beliefs about a subject. Ideally, in a debate, everyone agrees on the facts so that the debate can focus on opinions.

5 For each of the following points, write fact (F) or opinion (O).

1 The total bill for cleaning and repairs has come to more than £5,000. ______
2 Constantly cleaning and restoring a piece of art is not an appropriate way to spend public money. ______
3 We had 400,000 visitors to our art museum last year. ______
4 We don't know exactly how much the sculpture is worth. ______
5 We can replace the sculpture with something that will be popular. ______
6 I don't think we'll be able to find anything that everyone likes. ______
7 Kids have been damaging the sculpture almost every night. ______
8 The shopping centre will be a great place to display the sculpture. ______

6 Work with a partner. Look at the facts and take turns to form one positive and one negative opinion based on the information.

1 Over half the local population want a new leisure centre in the city.
2 It will cost £10,000 to relocate the sculpture in the shopping centre.
3 A national art collector is interested in buying the sculpture.
4 A security guard could be hired to watch the sculpture at night.

DISCUSSION

7 Work with a partner. Discuss the questions.

1 Which places in your city or country display public art?
2 Why do you think these places have chosen to put art on display?
3 What opinions do you think local people have about the artwork?

CRITICAL THINKING

At the end of this unit you are going to do the speaking task below.

> A public sculpture where you live divides the opinion of the community. It is regularly vandalized and is expensive to repair. The local government are now having an informal debate on selling it.

Debate statements and responses

In a debate, a statement is an expression of a position, opinion or suggestion on the topic. A response is a reaction to a statement that has been made. Participants in a debate respond to an initial statement and any further responses before a decision can be reached.

ANALYZE

1 Match the sentences (1–4) to the parts of a debate structure (a–d).

1 If we remove the sculpture, we'll need to replace it.
2 We won't be able to find anything that everyone likes.
3 Let's put together a proposal.
4 You could say that, but I think we could probably find something that would be popular.

a Statement
b Response 1
c Response 2
d Decision

2 Work with a partner. Rewrite the sentences using the prompts.

1 Statement: we should / I don't / our college campus / spend / money / think / on public art / for / .

____

2 Response 1: to increase / But / positivity / has been / public art / found / .

____

3 Response 2: education facilities / should / The money / probably / spent on better / be / .

____

4 Decision: on campus / the costs / Look at / and / further / benefits / of public art / .

____

CREATE

3 Work with a partner and look at the statements in the table. Think of a response to support each statement and write it in the response 1 box.

statement	response 1	response 2	decision
A: It costs too much money to repair the constant damage to the sculpture.			
B: The sculpture is now a danger to the public and should be moved.			

4 Think of a response against each statement and write it in the response 2 box on the previous page.

5 Looking at the statements and responses you have written, what possible decisions might be made? Write your ideas in the table on the previous page.

6 Work with another pair. Compare your tables. Did you make the same decisions? Why / Why not?

SPEAKING

PREPARATION FOR SPEAKING

1 Work in pairs. Take turns saying the two sentences, replacing the words in bold with other words or expressions in the box.

opinion the speaker disagrees with	**At first glance, it looks as if** Many people think that It looks like We take it for granted that Some people say It may seem like It seems as if ...		the painting is just graffiti,
speaker's opinion	**but** however	**in fact,** actually, in reality, the truth/fact of the matter is	it's the work of a talented artist.

2 Use the expressions from Exercise 1 to contrast the opinions below. You can use option A or B as the speaker's opinion.

opinion A	opinion B
Public art is a waste of money.	Art is an important part of any culture.
Graffiti has no place in cities.	Graffiti can make a city beautiful.
Learning a second language is very important.	Some people never use a second language.
Professional athletes are paid too much money.	Professional athletes work very hard to earn their pay.
Computer technology helps people communicate.	Computer technology isolates people.

EXPLANATION

Language for hedging

Hedging is used to make you sound less direct and more polite when responding to a statement that you do not agree with.

A: Public art is a waste of time and money.

B: Well, **I'm not an expert, but** I have read that it can benefit your health.

Hedges

Personally, I'm not really sure ...
I'm not an expert, but ...
All I know is ...
For me, ...

Hedges for responding

You could say that, however actually ...
That's true in part, but I think ...
You may be right, but I wonder if ...
I see what you're saying, but maybe ...

3 Work with a partner. Look at the table below. Take turns giving an opinion and responding. Use hedging to make your opinions and answers more polite.

	student A	student B
1	I don't think this picture represents anything important.	I disagree. It gives us something to think about.
2	Making art isn't as important as making money.	I disagree. Making art is an important form of human expression.
3	We shouldn't install this sculpture.	I disagree. It would be very popular with the students.
4	Graffiti is a crime.	All graffiti-style painting isn't a crime.

PRONUNCIATION FOR SPEAKING

EXPLANATION

Stress in hedging language

When using hedging language, the speaker usually stresses two elements in a sentence. One is the expression that acknowledges the other speaker's statement. This often contains a modal verb, which is usually stressed. The other is the speaker's opinion, where often the pronouns *I* or *me* are stressed.

That might be true, but I think ...

4 9.4 Listen to the hedging language. Underline the stress in each expression. The first one is done for you.

1 Personally, <u>I'm</u> not really sure ...
2 I'm not an expert, but ...
3 All I know is ...
4 For me, ...
5 You could say that, however actually ...
6 That's true in part, but I think ...
7 You may be right, but I wonder if ...
8 I see what you're saying, but maybe ...

5 Work with a partner. Practise saying the sentences in Exercise 4 with the correct stress.

Restating somebody's point

In an informal debate, speakers sometimes restate another person's point, either because they aren't sure they've understood it and they want to clarify it or because they want to call attention to it and argue against it.

6 Read the conversations and write clarification (C) or argument (A).

1 **A** I think we should start over again.
B Start over again? Do you mean reject all three of the applications?
A No, I think we should consider them all, but let's take a break first. ______

2 **A** It's clear to me that we shouldn't invest in art right now. We don't have the money.
B We don't have the money? So what you're saying is that public art isn't important. ______

3 **A** That painting is nothing but graffiti.
B Nothing but graffiti? In other words, you don't think it's art. ______

4 **A** We can spend 10,000 a year on art for the next three years.
B So, if I understand you correctly, our total artwork budget is 30,000, then?
A Yes, that's right. ______

7 Work in pairs. Take turns making statements and restating the point, either to clarify it or argue against it. Use the expressions in Exercise 4 to help you.

Possible opinions (or use your own):

1 The (type of car) is the best car in the world.
2 Fashion designers are artists and clothes are works of art.
3 I don't think the government should spend any money on public art.

SPEAKING TASK

A public sculpture where you live divides the opinion of the community. It is regularly vandalized and is expensive to repair. The local government are now having an informal debate on selling it.

PREPARE

1 Work in groups of three. Look at the photograph. What are the pros and cons of keeping a sculpture like this? Make notes and decide if your group is for or against the sculpture being sold.

2 Decide which of the ideas from Exercise 1 best support your group's view of the sculpture.

3 To present your ideas, think of two statements to use in the debate and write them in the table below.

4 People who don't agree with you may respond against your statements. Make notes on how other speakers might respond to your statement in the table.

PRACTISE

5 Practise your presentation as a group.

DISCUSS

6 Work with two people from different groups. Have the debate. Make notes in the table to help you to address other people's points. Could you come to any decisions or make any next steps in your debate? Why / Why not?

statement	responses	decision or next step

TASK CHECKLIST	✔
Have you used language to express contrasting opinions?	
Have you used hedging language while giving opinions?	
Have you used hedging language when responding to other people's opinions?	
Have you restated other speakers' points if relevant	

OBJECTIVES REVIEW

I can ...

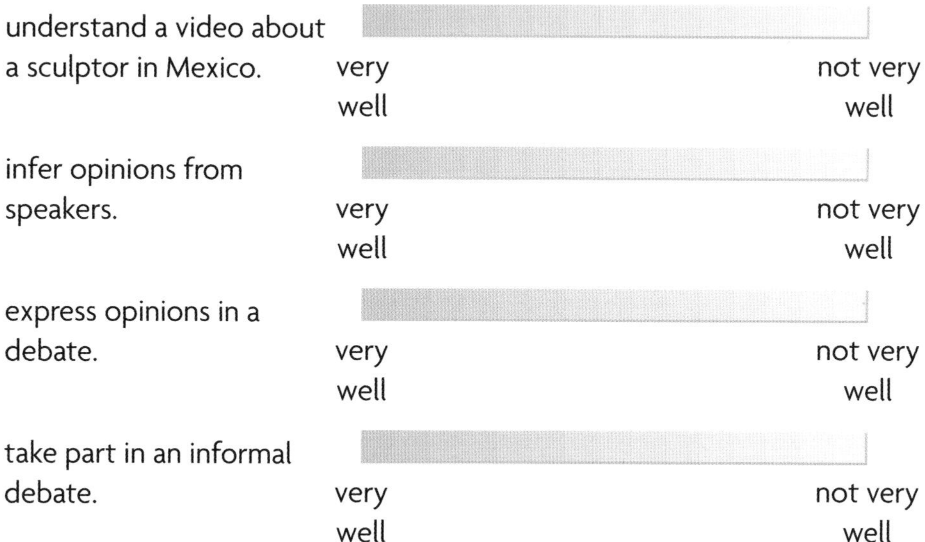

understand a video about a sculptor in Mexico. very well — not very well

infer opinions from speakers. very well — not very well

express opinions in a debate. very well — not very well

take part in an informal debate. very well — not very well

WORDLIST

UNIT VOCABULARY	ACADEMIC VOCABULARY
colour scheme (n)	analyze (v)
creativity (n)	appreciate (v)
criticism (n)	bold (adj)
crystal (n)	comment (v)
geometric (adj)	composition (n)
graffiti (n)	display (v)
inspiration (n)	focus (v)
junction (n)	intense (adj)
self-expression (n)	interpret (v)
street art (n)	mine (n)
vandalism (n)	reject (v)
	remove (v)
	restore (v)
	reveal (v)

LEARNING OBJECTIVES

Watch and listen	Watch and understand a video about the importance of the elderly in Egyptian families
Listening skills	Understand specific observations and generalizations
Speaking skills	Reference data in a presentation, make comparisons
Speaking task	Give a presentation to a seminar group

AGEING UNIT 10

UNLOCK YOUR KNOWLEDGE

Work with a partner. Discuss the questions below.

1 What do you think you will able to do when you reach old age that you cannot do now?
2 What can you do now that you will no longer be able to do when you reach old age?
3 Do you think older people should be allowed to continue working for as long as they like? Why / Why not?

WATCH AND LISTEN

PREPARING TO WATCH

UNDERSTANDING KEY VOCABULARY

1 You are going to watch a video about the importance of the elderly in Egyptian families. Before you watch, read the paragraph and match the words in bold (1–8) to the definitions (a–h).

> (1)**Approximately** 20% of people over the age of 65 are at risk of (2)**poverty** in the UK. This (3)**generation** has been badly affected by global economic problems. As the (4)**ageing** population leaves work, many find that they have not saved enough money for their retirement. For some, the only (5)**cost-effective** solution is to move into the (6)**households** of their children or other relatives. However, those who have lost touch with close relatives or are unable to arrange a (7)**reunion** with distant family members must rely on the government or charitable organizations for support. Members of these charities (8)**donate** time and money to help these elderly people who live difficult lives with no other means of support.

a a situation where people meet again after they have not seen each other for a long time ____
b good value for the amount of money paid for something ____
c a group of people, usually a family, who live together ____
d all of the people of about the same age within a society or family ____
e the condition of being extremely poor ____
f a person or thing that is getting older ____
g not exactly, but close to a particular number or time ____
h to give money or goods to help a person or organization ____

2 Work in pairs and discuss the questions below.

USING YOUR KNOWLEDGE TO PREDICT CONTENT

1 Do several generations of a family tend to live together in your country? Why / Why not?
2 Where do elderly people live in your country? Who looks after them?
3 At what age do young people usually leave home? Is this different in urban and rural areas?

WHILE WATCHING

UNDERSTANDING MAIN IDEAS

3 Watch the video. Write true (T) or false (F) next to the statements below.

1 Ali and his family are from Cairo. ____
2 Ali has worked at the bakery since he was 10 years old. ____
3 Ali lives with a relative in Cairo. ____
4 Ali is returning home to go to school. ____

LISTENING FOR KEY INFORMATION

4 Watch again. Read the answers to the questions. Write the questions for each answer.

1 ____
Approximately 17 million.
2 ____
Seven years old.
3 ____
20%.
4 ____
Six dollars, of which one dollar he keeps for himself.
5 ____
Ten hours, seven days a week.
6 ____
Ten months.
7 ____
81%.
8 ____
13%.

DISCUSSION

5 Work with a partner. Discuss the questions.

1 What are the lives of elderly people in your country like?
2 How do the lives of young people compare to older people?
3 In what ways do older people help and support younger people?
4 In what ways do younger people help and support older people?

LISTENING 1

PREPARING TO LISTEN

USING YOUR KNOWLEDGE

1 You are going to listen to a finance podcast. Before you listen, discuss the questions below in a group.

1 In your country, what are typical activities for older people?
2 Do you think you will do the same activities when you are older?

UNDERSTANDING KEY VOCABULARY

2 Complete the sentences below with the words from the box.

luxuries assets pension retirement investments consumer finance property

1 __________ is the time when you stop working permanently, usually because you have reached a particular age.
2 Expensive things bought for comfort and pleasure are __________ .
3 Sums of money put into companies in order to make more money are __________ .
4 A __________ is someone who buys and uses products and services.
5 The management of money is also called __________ .
6 A __________ is a regular income older people receive from a company or the government when they stop working.
7 A person's home, or a company's land and other buildings they own are their __________ .
8 __________ are all the things owned by a person, including money.

WHILE LISTENING

LISTENING FOR GIST

3 10.1 Listen and choose the subjects that are discussed in the podcast.

1 A comparison of retirement in the past with retirement today. ☐
2 The financial and social problems of caring for the elderly. ☐
3 An example of an enjoyable retirement. ☐
4 Problems experienced by the elderly travelling abroad. ☐
5 The effects of increased health and fitness on the elderly. ☐
6 The role the elderly play in their grandchildren's lives. ☐
7 A prediction about retirement in the future. ☐
8 Advice on how to save money for retirement. ☐

4 10.1 Listen to the podcast again. Complete the notes below.

LISTENING FOR DETAIL

The spending power of the over-60s (last year's data):
Assets: (1)£ ______________
Spent on leisure: (2)£ ______________ – more than (3) ______________% of all consumer spending
Money spent on eating out: (4)£ ______________
Money spent on travel: (5)£ ______________
Rick and Nadia Jones:
Retirement age: (6) ______________
Value of home: (7)£ ______________
The outlook for the next generation:
Fraction of parents who plan to leave their home, but no money, to their children: (8) ______________
Percentage of people aged over 65 in Europe who will still be working in 2030: (9) ______________%

POST-LISTENING

Understanding specific observations and generalizations

Specific observations are statements about particular people, things or facts. Generalizations are statements about the way things usually are. Listening for whether something is a specific observation or generalization can tell you if it is true just for the case the speaker is referring to, or in a large number of cases.

5 Read the sentences and write specific observation (S) or generalization (G).

1 Our daughters still see us as young. S
2 People nowadays don't usually think of 65 as old. G
3 Last year, 57% of retired people were looking for jobs. ______
4 By the year 2030, more than 20% of European people aged over 65 will still be working. ______
5 Retired people now want to do more exciting things! ______
6 We retired at 62, and since that time, we've travelled a lot and have had years of excitement and fun. ______
7 Today's generation is probably facing a more difficult retirement than their parents. ______
8 More retired people have to look for work now. ______

6 Match the specific observations and generalizations from Exercise 5.

specific observation	generalization
1	2

PRONUNCIATION FOR LISTENING

Elision and intrusion

When we speak naturally, we do not always pronounce individual words. Words connect with each other, new sounds can get added and other sounds get lost. *Intrusion* is when an extra sound is added between two words. *Elision* is when a sound between two words, usually the last sound of the first word, is lost.

7 10.2 Listen. Tick the correct category for the words in bold.

	/j/	/w/	lost sound
1 **And because** they worked hard and saved for their retirement, they have plenty of money to spend.			✓
2 According **to one** survey, 20 years ago, most of today's older people believed they would work in the garden, read and babysit their grandchildren.		✓	
3 We've talked **to our** daughters about it.			
4 I think our parents' generation thought it was really important to save for the **next generation**.			
5 **They understand** that the money is ours to spend.			
6 They **also understand** that as long as we're fit and healthy, we might as well enjoy life.			
7 **We are** not planning on selling it, so they'll get that eventually.			
8 People who have exercised **and eaten** a good diet throughout their lives have plenty of energy to enjoy life after work.			

8 Work in pairs. Take turns saying the sentences in Exercise 7 using the correct pronunciation.

DISCUSSION

9 Work with a partner. Discuss the questions.

1 Do you think parents should stop providing for their children at some point in their lives? Why / Why not?
2 What would you hope to give your own children in the future?
3 What can children do for their parents when they become adults?

LANGUAGE DEVELOPMENT

VERBS WITH INFINITIVES

EXPLANATION

Verbs followed by *to* + infinitive

Some verbs are usually followed by *to* + infinitive. Common examples are *agree, arrange, consent, manage, offer, refuse, threaten* and *want.*

We live close to both our daughters and **offer to babysit** our grandchildren regularly.

After certain verbs in active sentences an object is included before *to* + infinitive.

Our savings allow us to live the life we've always wanted.

Other verbs which follow this pattern are: *advise, cause, enable, entitle* and *persuade.*

1 Correct the sentences below.

1 We always advise our daughters live life to the full.

____

2 We want encourage to other people to retire early.

____

3 We managed for save enough money when we were working.

____

4 We would not to consent go into a retirement home.

____

5 We refuse for spend our retirement at home.

____

6 I won't force to my children take care of me.

____

2 Rewrite the sentences using the clues in brackets.

1 My children said they would let me live with them when I'm old. (offer)
My children offered to let me live with them when I'm old.

2 My wife didn't accept the idea at first. (agree)
____

3 Her pension was generous, so she could retire comfortably. (allow)
____

4 We would never leave our children without any inheritance. (threaten)
____

3 Compare your sentences with another pair.

ACADEMIC VERBS FOR SUPPORT AND ASSISTANCE

4 Match the less formal words (1–8) to the academic words (a–h).

Informal		Academic	
1 give	5 help	a permit	e assist
2 allow	6 make sure	b devote (oneself) to	f cooperate
3 work together	7 show	c contribute	g indicate
4 give (oneself) to	8 take part	d ensure	h participate

5 Complete each sentence below with an academic word from Exercise 4. Sometimes more than one answer is possible.

1 Local services need to ______________ with each other to ensure welfare standards.
2 We should ______________ elderly people to choose where they live.
3 The government should ______________ that care for the elderly is high quality.
4 Retired people shouldn't feel that they should have to ______________ money to their children.
5 Households often ______________ older members of the family to continue to live independently.
6 The figures ______________ that more elderly people now live in care homes.
7 People ______________ themselves to their children and expect care in return.
8 Elderly people need to be able to ______________ in local community activities.

LISTENING 2

PREPARING TO LISTEN

UNDERSTANDING KEY VOCABULARY

1 You are going to listen to three presentations on ageing in different countries. Before you listen, match the words (1–10) to the definitions (a–j).

1 nuclear family	a family consisting of parents and their children, not aunts/uncles, grandparents, etc.
2 provider	b look after someone or something
3 dependant	c people related to you who lived a long time ago
4 support	d something that it is your duty or job to deal with
5 institution	e a disadvantage, or negative part of a situation
6 drawback	f a large building or organization where people live and are cared for together
7 responsibility	g someone who needs to be taken care of
8 welfare	h a person's physical and mental health and happiness
9 ancestors	i someone who brings money and resources to a family
10 fertility rate	j the ratio of births in women able to have children in a population or country at a particular time

USING YOUR KNOWLEDGE

2 Work with a partner. Discuss the questions.

1 What are the challenges of having more old people in modern society?
2 What are the advantages and disadvantages of institutions for the elderly?
3 What are the advantages and disadvantages of caring for elderly relatives at home?

3 Compare your answers with another pair.

WHILE LISTENING

LISTENING FOR GIST

4 10.3 Listen to the three presentations. Match the countries to the fact files (a–c).

Egypt Turkey Japan

Country	Population 2012	% 65 or over 2012	Population 2050	% 65 or over 2050
a ______________	127 million	23%	106 million	35%
b ______________	85 million	4.7%	100 million	16.8%
c ______________	80 million	6.4%	92 million	20%

LISTENING FOR DETAIL

5 10.3 Listen to the presentations again. Tick the topics the students discuss. Some topics are discussed by more than one student.

	Fahad, Egypt	Mika, Japan	Ahmet, Turkey
1 family support system for caring for the elderly			
2 the government's role in caring for the elderly			
3 caring for an elderly aunt at home			
4 the lifestyle of 20- and 30-year olds			
5 changes in population size due to fertility rates			
6 the pros and cons of caring for an elderly person in the home			

POST-LISTENING

6 Work in pairs. Look at the words in bold in the sentences below. Write cause (C) or effect (E) next to each sentence.

1 This increase will **result in** more elderly people in the community that need care. ______
2 My father's aunt lives with us **because** she never married. ______
3 This **leads to** a child's role changing from being a dependent to supporting the family. ______
4 The population increase **stems from** the fact that people are living longer. ______
5 Living closely together can **give rise to** tensions. ______
6 Moving old people into nursing homes **allows** the younger generation to continue their lives. ______

DISCUSSION

7 Work with a partner. Discuss the questions.

1 How are the elderly cared for in your country?
2 Has this changed in the past 20 years? If so, how?
3 Do you think it will change in the next 20 years? Why / Why not?

CRITICAL THINKING

At the end of this unit you are going to do the speaking task below.

Give a presentation on how ageing has changed a country's population over time and the impact this is likely to have on its society in the future.

Line graphs

Line graphs are used to show changes in data over time. It is important to look at any significant or unusual features in a line graph as well as the main data trends.

ANALYZE

1 Look at the line graph below. Answer the questions.

1 What do the numbers on the left side of the graph represent?

____

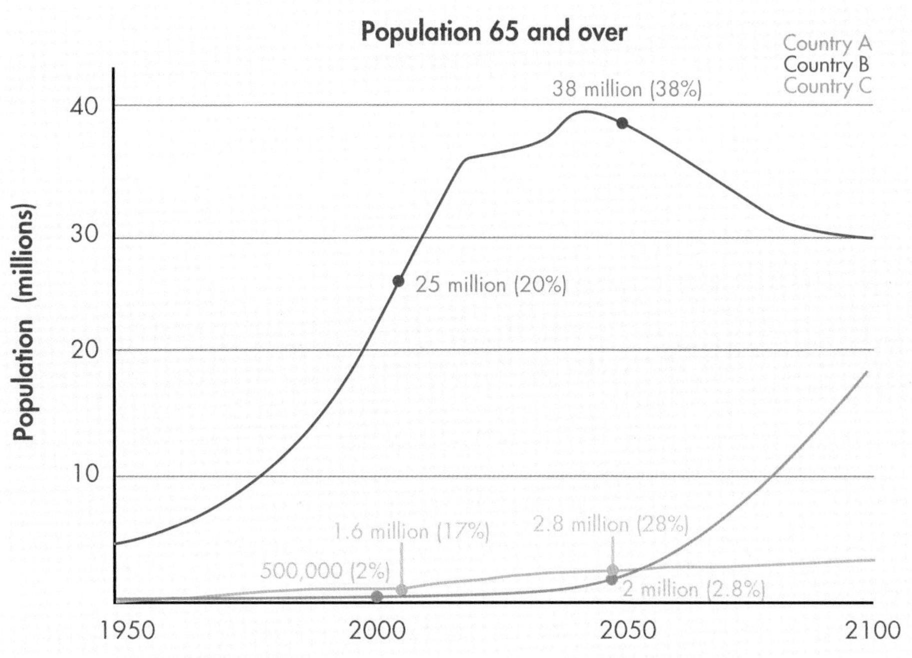

2 What do the numbers along the bottom of the graph represent?

____

3 Which two lines have a similar shape? Which line has a different shape?

____

4 What percentage of Country A's population was over 65 in the year 2000?

____

5 What percentage of Country B's population was over 65 in 2000?

____

6 What percentage of Country C's population will be over 65 in 2050?

____

EVALUATE

2 Match the statements to the correct countries (A–C) in the graph.

1 The population aged over 65 has been growing steadily since 1950 and will continue to grow rapidly. ______
2 The population aged over 65 has mainly been growing steadily and will continue to increase at a similar rate. ______
3 The population aged over 65 was growing rapidly, but will decrease in the future. ______

3 Match the statements about the data with the correct countries (A–C).

1 The population aged over 65 in 2100 is predicted to be 30 million. ______
2 By 2100, the population aged over 65 will be about 3.2 million. ______
3 The population aged over 65 is expected to reach 20 million by the year 2100. ______
4 A steady increase in the population aged over 65 to 38 million in 2050 will be followed by a steady decrease. ______
5 The population aged over 65 will increase from about half a million today to two million in 2050. ______
6 The population aged over 65 fell by around 500,000 people just after the year 2000. ______

UNDERSTAND

4 Look at the graph again. Answer the questions.

1 Do any of the graphs have similar patterns?

____

2 Are any of the figures the same?

____

3 Are any of the graphs different to the other two graphs? Why?

____

5 Work with a partner. Write the similarities and differences you noted in Exercise 4 in the table below.

similarities	differences

6 Compare your answers with another pair. Did you have the same answers? Why / Why not?

SPEAKING

PREPARATION FOR SPEAKING

REFERENCING DATA IN A PRESENTATION

1 Look at the line graphs. Match the descriptions (1–6) to the correct countries (A–B).

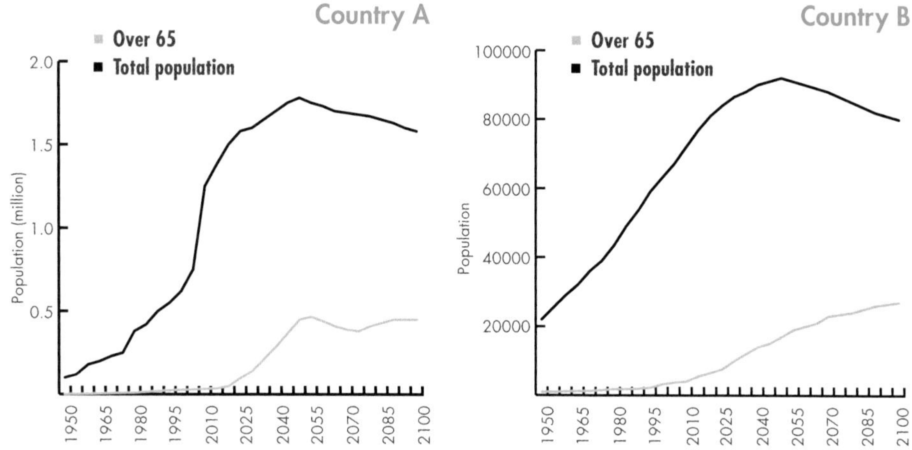

1 As you can see in the graph, between 2010 and 2080, the population of over-65s will shoot up from 4,000 to 24,000 people. ______
2 If you look at the graph, we can see the population peaks at 1.78 million people in 2050. ______
3 Between 2055 and 2070, the population of over-65s is due to plummet from 466,000 to 390,000. ______
4 If you look at the data provided, you can see that the growth in population remains steady from 1950 to 2050. ______
5 After peaking in 2055, the population of over-65s in will fluctuate and then stabilize at about 450,000 people. ______
6 After a steady increase in population between 2010 and 2050, the population is due to fall slowly. ______

2 Work with a partner. Use the language from Exercise 1 to describe other parts of the graphs above.

After an increase in the population over 65 ...

Explaining causes and effects

Explaining cause and effect to your audience helps them understand why information is important and how different pieces of information are connected.

3 Match the sentence halves.

1 The steady increase in population between 1950 and 2000 was the result of ...
2 The sharp rise in population between 2005 and 2010 was brought about by ...
3 The predicted decrease in population from 2050 onwards can be traced back to ...
4 The number of over-65s will increase steeply after 2020 owing to ...
5 Immigration and improvements in healthcare between 1950 and the present account for ...

a ... families deciding to have fewer children today. ______
b ... huge improvements in healthcare today. ______
c ... a high level of immigration during that period. ______
d ... a steady population increase from 22 million to nearly 80 million. ______
e ... a large number of young people deciding to have children. ______

4 For each expression below, use words in the table to write cause and effect sentences. More than one answer is possible in most cases.

people living longer	1 was the result of	improvements in medical care
a population decrease	2 was brought about by	increase in over-65s
a population increase	3 can be traced back to	people moving out of the country
the steady population	4 accounts for	the high number of over-65s
	5 owing to	

PRONUNCIATION FOR SPEAKING

Contrastive stress in comparisons

A speaker comparing numbers usually stresses the numbers and the comparison word to emphasize the importance of the figures.

5 10.4 Listen to the sentences. Underline the words that are stressed. The first one is done for you.

1 Today, the over-65s make up <u>2.5</u>% of Country A's total population. This figure is <u>smaller than</u> the figure of <u>7</u>% for Country B.
2 The population of Country B will be 77 million in 2050. This number is much larger than the figure of 1.4 million for Country A in 2050.
3 By 2050 Country A's population will have risen to 1.78 million people. The population for Country B also peaks in 2050 with 9.2 million.

6 Work with a partner. Practise saying the sentences with contrastive stress.

SPEAKING TASK

Give a presentation on how ageing has changed a country's population over time and the impact this is likely to have on its society in the future.

Split into three groups. Each group will look at one country: A, B or C.

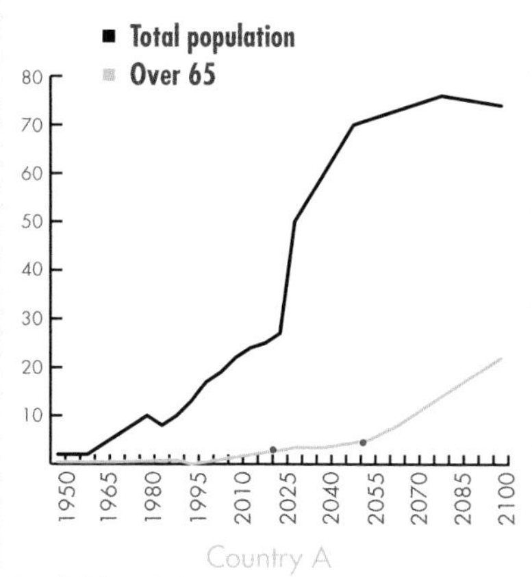

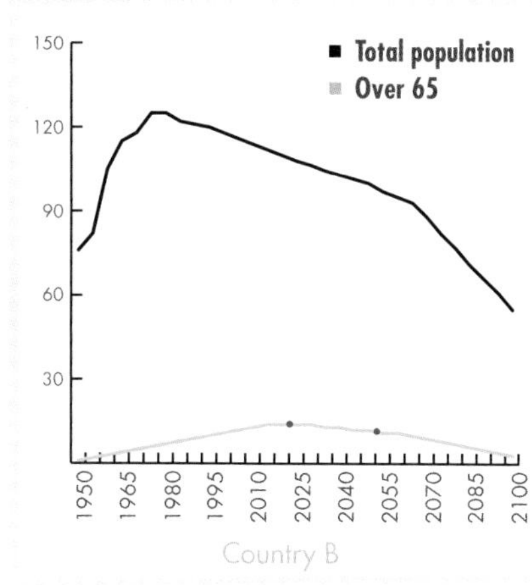

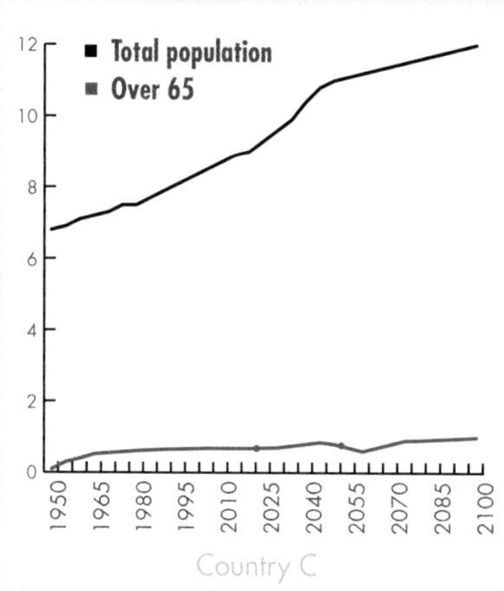

PREPARE

1 In your group, look at the graph for your country. Answer the questions and take notes.

1 What are the main points or trends that your graph shows?
2 Is there a relationship between any of the data in your graph?

2 Look at the additional information about your country below. Answer the questions in your group and take notes.

1 How does this information correspond with the data on the graph?
2 Is it supported by the main points that you found?
3 Is it supported by any significant or unusual features in the graph?

Country A

- In Country A many young people have recently begun moving to the city, so rural populations are becoming more elderly.
- At 2%, the percentage of the population aged over 65 is relatively small and almost all elderly people are cared for by their families.
- The government has no plans to provide institutions for elderly people.

3 Look at the graphs and additional information for the other two countries. Write two statements that compare the data of your country to the data of the other countries.

Country B

- For people in Country B it is normal for adult children to leave home and live away from their parents.
- Most elderly people are cared for by institutions which enables younger generations to continue working knowing they are well-cared for.
- The government provides institutions for elderly people for families who cannot afford to pay for their care.

Country C

- For people in Country C adult children usually settle near their parents so they can look after them in old age.
- About 30% of elderly people are cared for by institutions.
- Because of a predicted increase of the population aged over 65 in the next 50 years, the government has started a programme of building institutions for elderly people.

4 Write notes for your talk on the following areas:

1 Presenting your data
2 Talking about the causes and effects of your data
3 Comparing your data to that of the other countries

PRACTISE

5 Practise your presentation in your group.

6 Form a new group with people who have looked at the other two countries. Perform your presentation to your new group. Were your presentations similar? Why / Why not?

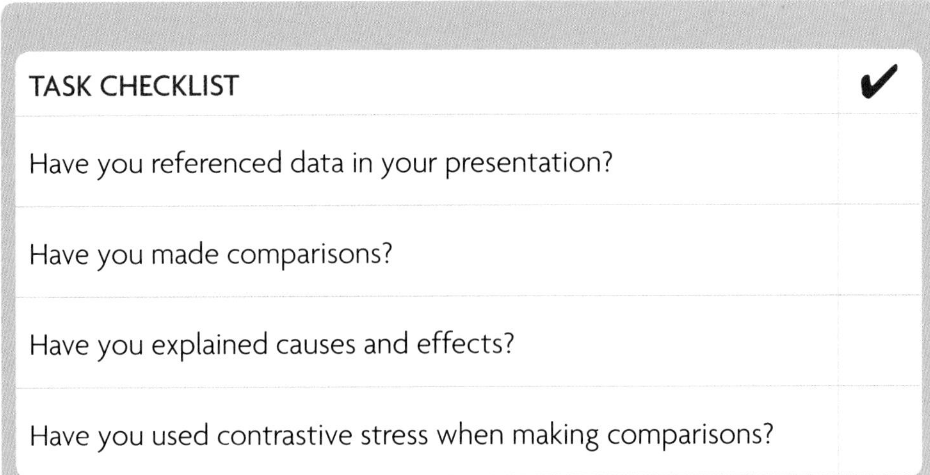

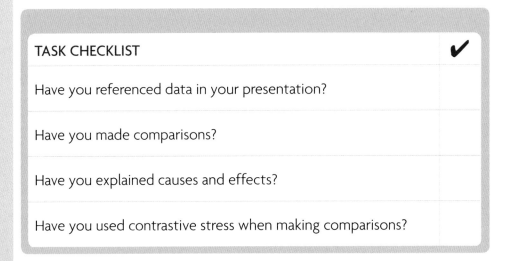

TASK CHECKLIST	✔
Have you referenced data in your presentation?	
Have you made comparisons?	
Have you explained causes and effects?	
Have you used contrastive stress when making comparisons?	

OBJECTIVES REVIEW

I can ...

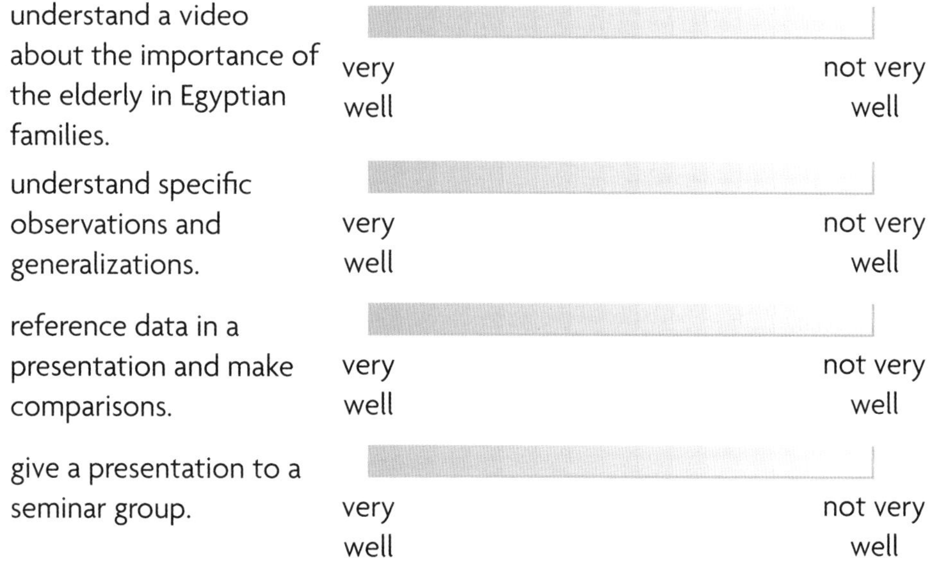

understand a video about the importance of the elderly in Egyptian families.	very well	not very well
understand specific observations and generalizations.	very well	not very well
reference data in a presentation and make comparisons.	very well	not very well
give a presentation to a seminar group.	very well	not very well

WORDLIST

UNIT VOCABULARY	ACADEMIC VOCABULARY
ageing (adj)	approximately (adv)
ancestor (n)	assist (v)
asset (n)	cooperate (v)
cost-effective (adj)	dependant (n)
donate (v)	devote (v)
fertility rate (n)	finance (n)
household (n)	generation (n)
institution (n)	indicate (v)
investment (n)	participate (v)
luxury (n)	permit (v)
nuclear family (n)	poverty (n)
pension (n)	property (n)
retirement (n)	responsibility (n)
reunion (n)	support (v)
	welfare (n)

GLOSSARY

Vocabulary	Pronunciation	Part of speech	Definition
UNIT 1			
agricultural	/ægrɪˈkʌltʃərəl/	(adj)	used for farming or relating to farming
agriculture	/ˈægrɪkʌltʃə/	(n)	farming
carbon dioxide emission	/ˈkɑːbən daɪˈɒksaɪd ɪˈmɪʃən/	(n)	the amount of carbon dioxide gas that is sent out
carbon footprint	/kɑːbənˈfʊtprɪnt/	(n)	a measure of the amount of carbon dioxide someone's activities produce
climate change	/ˈklaɪmət tʃeɪndʒ/	(n)	the way the Earth's weather is changing
consumer	/kənˈsjuːmə/	(n)	a person who buys goods or services for their own use
crop	/krɒp/	(n)	a plant such as a grain, fruit or vegetable that is grown in large amounts
environment	/ɪnˈvaɪrənmənt/	(n)	the air, water, and land in or on which people, animals, and plants live
export	/ɪkˈspɔːt/	(v)	to send goods to another country for sale
imported	/ɪmˈpɔːtɪd/	(adj)	brought in from another country
processing	/ˈprəʊsesɪŋ/	(n)	to prepare, change, or treat food or natural substances as a part of an industrial operation
produce	/ˈprɒduːs/	(n)	food that is grown or made in large quantities to be sold
produce	/prəˈdjuːs/	(v)	to make something or bring something into existence
provider	/prəˈvaɪdə/	(n)	someone who provides something
purchase	/ˈpɜːtʃəs/	(v)	to buy
rice paddy	/raɪs ˈpædi/	(n)	a field full of water in which rice is grown
supply chain	/səˈplaɪ tʃeɪn/	(n)	the system of people and things that are involved in getting a product from the place where it is made to the person who buys it
transportation	/trænspɔːteɪʃən/	(n)	a vehicle or system of vehicles for getting from one place to another
UNIT 2			
academic	/ækəˈdemɪk/	(adj)	relating to schools, colleges and universities, or connected to thinking and studying and not practical skills
acquire	/əˈkwaɪə/	(v)	to learn or get something
apprentice	/əˈprentɪs/	(n)	someone who has agreed to work for a skilled person for a particular period of time, often for low payment, in order to learn that person's skills
arc	/ɑːk/	(n)	the shape of part of a circle, or other curved line
careers adviser	/kəˈrɪəz ədˈvaɪzə/	(n)	someone whose job is to give people advice and information about what type of work they could do or how they could progress to a better job
complex	/ˈkɒmpleks/	(adj)	involving a lot of different but connected parts
exhausted	/ɪgˈzɔːstɪd/	(adj)	extremely tired
manual	/ˈmænjuəl/	(adj)	involving physical work rather than mental work
mechanical	/məˈkænɪkəl/	(adj)	relating to or operated by machines
mission	/ˈmɪʃən/	(n)	an important job, usually travelling somewhere
nuclear	/ˈnjuːklɪə/	(adj)	relating to the energy that is released when the nucleus of an atom is divided
partner	/ˈpɑːtnə/	(n)	someone that you do something with, for example working in class
physical	/ˈfɪzɪkəl/	(adj)	related to the body
practical	/ˈpræktɪkəl/	(adj)	relating to experience, real situations or actions rather than ideas or imagination
professional	/prəˈfeʃənəl/	(adj)	relating to a job that needs special training or education
secure	/sɪˈkjʊə/	(adj)	safe from danger or harm or not likely to end
space station	/speɪsˈsteɪʃən/	(n)	a vehicle in which people can travel round the Earth, outside its atmosphere, doing scientific tests
specialist	/ˈspeʃəlɪst/	(n)	someone who has a lot of experience, knowledge, or skill in a particular subject
technical	/ˈteknɪkəl/	(adj)	relating to the knowledge, machines or methods used in science and industry
theoretical	/θɪəˈretɪkəl/	(adj)	based on ideas rather than practical experience
understanding	/ʌndəˈstændɪŋ/	(n)	knowledge about a subject, situation, etc. or about how something works
vocational	/vəʊˈkeɪʃənəl/	(adj)	Vocational education and skills prepare you for a particular type of work.
weightless	/ˈweɪtləs/	(adj)	having or appearing to have no weight

Vocabulary	Pronunciation	Part of speech	Definition
UNIT 3			
antibiotic	/æntibaɪ'ɒtɪk/	(n)	a medicine which cures infections by destroying harmful bacteria
clinical	/'klɪnɪkəl/	(adj)	relating to medical treatment and tests
contract	/kɒn'trækt/	(v)	to get a serious disease
controlled	/kən'trəʊld/	(adj)	limited
data	/'deɪtə/	(n)	information or facts about something
diagnose	/'daɪəgnəʊz/	(v)	to say what is wrong with someone who is ill
disease	/dɪ'ziːz/	(n)	(an) illness caused by infection or by health failure rather than by an accident
inhale	/ɪn'heɪl/	(v)	to breathe air, smoke, or gas into your lungs
occur	/ə'kɜː/	(v)	to happen, often without being planned
outbreak	/'aʊtbreɪk/	(n)	a time when something suddenly begins, especially a disease
precaution	/prɪ'kɔːʃən/	(n)	something that you do to prevent bad things happening in the future
proven	/'pruːvən/	(adj)	something that has been shown to be true
recovery	/rɪ'kʌvəri/	(n)	when you feel better again after an illness or injury
researcher	/rɪ'sɜːtʃə/	(n)	someone who does research as a job
scientific	/saɪən'tɪfɪk/	(adj)	relating to science, or using the organized methods of science
spore	/spɔː/	(n)	a reproductive cell produced by some plants and simple organisms
treat	/triːt/	(v)	to give medical care to someone for an illness or injury
trial	/traɪəl/	(n)	a test of something new to find out if it is safe, works correctly, etc.
UNIT 4			
adequate	/'ædəkwət/	(adj)	enough
apparent	/ə'pærənt/	(adj)	obvious or easy to notice
appropriate	/ə'prəʊpriət/	(adj)	suitable or right for a particular situation or occasion
blizzard	/'blɪzəd/	(n)	a severe snow storm with strong winds
burn	/bɜːn/	(v)	to hurt a part of the body with fire or heat
bury	/'beri/	(v)	to cover something or someone completely with a large quantity of something
collapse	/kə'læps/	(v)	to fall down suddenly because of pressure or having no strength or support
collision	/kə'lɪʒən/	(n)	an accident that happens when two vehicles hit each other with force
considerable	/kən'sɪdərəbl/	(adj)	large or important enough to be noticed
crash	/kræʃ/	(n)	an accident in which a vehicle hits something
cut	/kʌt/	(v)	to injure yourself on a sharp object which makes you bleed
fall	/fɔːl/	(v)	to move down towards the ground, sometimes by accident
fierce	/fɪəs/	(adj)	very strong or powerful
goggles	/'gɒglz/	(n)	special glasses that fit close to the face to protect the eyes
gust	/gʌst/	(n)	a sudden strong wind
harness	/'hɑːnəs/	(n)	a piece of equipment with straps and belts, used to control or hold in place a person, animal, or object
heatstroke	/'hiːtstrəʊk/	(n)	a condition that can lead to death, caused by being too long in a very hot place
helmet	/'helmət/	(n)	a hard hat that protects your head
injury	/'ɪndʒəri/	(n)	damage to someone's body in an accident or an attack
irritate	/'ɪrɪteɪt/	(v)	to make a part of your body sore or painful
major	/'meɪdʒə/	(adj)	more important, bigger or more serious than others of the same type
minor	/'maɪnə/	(adj)	not important or serious
potential	/pə'tenʃəl/	(adj)	possible when the necessary conditions exist
protection	/prə'tekʃən/	(n)	the act of protecting or state of being protected
scald	/skɔːld/	(v)	to burn the skin with boiling liquid or steam
sea level	/siː 'levəl/	(n)	the average height of the sea where it meets the land
slip	/slɪp/	(v)	to slide by accident and fall or almost fall
straightforward	/streɪt'fɔːwəd/	(adj)	easy to understand or simple
strain	/streɪn/	(v)	to injure part of your body by using it too much
sunburn	/'sʌnbɜːn/	(n)	a condition in which your skin is sore and red because you have spent too long in the strong heat of the sun
sunscreen	/'sʌnskriːn/	(n)	a cream that you put on your skin to stop it from being burned by the sun

Vocabulary	Pronunciation	Part of speech	Definition
trap	/træp/	(v)	If someone or something is trapped, they are unable to move or escape
trek	/trek/	(v)	to walk a long distance, usually over land such as hills, mountains, or forests
UNIT 5			
apply	/ə'plaɪ/	(v)	to spread or rub a substance such as cream or paint on a surface
approach	/ə'prəʊtʃ/	(n)	a way of doing something
assemble	/ə'sembl/	(v)	to put the parts of something in the correct places and join them to each other
concept	/'kɒnsept/	(n)	a principle or idea
cost	/kɒst/	(n)	the amount of money that you need to buy or do something
dip	/dɪp/	(v)	to put something into a liquid for a short time
ensure	/ɪn'ʃɔː/	(v)	to make something certain to happen
handmade	/hænd'meɪd/	(adj)	made using the hands rather than a machine
high-quality	/haɪ' kwɒlɪti/	(adj)	high-quality products or services are very good, well-made, etc.
identical	/ɑɪ'dentɪkəl/	(adj)	exactly the same
individually-produced	/ɪndɪ'vɪdjuəli prə'djuːst/	(adj)	made one at a time
industrial	/ɪn'dʌstriːəl/	(adj)	connected with industry, or having a lot of industry and factories, etc.
management	/'mænɪdʒmənt/	(n)	the control and organization of something
manager	/'mænɪdʒə/	(n)	someone in control of an office, shop, team, etc.
mass-produced	/mæs prə'djuːst/	(adj)	produced in large numbers, cheaply in a factory
method	/'meθəd/	(n)	a way of doing something, often one that involves a system or plan
phase	/feɪz/	(n)	a stage or period which is part of a longer period
process	/'prəʊses/	(n)	a series of actions that you take in order to achieve a result
production	/prə'dʌkʃən/	(n)	when you make or grow something
scratch	/skrætʃ/	(v)	to rub a hard surface with a sharp object, often making a noise
seal	/siːl/	(v)	to cover a surface with a special liquid to protect it
small-scale	/smɔːl skeɪl/	(adj)	describes an event or activity that is small in size
volume	/'vɒljuːm/	(n)	the number or amount of something, especially when it is large
UNIT 6			
adapt	/ə'dæpt/	(v)	to change your behaviour so that it is suitable for a new situation
affect	/ə'fekt/	(v)	to have an influence on someone or something, or to cause them to change
capture	/'kæptʃə/	(v)	to take someone as a prisoner, or to take something into your possession, especially by force
coastal	/'kəʊstəl/	(adj)	situated on, or relating to the coast
conservation	/kɒnsə'veɪʃən/	(n)	the protection of nature
conservationist	/kɒnsə'veɪʃənɪst/	(n)	someone who works to protect nature
copper	/'kɒpə/	(n)	a reddish-brown metal used especially for making wire and coins
decline	/dɪ'klaɪn/	(v)	to gradually become less or worse
destruction	/dɪ'strʌkʃən/	(n)	when something is destroyed
diamond	/'daɪəmənd/	(n)	an extremely hard valuable stone which is used in jewellery, and in industry for cutting hard things
dust storm	/dʌst stɔːm/	(n)	a strong wind that carries clouds of fine dust, soil, and sand over a large area
endangered species	/ɪn'deɪndʒəd 'spiːʃiːz/	(n)	animals or plants that may soon not exist because there are very few now alive
exploit	/ɪk'splɔɪt/	(v)	to use someone or something unfairly for your own advantage
extract	/ɪk'strækt/	(v)	to remove or take out something
habitat	/'hæbɪtæt/	(n)	the natural environment of an animal or plant
impact	/'ɪmpækt/	(v)	to affect something or someone
logging	/'lɒgɪŋ/	(n)	the activity of cutting down trees for wood
mineral	/'mɪnərəl/	(n)	a valuable or useful chemical substance that is formed naturally in the ground
mining	/'mɑɪnɪŋ/	(n)	the industry or activity of removing substances such as coal or metal from the ground by digging
natural gas	/'nætʃərəl gæs/	(n)	gas, found underground, that is used as a fuel
orangutan	/ə'ræŋutæn/	(n)	a large ape with reddish-brown hair and long arms
rainforest	/'reɪnfɒrɪst/	(n)	a forest in a tropical area which receives a lot of rain

Vocabulary	Pronunciation	Part of speech	Definition
rescue centre	/'reskjuː 'sentə/	(n)	a place where sick animals are taken care of
resource	/rɪ'zɔːs/	(n)	something useful that a country, person, or organization has which they can use
source	/sɔːs/	(n)	where something comes from
species	/'spiːʃiːz/	(n)	a group of plants or animals which share similar characteristics
surface	/'sɜːfɪs/	(n)	the top or outside part of something
survive	/sə'vaɪv/	(v)	to continue to live or exist, especially after almost dying or being destroyed
waste	/weɪst/	(n)	unwanted matter or material of any type
UNIT 7			
abandon	/ə'bændən/	(v)	to leave a place, thing, or person for ever
ambitious	/æm'bɪʃəs/	(adj)	requiring a lot of work and difficult to achieve.
beam	/biːm/	(n)	a long, thick piece of wood, metal, or concrete, especially used to support weight in a building or other structure
brick	/brɪk/	(n)	a small, hard, rectangular block used for building walls and houses
concerned	/kən'sɜːnd/	(adj)	worried
concrete	/'kɒŋkriːt/	(n)	a very hard building material made of cement, sand, stones and water
contribute	/kən'trɪbjuːt/	(v)	to give something, especially money in order to provide
controversial	/kɒntrə'vɜːʃəl/	(adj)	causing disagreement or discussion
convert	/kən'vɜːt/	(v)	to (cause something or someone to) change in form or character
current	/'kʌrənt/	(adj)	happening or existing now
development	/dɪ'veləpmənt/	(n)	an area on which new buildings are built in order to make a profit
existing	/ɪg'zɪstɪŋ/	(adj)	describes something that exists now
expand	/ɪk'spænd/	(v)	to increase in size or amount, or to make something increase in this way
extension	/ɪk'stenʃən/	(n)	a new part added to a house or other building
feature	/fiːtʃə/	(n)	a part of a building or of an area of land
foundation	/faʊn'deɪʃən/	(n)	the structures below the surface of the ground that support a building
heritage	/'herɪtɪdʒ/	(n)	the buildings, paintings, customs, etc. which are important in a culture or society because they have existed for a long time
landmark	/'lændmɑːk/	(n)	a building that you can easily recognize, especially one that helps you to know where you are
maintain	/meɪn'teɪn/	(v)	to keep something in good condition
preserve	/prɪ'zɜːv/	(v)	to keep something the same or prevent it from being damaged or destroyed
steel	/stiːl/	(n)	a very strong metal made from iron, used for making knives, machines, etc.
stone	/stəʊn/	(n)	a hard, solid substance found in the ground, used for building
structure	/'strʌktʃə/	(n)	a building or something that has been built
supporting wall	/sə'pɔːtɪŋ wɔːl/	(n)	a wall that carries the weight of the ceiling in a building
sympathetic	/sɪmpə'θetɪk/	(adj)	being in harmony
transform	/træns'fɔːm/	(v)	to change something completely, usually to improve it
UNIT 8			
capacity	/kə'pæsəti/	(n)	the total amount that can be contained or produced
challenge	/'tʃælɪndʒ/	(n)	something that is difficult and that tests someone's ability or determination
complex	/'kɒmpleks/	(adj)	involving a lot of different but related parts
consumption	/kən'sʌmpʃən/	(n)	the amount eaten or used
dam	/dæm/	(n)	a wall built across a river that stops the river's flow and collects the water, especially to make a reservoir (=an artificial lake) that provides water for an area
element	/'elɪmənt/	(n)	a part of something
energy-efficient	/'enədʒi ɪfɪʃənt/	(adj)	using little electricity, gas, etc.
environmentally friendly	/ɪnvaɪərən'mentəli 'frendli/	(adj)	not harmful to the environment
experimental	/ɪksperɪ'mentəl/	(adj)	relating to tests, especially scientific ones
function	/'fʌŋkʃən/	(n)	the purpose of something or the particular responsibility of someone
generation	/dʒenə'reɪʃən/	(n)	the production of energy in a particular form
generator	/dʒenəreɪtə/	(n)	a machine that produces electricity
limitation	/lɪmɪ'teɪʃən/	(n)	a rule or situation that limits something
maintenance	/'meɪntɪnəns/	(n)	the work needed to keep a road, building, machine, etc. in good condition

Vocabulary	Pronunciation	Part of speech	Definition
network	/ˈnetwɜːk/	(n)	a system or group of connected parts
pipe	/paɪp/	(n)	a long tube inside which liquid or gas can move through
reservoir	/ˈrezəvwɑː/	(n)	a place for storing liquid, especially a natural or artificial lake providing water for a city or other area
shaft	/ʃɑːft/	(n)	a rod forming part of a machine such as an engine, that turns in order to pass power on to the machine
tower	/ˈtaʊə/	(n)	a tall, narrow structure, often square or circular, which either forms part of a building or stands alone
turbine	/ˈtɜːbaɪn/	(n)	a type of machine through which liquid or gas flows and turns a special wheel with blades in order to produce power
UNIT 9			
analyze	/ˈænəlaɪz/	(v)	to study or examine something in detail, in order to discover more about it
appreciate	/əˈpriːʃieɪt/	(v)	to understand how good something or someone is and be able to enjoy them
bold	/bəʊld/	(adj)	strong in colour or shape and therefore easy to notice
colour scheme	/kʌlə skiːm/	(n)	a combination of colours that has been chosen for a particular room
comment	/ˈkɒment/	(v)	to make a comment
composition	/kɒmpəˈzɪʃən/	(n)	the way that people or things are arranged in a painting or photograph
creativity	/kriˈeɪtɪvɪti/	(n)	the ability to produce new ideas or things using skill and imagination
criticism	/ˈkrɪtɪsɪzəm/	(n)	when you say that something or someone is bad
crystal	/ˈkrɪstəl/	(n)	clear, transparent rock that is used in jewellery, or a piece of this
display	/dɪˈspleɪ/	(v)	to arrange something somewhere so that people can see it
focus	/ˈfəʊkəs/	(v)	to concentrate
geometric	/dʒiːəˈmetrɪk/	(adj)	describes a pattern or arrangement that is made up of shapes such as squares, triangles, or rectangles
graffiti	/grəˈfiːti/	(n)	writing or pictures painted on walls and public places, usually illegally
inspiration	/ɪnspɪˈreɪʃən/	(n)	someone or something that gives you ideas for doing something
intense	/ɪnˈtens/	(adj)	extreme or very strong
interpret	/ɪnˈtɜːprɪt/	(v)	to decide what the intended meaning of something is
junction	/ˈdʒʌŋkʃən/	(n)	a place where things, especially roads or railways, come together
mine	/maɪn/	(n)	an underground system of holes and passages where people dig out coal or other minerals
reject	/rɪˈdʒekt/	(v)	to refuse to accept or agree with something
remove	/rɪˈmuːv/	(v)	to take something or someone away from somewhere, or off something
restore	/rɪˈstɔː/	(v)	to repair and clean something old
reveal	/rɪˈviːl/	(v)	to allow something to be seen that, until then, had been hidden
self-expression	/self ɪkˈspreʃən/	(n)	expression of your personality, emotions, or ideas
street art	/striˈːt ɑːt/	(n)	art in public spaces, usually refers to illegal art
vandalism	/ˈvændəlɪzəm/	(n)	the crime of intentionally damaging property belonging to other people
UNIT 10			
ageing	/ˈeɪdʒɪŋ/	(n)	the process of becoming older
ancestor	/ˈænsestə/	(n)	a relative who lived a long time ago
approximately	/əˈprɑksɪmətli/	(adv)	close to a particular number or time although not exactly that number or time
asset	/ˈæset/	(n)	something which a person or company owns which has a value
assist	/əˈsɪst/	(v)	to help
cooperate	/kəʊˈɒpəreɪt/	(v)	to work together with someone in order to achieve the same aim
cost-effective	/kɒst ɪˈfektɪv/	(adj)	If an activity is cost-effective, it is good value for the amount of money paid.
dependant	/dɪˈpendənt/	(n)	someone who depends on you for financial support
devote	/dɪˈvəʊt/	(v)	to give all of something, especially your time, effort, love, or yourself, to something you believe in or to a person
donate	/dəʊˈneɪt/	(v)	to give money or goods to help a person or organization
fertility rate	/fəˈtɪlɪti reɪt/	(n)	the number of births in an area
finance	/ˈfaɪnæns/	(n)	(the management of) a supply of money
generation	/dʒenəˈreɪʃən/	(n)	all the people in a society or family who are approximately the same age
household	/ˈhaʊshəʊld/	(n)	a family or group of people who live together in a house

Vocabulary	Pronunciation	Part of speech	Definition
indicate	/ˈɪndɪkeɪt/	(v)	to show that something exists or is likely to be true
institution	/ɪnstɪˈtjuːʃən/	(n)	a building where people are sent so they can be looked after
investment	/ɪnˈvestmənt/	(n)	the money that you put in a bank, business, etc. in order to make a profit
luxury	/ˈlʌkʃəri/	(n)	something expensive which is pleasant to have but is not necessary
nuclear family	/ˈnjuːklɪər ˈfæməli/	(n)	a family consisting of two parents and their children, but not including aunts, uncles, grandparents, etc
participate	/pɑːˈtɪsɪpeɪt/	(v)	to take part in or become involved in an activity
pension	/ˈpenʃən/	(n)	a sum of money paid regularly by the government or a private company to a person who has stopped working because they are old or ill
permit	/pəˈmɪt/	(v)	to allow something
poverty	/ˈpɒvəti/	(n)	the condition of being extremely poor
property	/ˈprɒpəti/	(n)	a building or area of land
responsibility	/rɪspɒnsɪˈbɪlɪti/	(n)	something that it is your job or duty to deal with
retirement	/rɪˈtaɪəmənt/	(n)	when you leave your job and stop working, usually because you are old
reunion	/riːˈjuːniən/	(n)	an occasion when people who have not met each other for a long time meet
support	/səˈpɔːt/	(v)	to look after someone by paying for their food, clothes, etc.
welfare	/ˈwelfeə/	(n)	physical and mental health and happiness, especially of a person

VIDEO AND AUDIO SCRIPTS

UNIT 1

The globalization of food

Narrator: International trade is the activity of buying, selling and exchanging goods and services between countries.

In the 21st century, industrialization, modern transportation, multinational corporations and outsourcing are all having a major impact on the international trade system.

Increasing international trade powers the continued growth of globalization. Food is one commodity that is traded worldwide.

In Longsheng, China, rice farmers have worked in these rice paddies for almost 800 years. The rice they grow feeds people all over the world.

Countries trade produce with each other to sell what they grow in excess and they buy commodities that are cheaper elsewhere, or that they cannot produce themselves.

France, for example, is only the 43rd largest country in the world, but it is the world's second largest exporter of agricultural products, selling wheat, dairy and meat products to countries worldwide.

Competition is fierce between countries to gain a competitive advantage in the international trade market and to get a good price for their produce.

In Australia, goods are transported far across the country by road and worldwide by ship.

Australian farmers export around 60% of what they produce, earning the country more than 30 billion Australian dollars per year. The transport involved in international trade can, however, have massive effects on pollution and the environment.

International trade can also make countries more economically reliant on non-domestic trade for the production, processing and purchase of goods.

These Mexican prickly pear farmers rely on selling their product in specialist food shops across the world.

However, this export business has brought money – and hope – to an entire community by creating jobs.

Without international trade, nations would be limited to the goods and services within their own borders and the food produced here, wouldn't end up on a plate here.

1.1

Voice-over: Today on Food Close Up – The 49,000 Kilometre Fruit Salad. We're looking at what shoppers are purchasing and finding out the true environmental cost of the produce that we buy everyday. Our reporter has gone to Freshmart in central London to investigate this issue and see just what shoppers are putting in their baskets.

Presenter: Hello listeners. I'm standing in the fruit and vegetable aisle of Freshmart, in central London. There are a lot of healthy eaters here and David Green is one of them. David, can we have a look in your basket? What are you buying today?

David: Mostly fruit and vegetables. I've got a bunch of grapes, some bananas, some kiwis, a small packet of blueberries, tomatoes and a lettuce. I'm making a fruit salad for lunch, as I'm watching my weight. I'm trying to eat healthily.

Presenter: I notice on the label that the bananas are from Thailand.

David: Yeah ... so?

Presenter: Do you mind if I check the grapes? Hmmm ... they're from South Africa. The kiwi comes from ... New Zealand and the blueberries are from Argentina. David, did you realize that all this fruit is imported from overseas?

David: Well, I guess as it's winter we can't grow these fruits in our country. They *have* to be imported. If we didn't then how would we get fresh fruit in winter?

Presenter: Good point. The global food industry – and the speed of shipping fresh foods by aeroplane – allows people all over the world to eat a huge variety of fresh fruit and vegetables all year round.

David: It's just more convenient, isn't it? Most of the fruit and vegetables I like, like peppers, oranges and cucumbers, grow in hotter countries. A lot of the fruit and veg that grows here in the UK is so boring.

Presenter: It *is* possible to grow fruits and vegetables from hot countries here, but they have to be grown in greenhouses, which increases production costs. If you look at these tomatoes, which were grown on a local farm, they're almost twice the cost of the tomatoes you've got here from Turkey, over 3,500 kilometres away.

David: I'd never pay that for a few tomatoes!

Presenter: I know, but cheap food comes at a price. Let's look at the figures. The bananas from Thailand travelled more than 9,500 kilometres to reach Freshmart, the grapes from South Africa came more than 9,600 kilometres and the Argentinean blueberries 11,100 kilometres. The kiwi from New Zealand? That was flown about 18,800 kilometres. So, that's ... 49,000 kilometres of air travel in one bowl! That's an incredibly long food supply chain and a huge carbon footprint, which means a huge amount of pollution was produced to get this food to the shelves. When food travels, a lot of carbon dioxide pollution is produced and most people now believe that carbon dioxide in the air is causing climate change – causing the Earth to get generally warmer.

David: I've never really thought about it that much. What about this lettuce? It's local.

Presenter: Even something that looks like it's local can have a big impact on the environment. It's far cheaper for supermarkets to have several large factories than lots of small ones all over the country, so food grown around the country is transported to large factories to be packaged or processed. This lettuce may be local, but it could have been transported across the country to be put into this plastic packaging. It's sometimes then transported back to the place it was grown in the first place.

David: So, before arriving in Freshmart, this local lettuce may have travelled ...

Presenter: ... maybe up to 500 kilometres? You can only really be sure how far something has travelled if you buy it directly from a farm or if you grow it yourself.

David: Wow. I can't believe it. Maybe I'll just have a pizza for lunch instead ...

Presenter: Thanks for your time, David. A 49,000 kilometre fruit salad and it isn't even very expensive for the consumer. The question is: what's the true environmental cost of David's healthy lunch? That's all for today. Thanks for listening to Food Close Up.

1.2

1 These agricultural products are already going abroad.
2 We grow many kinds of tea on this plantation.
3 The police regularly find illegal imports.
4 The company sewed more clothes overseas last year.
5 The bananas are timed so that they ripen together.
6 Flying the crops causes air pollution.
7 The products pass through customs easily.
8 I want to know why these routes cost more.

There hasn't been much support from the government over the issue of imported agricultural crops. There are three issues with this. First, nearly a sixth of all imported fruit cannot grow in our climate. Secondly, the state should help our own farmers rather than foreign growers. Finally, we should not fall into the trap of not growing enough food. What would happen if it didn't rain and we were left with a food shortage?

1.4

Due to general changes in lifestyle, people these days are increasingly eating a healthier diet, consisting of plenty of fruit and vegetables, along with milk and other dairy products, protein in the form of meat, fish, eggs or beans, and starchy foods such as rice, potatoes and pasta.

As a result, it's easier than ever to find food that's good for you at the supermarket, but are some of these foods actually unhealthy for the environment?

There's been a lot of discussion in the media about imported foods. Many people say that imported products harm the environment because they're shipped long distances by aeroplane. It has been suggested that we should choose domestic foods over overseas foods, because of aeroplanes creating pollution that causes environmental problems.

Experts argue that foods that are the least damaging to the environment are usually the ones grown locally. Consequently, some people believe that local foods are always more environmentally friendly and are therefore always the most appropriate choice, but is this really true? Let's look at some data.

This pie chart shows the carbon footprint of the UK food system. Firstly, as you can see, the largest part of the carbon footprint is the section called *Households*, meaning the energy used in homes to store and prepare food – mostly refrigeration or cooking with gas or electrical appliances. This accounts for more than a quarter of the total carbon footprint. Secondly, according to the chart, the next main source of carbon in the UK food system is processing. Examples of this would be putting vegetables in tins, or turning ingredients into ready-meals, like frozen pizza. This makes up about one fifth of the total. After processing, agriculture is the next main source of carbon emissions. The UK is a cool and rainy country, which means that tomatoes in the UK must be grown in greenhouses. These greenhouses are heated, which therefore produces carbon dioxide. Tomatoes grown in Spain require less energy to grow because the climate in Spain is milder and greenhouses aren't needed.

After agriculture, wholesale and retail food sales account for 14% of the food carbon footprint. This refers to the energy used to store and sell foods in warehouses and supermarkets and so on.

After that comes food service. This basically means the energy used by restaurants and cafés to supply food to customers. Next comes emissions linked to packaging such as the containers that food is put in to be sold or transported. For example, when you buy chicken in a UK supermarket, it comes in a tray, usually wrapped in plastic. Finally, the smallest portion of energy in the UK food system goes to transportation.

So, what does this tell us about food kilometres? In summary, the data shows that transporting food definitely uses energy and produces carbon emissions, but from this evidence, that it makes up the very smallest part of the carbon footprint from food.

I'd like to talk about where your money goes when you buy a cup of coffee. There has been a lot of discussion in the media recently about fair prices for the people in countries who grow crops like coffee. Many people believe that it's not right that a cup of coffee can cost £3 or more, of which the farmers only get a few pennies. However, others have pointed out that the coffee beans are only one part of the cost of supplying a cup of coffee. They say that the other ingredients, such as milk and sugar, are also a big part of the cost of a cup of coffee. However, I would like to show that in a typical coffee house, the ingredients are only a small part of the overall cost. Let's look at some data. If you consider the information on this chart ...

This pie chart shows where your money goes when you buy a cup of coffee. Firstly, as you can see, the largest part of the cost is administration, at 26%. That's more than a quarter of the cost per cup. Secondly is labour, which you'll notice accounts for 18% of the cost. Next, tax, profit, and rent each make up about 14% of the cost, or a total of 42% of the price of your cup of coffee.

Finally, I'd like to draw your attention to the three parts that are related to the product you take away – milk at 6%, the cup, sugar and lid at 4% and the coffee itself at 2%. Together, they make up 12% of the price you pay.

UNIT 2

Astronaut training

Narrator: Clay Anderson wears a suit to work. A space suit! Clay has been training for the past nine years to work on NASA's International Space Station.

His training is very practical, but it also needs to be theoretical – he needs maths and physics to understand the science of space travel before he leaves Earth.

Preparing for work in space is a huge challenge. In space, astronauts are weightless – they float freely in the air. How can you prepare for that?

Clay trains for this part of the mission in an aeroplane, but how does it work?

The plane is flown in a series of arcs – taking a curved path up and then down again. This allows the student astronauts to be weightless for about 30 seconds at a time.

Thirty seconds is long enough to see what working whilst weightless feels like, but for proper training, Clay and the other trainees need hours of practice.

And for that, they come here. This training pool is 60 metres long, 30 metres wide and 12 metres deep. It holds more than 22 million litres of water and is the largest indoor pool in the world.

The facility has 200 employees and more than 60 divers who help with astronaut training.

Clay and his mission partner are lowered into the pool and their suits are checked for leaks.

For every hour Clay plans to work in space, he needs to practise for seven hours in the pool.

The work area in the pool is an exact copy of the space station. This gives Clay very practical experience with the station and with the tools he needs.

Clay practices every part of the job he will need to do in space. He will work long hours and so he needs to be physically strong to do the job.

After seven hours in the training pool, Clay is clearly exhausted, but happy with the progress of his training.

Clay: Long day, lots to do, tired hands, but it was all good.

Narrator: After his training, Clay will be ready for his six month space mission. When he goes to work on the International Space Station, he will hopefully have prepared enough to find time to enjoy the view.

2.1

Adviser: Hello, Bahar. Welcome to the careers office. Good to see you.

Bahar: Hello.

Adviser: Now, I saw from your file that you're looking for advice on what to do when you graduate. You're considering university, aren't you?

Bahar: Yes, that's right, but I'm not really sure which course to apply for.

Adviser: Well, what are you considering?

Bahar: I like Maths and Physics, and I'm doing well in those classes.

Adviser: Looking at your file, I couldn't agree more! You should make use of your Maths and Physics abilities. Any ideas?

Bahar: Well, I'm considering studying Engineering.

Adviser: Ah, Engineering. That's a big field. Engineering jobs are secure though. The world will always need engineers! What sort of Engineering are you interested in? Electrical? Civil? Nuclear?

Bahar: I'm not sure. I've always been interested in the way things work, you know, cars and other machines. So, I'd like to study something technical, that's for sure. Actually, I'm quite interested in space flight. Space shuttles are really cool.

Adviser: Maybe you should consider Mechanical Engineering then. As a start, anyway. That's a good, basic Engineering degree – it covers the core subjects. Mechanical engineers often go on to become specialists in lots of different jobs – Aerospace Engineering is just one of them. It would definitely be a way to use your talent for Maths and Physics and acquire some really useful skills and an in-depth understanding of the field.

Bahar: Right, but I'm not sure if that would be for me. An Engineering degree would be very academic. I wonder if I should try something more vocational. Maybe a diploma course? I actually quite like manual work. I'd rather make something than write about it! Is it possible to become an apprentice engineer and then study for professional qualifications?

Adviser: Have you done much research on different courses that are available?

Bahar: Not yet.

Adviser: How about trying to find out more about Engineering courses, then? I could give you the names of some universities and colleges that teach Engineering in Istanbul. You could visit them and discuss their courses in detail.

Bahar: Yes, that's a good idea. I think I could do that. I'd like to know more about what engineers actually do and I'd rather talk to someone than just read their website. Thanks.

Adviser: In that case, have you considered talking to some engineers about their work?

Bahar: I don't know any engineers.

Adviser: Well, I know that some of the parents of students here are engineers. I'm sure we could arrange for you to talk with them. You could ask them what their job is like.

Bahar: That would be great. I really want to know how practical Engineering work is. I wouldn't mind the theoretical side of Engineering, the Maths and the Physics, but I think I'd really enjoy the practical side of Engineering. You know, designing and making things. Manufacturing Engineering could be really interesting.

Adviser: You might want to try contacting a manufacturing Engineering firm here in the city, then. In fact, I could help you with that. We could probably set up a visit for you.

Bahar: That would be fantastic. Thank you.

 2.2

See script on page 38.

 2.3

Adviser: Hello, Adam. Come in. Sit down.

Adam: Thank you, sir.

Adviser: Have you finished your research into the medical courses I suggested last time we met?

Adam: Not entirely. I've done some, but I'm having a hard time deciding what I want to do.

Adviser: I see. That's understandable. There's a lot to think about. Is studying medicine the most important consideration for you?

Adam: Yes and no. The most important thing is probably that I go on a medical course of some kind, but not necessarily one that involves a lot of study.

Adviser: OK.

Adam: Getting a secure job after I finish my course is important, though, and I really want to help people.

Adviser: What about location? Do you care about where you study?

Adam: Not really. That's probably the least important factor.

Adviser: OK, good. Well, I think we're getting somewhere. With your good marks, you should consider studying to become a doctor.

Adam: I'm not sure about that.

Adviser: Really? Why not?

Adam: Well, I guess another one of my criteria is that the job is very practical.

Adviser: Sorry, but I have to disagree. I think being a doctor is a very practical job!

Adam: Yes, but I'd rather not have to study for so many years.

Adviser: Maybe you should consider becoming an emergency room nurse.

Adam: I've looked into that. It's a degree course.

Adviser: You don't sound too keen. If you're not interested in that, what else are you considering?

Adam: It depends. I'm not sure what I can apply to study. There are a few courses where you can study to become an emergency medical technician – an EMT. They're the people who work on ambulances, assessing patients' conditions, performing emergency procedures, attending accidents and so on.

Adviser: That's a tough job. Exciting, but tough, and very physical.

Adam: Yes, but it seems like a great way to really help people when they need it.

Adviser: So, what's the difference between the two courses?

Adam: The EMT course is very practical. When you work in an ambulance, you need a lot of practical skills to help people. You have to be very independent and self-confident to make decisions on your own, and of course there's the driver training, too!

Adviser: OK, I see your point.

Adam: The emergency room nursing course is also practical, but it includes more theoretical work. Especially when you study the core subjects – learning about the human body and about medicines and so on. It would involve a lot more complex study. You have to work closely with hospital staff. It's a degree course.

Adviser: And the EMT course?

Adam: It's a diploma course. So, it would take a lot less time and I'd be able to start work quickly. It would be great to actually work after so much study. I've been studying my whole life. I'm ready to *do* something, have some adventures, so I'm not too sure about nursing.

Adviser: Yes, I can see that. It may not be the ideal course.

Adam: EMTs need in-depth understanding of how to deal with emergencies and they need the ability to make quick decisions.

Adviser: I think you'd be good at it.

Adam: And if I wanted to continue my training, after working as a basic EMT, I could study to become an EMT specialist. That's another diploma course.

Adviser: But, wouldn't you rather study to be a nurse? I imagine the pay would be better.

Adam: You're probably right, but I don't think it's for me.

Adviser: Why don't we get some more information about EMT courses, then and find out which colleges offer that diploma.

Adam: That would be a great idea.

Adviser: I guess you've made a decision, then. You're going to apply for EMT training.

Adam: I think that's really what I want to do.

 2.4

A: I think the most important factor is probably financial need.

B: I'm not sure about that. What if we say that financial need is number two?

C: So, what's number one?

B: I feel it's important to really focus on the applicants' potential contribution to society.

C: I think that's right. Why don't we rank the proposed courses of study according to their contribution to society?

A: OK, I can see your point, but why don't we just say that the interview is number one and financial need is number two?

C/D: OK.

B: Wait a minute. I don't agree with that at all. Academic ability is much more important. What if we say that academic score is the most important factor?

A: I think the rest of us are in agreement about the most important factors.

D: Well, I think the least important thing is the student's written application.

C: Sorry, I don't think I agree. They need to be able to write well.

B: Wait! Have you considered taking the applicants' family situations into account?

2.5

1 **A:** Students need to be good at both writing and speaking.
B: I see. That's understandable.

2 **A:** Hotel workers are important, but emergency medical technicians save lives.
B: OK, I see your point.

3 **A:** The Chinese language is becoming more important all the time.
B: You might be right about that.

4 **A:** Why don't we say emergency medical technicians have the most important job?
B: OK, I think we all can live with that.

5 **A:** What if we agree that financial need is the most important factor?
B: Right. We've made a decision.

6 **A:** Can we agree that academic score is the most important factor?
B: I think we've come to an agreement.

UNIT 3

 Anthrax

Narrator: In 2006, a New York drummer and drum-maker, named Vado Diomande, became seriously ill.

The doctors did tests to diagnose the problem and were shocked by the results. Vado had anthrax.

Anthrax is one of the world's most dangerous diseases. Whenever a case of anthrax is discovered, government authorities are notified immediately.

Government scientists, doctors and experts must protect the health and safety of the public.

Anthrax spores occur naturally, found in soil and in animal products. Animals can carry the disease without being ill, but humans can't.

The spores are invisible, but if inhaled, humans can become extremely ill very quickly.

Inhaled anthrax spores replicate and produce chemicals that destroy the human body.

Anthrax can only spread through spores, so Vado couldn't infect other people.

Anthrax is rare, but an outbreak could kill tens of thousands of people in just days. It is important to identify cases of anthrax quickly.

Fortunately, the disease can be treated if it is identified early.

The doctors had to act quickly.

The disease was treated with antibiotics and special anthrax drugs.

The experts couldn't understand how Vado had contracted anthrax, and equally, whether other people were going to catch it.

They searched Vado's home for clues and found a trace of anthrax in his apartment – but it wasn't the source. But when they checked Vado's drum-making workshop, they discovered the source of the disease: animal skins that had been used for making drums.

The skins, with the anthrax, had come from Africa.

Fortunately, Vado's treatment worked and he made a full recovery.

3.1

Teacher: Throughout history there have been many pandemics around the world: measles, malaria, cholera, flu. So, how does a common disease turn into a pandemic? Any ideas?

Student 1: People's general health and how close they live to each other can be major factors in the spread of disease, can't they?

Student 2: Yeah, so governments need to make sure people are in good health and live in good conditions to stop diseases spreading.

Teacher: Well, that's a good idea, but there's a limit to what governments can do, especially in times of economic difficulty.

Student 2: And governments don't always have the power to say exactly how everyone should live.

Teacher: So what factors do you think would make a country at a high-risk of pandemic?

Student 3: Well, countries with large populations are probably at risk, especially where large numbers of people live close together.

Student 1: And countries where a lot of international travellers pass through, like the UK and other countries in dark and medium blue on the map.

Teacher: That's right. The countries most at risk of a pandemic these days are more wealthy countries like Singapore, the UK, South Korea, the Netherlands and Germany. What do those countries have in common?

Student 2: They're not all large countries, but they do all have large cities with big populations.

Student 1: And they're all places where a lot of international travellers might go. They have a lot of airports and potentially thousands of people coming in every day, from all over the world.

Teacher: Correct. If you look at those countries in light blue and white, they're at a medium and low risk of pandemic because they have less dense populations, less international travel, fewer borders, etc. OK, so imagine you're an adviser to your government. You want to protect your country from a pandemic. What should you do?

Student 1: You should give everyone a vaccine.

Teacher: A vaccine. OK, good idea. Can anyone explain what that is?

Student 2: It's a kind of medicine, isn't it?

Teacher: Yes, sort of. Most medicines are given to patients after they have the illness, to make them well again, but a vaccine is different. A vaccine provides disease prevention. It's given to patients to stop them becoming infected.

So if we want to avoid pandemics, then governments need to implement vaccination programmes for common diseases, don't they?

Student 3: The government should force everyone to have vaccines. They should get a vaccine to people as soon as an outbreak occurs because prevention is generally much easier than treatment.

Student 2: I'm not sure I agree. The trouble is, viruses change every year. So a vaccine that worked really well last year may not be effective this year.

Student 1: There's another thing to consider, too; a lot of people don't want to have a vaccine that might not work. They can't force people to have it, can they?

Teacher: Well, I don't think any governments do, but in the event of a pandemic, they definitely encourage people to have it, and a lot of people do. People don't want to catch a disease, do they? So other than vaccination what other ways are there of stopping the spread of disease?

Student 1: International travel is a big risk to a disease spreading quickly. We shouldn't allow people with diseases into the country.

Student 3: I'm not sure I agree. The trouble is, most people spread diseases before they even know they have them.

Student 2: And there's another problem. How could people prove whether or not they have diseases? It would be impossible to set up a system for checking it.

Student 1: During a pandemic, we should stop all flights from countries that are affected, shouldn't we? If we don't let people into the country, then the disease won't get here.

Student 2: But there's another side to that argument. People travel all the time for business. It would have a terrible effect on the economy, wouldn't it?

Student 3: But also, in most countries, people who live near the border travel back and forth, sometimes every day. It would stop a lot of people going to work, and could separate families.

Teacher: Well, there are some really interesting views there from all of you. Can anyone think of some simpler suggestions for decreasing the risks of pandemics, then? Perhaps not as large-scale as closing down country borders?

Student 1: Well, people who have flu should stay at home from school or from work, shouldn't they? ...

See script on page 56.

Flu season is here, but experts and the public are divided on the subject of vaccination. Those in favour of the flu vaccination say that it may help you avoid becoming ill and may also help stop the spread of the disease. They point out that this may save lives. Those experts against the flu vaccination argue that there is no proof that it works. Some go as far as to say that it may be unsafe, because it is produced very quickly, though there is no evidence to support this claim.

The fact is that there is no research or clinical evidence to show that either side is correct. As the debate continues, statistics show that only about 30% of us choose to have the flu vaccination each year.

Host: Since the news that this year's flu vaccination is ready, the government has advised that the old, young, and people with medical problems be vaccinated.

However, not everyone thinks vaccination is a good idea. About 30% of us get the flu vaccination as a precaution each year, but 70% don't. Of that 70%, some are actively against the flu vaccination.

In today's debate, we'll begin with flu expert Dr Sandra Smith in favour of flu vaccination. After that, we'll hear from alternative medicine practitioner Mark Li, who is against flu vaccination.

Dr Smith will now begin. Dr Smith.

Sandra: Thank you. Well, influenza, or the flu, is a respiratory disease that can make you feel extremely ill. Ninety-eight percent of people who get the flu recover after several days. While they may feel terrible, there are usually no lasting problems. However, the flu can cause severe illness or worse for about 2% of the people who get it. It may not sound like a lot, but actually, this is hundreds of thousands of people around the world each year. It can be especially serious for the very old and the very young. Obviously, we want to do everything in our power to stop the infection spreading. This brings us to vaccination.

Vaccines have saved millions of lives. They're a proven method of disease prevention. Scientists have been developing flu vaccines from the 1930s up to today, so we have a lot of experience with them. Researchers make new flu vaccines every year based on the previous year's flu virus. The government recommends that children between the ages of 2 and 17, people over 65 and anyone who already has a serious illness have the flu vaccine.

To finish up, let me say this: I'm a flu specialist. I research the virus and work closely with flu patients all the time, so I'm constantly exposed to the virus. I've had the vaccination. All of my colleagues have had the vaccination and none of us have got flu. There's no guarantee that vaccination will prevent you getting flu, but it won't hurt you and there's a chance it could save your life. How would you feel if someone in your family passed up the chance for vaccination, and then became really ill? Thank you.

Host: We'll now have the statement against vaccination, from Mr Mark Li.

Mark: Thank you and thank you, Sandra. Let me start by saying that I'm not against all vaccination. Dr Smith is absolutely right that many vaccines work very well and that millions of lives have been saved by vaccination. There's plenty of good scientific data that proves that, but let me ask you this: has the flu vaccine been properly tested? Have there been proper scientific trials to prove that it works, that it stops infection? Does it really provide prevention of the disease?

For most medicines, the government makes sure that proper tests are carried out, but this isn't the case with the flu vaccine. There isn't one single scientific study that proves that this year's flu vaccine works. The packaging on this flu vaccine clearly states that 'No controlled trials have been performed that demonstrate that this vaccine causes a reduction in influenza.' It's here in black and white.

If it says on the package that there's no proof that it's an effective prevention, why are we using it? Yes, vaccination can be good, but flu vaccination is just a big experiment and it may actually be doing more harm than good. Thank you.

Host: Thank you, Mr Li. So, we'll now have Dr Smith's response.

Sandra: Thank you. You have some interesting points, Mark. It's true that when the flu emerges every year it's a bit different to the year before. When making a vaccine, we have to try to work out how the flu is going to change and adjust it to the new virus; we can't wait until the new virus emerges. It would be too late.

So while Mr Li is right – we don't do trials of the flu vaccine in the way that we do trials for other medicines – that doesn't mean we aren't scientific in our methods. I'd definitely like to challenge the idea that there's no scientific basis for our work. I disagree with Mr Li on that point. Let me tell you more about my work in that area.

We can prove in the laboratory that vaccines can reduce the risk of getting a disease, generally. What we don't know is exactly how this year's flu virus will change, but we can use our experience to make a prediction. As for the question of the vaccine being dangerous: it doesn't contain a live virus, so you definitely can't get flu from the vaccine. If someone is vaccinated and then they happen to become ill, that doesn't logically mean the vaccination caused the illness. They were most likely exposed to the virus before they were vaccinated. Thank you.

Host: Thank you, Dr Smith. Mark Li will now make the final response.

Mark: Well, I'm sure Dr Smith is a very good doctor, but I think the flu vaccine package I mentioned earlier is clear. It's obvious that the vaccine hasn't been properly tested.

The other big concern, of course, is safety. A lot of us believe that the vaccine actually makes people ill rather than making them well – so she and I disagree on that point. I'm talking about side effects. Some people have become really ill after being vaccinated. This can be anything from headaches to stomach problems. Do you really want to use a medication that may make you ill? Supposing you gave your kids the vaccine and it made them worse rather than better? Some people also believe that the vaccine may give you the flu rather than stopping you from catching it. I've had patients who were healthy, then took the flu vaccine and became ill. Medicines shouldn't make us ill. That's why I'm against the flu vaccine, and that's why I don't think anyone at all should have it. Thank you.

Host: Thank you both.

UNIT 4

Andes mountain trek

Narrator: The Andes Mountains in Patagonia rise from sea level to over 4,000 metres.

In 2004, Steve Ogle and Chad Sayers went there to go trekking.

Trekking is risky. One of the biggest dangers trekkers face is the weather.

The way the wind moves in Patagonia … it comes sometimes in fierce gusts … you know, you just can't predict it.

Steve and Chad planned to ski a route across the snow and ice where no one had ever been before.

The trip began well.

The weather was incredible. It was calm, clear, warm. Uh, it was like paradise.

But in Patagonia, the weather can change suddenly.

In a storm, winds can reach speeds of 200 kilometres per hour. Not long into their trip, Steve and Chad saw – and felt – a storm coming.

And just like that, it got black.

The wind began to blow.

They set up their tent for protection.

The wind reached a speed of 160 kilometres per hour.

The wind blew the snow and created a ground blizzard. Steve and Chad were trapped.

For three days, the men stayed in the tent as the snow slowly covered it.

The situation was dangerous. Their tent was disappearing under the snow and the risk of it collapsing was high, so they had to remove the snow.

It was just so powerful.

The men were trapped in their tent for ten more days while the snow continued to bury it.

When we were in that tent, and that storm was hitting us so hard, we really felt like we could just disappear out there.

The storm continued for two weeks.

The men began to worry about running out of food …

… but then the storm ended. It had dropped 2.5 metres of snow on the tent.

Ground blizzards are not unusual in Patagonia.

Chad and Steve certainly now have a clearer understanding of the risks of trekking in the Andes.

Since the men left, no one has returned to this part of Patagonia.

Guide: Welcome everyone. My name is Emir and I'm your guide today. Now, before we go out on the dunes, we need to go over some important safety information.

First, you need to wear appropriate shoes. Can I check that everyone has appropriate shoes? What I mean is shoes that won't fall off, that really protect your feet. The sand is hot and you always have to be prepared to walk. Foot injuries are a real hazard, but if you're wearing closed shoes then your feet will be protected.

Student 1: Are these OK?

Guide: Ummm. Sandals aren't so good, actually. They can come off so you mustn't wear them. Do you have anything else?

Student 1: I have some trainers in the coach.

Guide: OK, you should put those on. You definitely need good foot protection. Does everyone else have suitable shoes? Because a lot of people think that because they're in a car, a dune buggy, shoes aren't important, but they really are. You have to protect yourself from foot injuries and you have to be prepared to walk. Trainers are perfect for this. Right. The sun is hot and the risk of sunburn is high, so you are to wear adequate sun protection. I'm talking about using plenty of sunscreen and wearing sun-protective clothing; clothes that cover your skin. There's sunscreen available in the reception area, so you can get some there before we go out. Ideally, you should have long sleeves to cover your arms and long trousers.

Heat stroke is also a danger, so you should try to stay as cool as possible or you're sure to have a pretty bad day. Remember, if you don't have adequate sun protection you will get severely burned, or get heatstroke and it could ruin your day, and also the rest of the week.

Student 2: What about sunhats?

Guide: Not necessary. I'm going to give you a helmet to wear. It doesn't usually happen, but if you have a crash or a collision, you're likely to injure your head unless you're wearing the helmet.

Student 3: What about sunglasses?

Guide: You can wear sunglasses, but I'm also going to give everyone goggles. The goggles will fit over your glasses, or sunglasses. They are to be worn at all times and will protect your eyes. Finally, there's one other very important piece of safety equipment, and that's the harness. If you don't wear a harness when we drive off the road, you bounce around in your seat and you could lose control or you could fall out. So everyone needs to wear a harness and the harness needs to be nice and tight. I'll help you with that when we go to the dune buggies. Remember, the harness is not to be removed at any time while you are in the buggy. Now let's get our helmets and goggles. ... Can everyone come over here and find a helmet and a pair of goggles? We'll need to adjust them to fit, but that's a very straightforward procedure. I'll show you how it's done. So to summarize, wear a helmet and goggles and use your harness to stay safe. That's pretty simple, isn't it? As long as everyone follows the rules, we're all bound to have a great day.

Now let's go to the buggies. ...

OK, now we need to talk about what happens if we have a crash or a collision. It doesn't usually happen, but it's possible and we need to be prepared. If your dune buggy rolls over, don't panic. If you are wearing your harness correctly, you will stay with the dune buggy. You are not to get out of the buggy as you could get run over. One of the guides will stop and make sure the area is safe, and we'll help you get out. We'll make sure the dune buggy is safe to drive and then we'll continue on.

It's the same if you have a collision. Stop the dune buggy, if it isn't already stopped, and we'll come and check to make sure everyone is OK and it's safe to move on. Right, so, in case you missed that, or you weren't paying attention, in a crash don't panic and stay in the dune buggy. We'll make sure it's safe and then we'll get you out. In a collision, it's the same thing. Don't panic, wait for help, we'll check you and the vehicle and then we'll go on.

1 The sand is hot, and you always have to be prepared to walk.

2 You definitely need good foot protection. Does everyone else have suitable shoes?

3 I'm talking about using plenty of sunscreen and wearing sun-protective clothing; clothes that cover your skin.

4 If you don't wear a harness when we drive off the road, you bounce around in your seat and you could lose control, or you could fall out.

Hassan: Hello, welcome. My name's Hassan Ali. I'm the owner of this restaurant.

Peter: Hello Mr Ali. I'm Peter Jones from the Health and Safety Office. We spoke on the phone.

Hassan: Yes. And this is my head chef, Mehmet Usman.

Mehmet: Hello.

Peter: Hello. Nice to meet you. Shall we get started? Now, your restaurant has five stars for hygiene, one of the best records in the city, and we also know you've got one of the safest kitchens in town, only eight incidents in the whole of the last year. Your safety record is outstanding.

Hassan: Yes, thank you. It's very important to us.

Peter: But I also understand that one of your kitchen workers fell off a ladder recently and had to go to hospital with a back injury.

Hassan: Yes, that's right. He strained his back. Actually, he's back at work now, but the accident was very unfortunate.

Peter: Yes, indeed. I've read the insurance report and I just wanted to check a few details with you about exactly what happened, as I need to complete some paper work. After that, we'll go through the risk assessment procedure, if that's all right?

Hassan: Yes, absolutely.

Peter: Great. It's very straightforward. We'll look at the kitchen and identify hazards and risks, and then we'll make sure you're taking adequate precautions to keep your staff safe.

Hassan: Yes, that's fine.

Peter: So, why don't we start with the ladder accident?

Hassan: OK. Mehmet, can you explain about our storage?

Mehmet: Sure. We keep some of our supplies on a high shelf and we use a small ladder to reach them. When Omar fell, he was using a ladder to get some boxes down. The ladder might have slipped on the wet floor. We aren't sure.

Peter: OK, I see. Well, we want to avoid this happening again. It could have been a considerable injury. So, in terms of risk assessment, the main thing is you need to make sure that the floor is dried after it has been cleaned and that people aren't lifting boxes down from higher than their head height. Without these changes there's a high risk of serious injury from a falling hazard. Almost 25% of accidents in professional kitchens occur when staff are lifting things off shelves.

Mehmet: Well, we've already made changes to our storage area. As you can see, we now don't use the top shelf, as it was too high to get things down easily and we make sure that there is always someone holding the ladder steady. We also make sure that the floor is dried after it has been cleaned.

Peter: Well, I can see from the paperwork that you've made sure that your new safety procedures are being followed. It's the first fall you've had in the kitchen in ten years and with the new procedures the risk of it happening again is very low.

Mehmet: We just need to remind people to do it, and not to rush too much.

Peter: You should also make sure that whoever cleans the floor wears gloves as cleaning products can irritate your skin.

Hassan: Yes, we already do that.

Peter: OK, I've noticed a few other potential hazards in the kitchen. According to your accident book there have been a few incidents of staff burning themselves on the stove and scalding themselves with hot liquid. In fact, it's ... five out of the eight incidents in the last year. Although nothing serious has happened so far, there is risk of a major injury if changes aren't made.

Hassan: First of all, we know that burns happen every day in a kitchen. It's just the nature of the job, but we have had more cases than usual lately.

Mehmet: They can be a major injury. I know, I've burnt and cut myself hundreds of times. It's part of being a chef! The most important thing is we've never had a major injury.

Peter: I'd say that with your current procedures the risk is medium. The main thing I'd like to see is that you get that risk of burns down to low. I'd recommend that the hobs are always turned off when they're not being used, even if it's just for a few seconds, to really get the risk level down.

Hassan: OK. I'll make sure that the kitchen staff follow that procedure.

Peter: Secondly, I'd like to look at the risk of scalds. A scald can be a serious injury, much worse than a burn. Twice as many kitchen staff in the city are admitted to hospital with scalds than they are with burns. Looking at your accident book and current working procedures, I'd say that the current risk level of a scald is high.

Mehmet: We've had a few scalds through the years, but nothing that required medical attention.

Peter: OK, but we need to reduce the risk of scalding. The most important thing is that the chefs shouldn't fill the pots too full. Scalds can happen when you move or tip over a pot that's too full. This needs to be made apparent to all staff members.

Hassan: So they should use big pots, but not fill them?

Peter: Right. That reduces the risk to low and makes scalding extremely unlikely. I also have a few concerns with the smoke and fumes coming from the hob. A fire or something burning could cause breathing problems or damage to the lungs if the smoke is inhaled, which is a minor injury. Do you always use your extractor fans?

Mehmet: Not always. They're high-power and very noisy. It's hard enough to hear in a busy kitchen as it is.

Peter: Despite the noise, they are useful. The current risk of injury is high. The extractor fans always need to be on. OK, so for the stove, three things, right?

Mehmet: Always turn off the hob when we're not using it, avoid overfilling the pots and always use the extractor fans.

Peter: Right, good. First of all, you're generally running a really safe kitchen here, but there are some improvements to be made. I need to write up the risk assessment form and send you a copy, but overall I'm very happy with the way you're running things here.

4.4

A: What are you reading?

B: It's an article about risks in the work place.

A: Oh yeah? What does it say?

B: I'm just reading about the hazards of working in a kitchen.

A: My brother worked in a kitchen. He was a chef and he cut his hands a lot with knives. I'm sure cuts must be one of the biggest risks in a restaurant kitchen.

B: Actually, this article says that research shows wet floors are the biggest hazard. In one study, more than 50% of kitchen injuries were from falls on wet floors.

A: Hmmm. What about knives?

B: It says here that only about 12% of injuries were cuts. Burns from cooking were more common, about 20% of the total injuries.

A: Guess I was wrong then!

4.5

2,290,010 people visited the theme park last year and we had 4,107 medical incidents. We calculate only 0.18% of visitors had any kind of medical issue. Or putting it another way, 982 people in every thousand visitors had a safe visit. By far, the most common incidents were minor. 32.2% of the medical issues were minor cuts and scrapes. After that, the next most common issue was heat stroke, with 1,117 cases last year. That's five cases per thousand visitors, or 27.3% of all medical issues. Fortunately, the three most serious problems – falling off a ride, choking on food, and getting burned by fireworks – were the least common. Together, they made up 18.4% of the issues we treated.

UNIT 5

 Making a running shoe

Narrator: New Balance running shoes are designed using cutting-edge technology, based on the idea of William J. Riley, who started the business in 1906.

The original inspiration for the running shoes came from chickens. Riley noticed that chickens have four parts of their feet on the ground at the same time and this gives them stability.

Running puts a lot of strain on many different parts of the body. Today, New Balance use computers to make sure that their shoes support the whole body.

The shoes need to be strong enough to take the impact of running, but comfortable enough to give the foot flexibility and speed. They cushion the parts of the foot that hit the ground, but also give the shoes stability, so that the foot is supported.

New Balance perform tests and review feedback from runners, to design the shoes on a computer.

They then print in 3D to make a quick full-size model. The 3D printing machine uses information from the computer to heat sand and mould it to make the model.

This model will be used to make thousands more shoes that will be sold around the world.

This factory makes 300,000 pairs of shoes a year.

The shoe uppers are made by hand.

The upper starts with one piece of leather which is cut out into 29 pieces to make the top of the shoe.

A robot sews the pieces together but the logo must be sewn by hand, taking special attention to get it just right.

Sewing the upper into three dimensions is a skilled job that can also only be done by human hand.

The upper is then ready to be glued to the sole.

Finally, the shoes are checked for quality, ready for their laces and box.

New Balance say 'a better fit produces better performance'. It takes testing, design and high-tech manufacturing to make a better fitting shoe.

Hello, and welcome to today's lecture. Our topic is clothes manufacturing, and I'll divide the lecture into three parts. The first part of the talk will look at the history of clothes manufacturing. I'll then move on to look at the development of mass-manufacturing, and we'll end with modern alternatives to this style of production. OK, let's begin. Now, the first factories began to appear in the UK in the 1700s and by the 1800s industrial advances were really changing how products, such as materials and clothing, were made. Before the 1800s, almost everything was handmade using simple tools, including clothing. Cheap clothes were individually produced in the home and finer, more expensive clothing was made by tailors. These tailors might make copies of the same suit or a shirt, but they made them one at a time. Both processes were fairly slow and things were produced in small quantities.

Sewing machines were developed in the 1800s, which made the manufacture of clothing much quicker. It was during this time that the industrial production of clothing began. Groups of factory workers started making identical items of clothing in high-volumes using sewing machines. By the end of the 19th century lots of everyday items such as shirts, trousers and dresses were mass-produced.

Nowadays, this is true of almost all of the clothes we wear. However, when we talk about clothing being mass-produced, that doesn't mean that items today are produced completely by machines. In fact, clothes made today in factories almost always have to be sewn by people, though of course they are usually operating the latest sewing machines. There are huge financial advantages to mass-produced clothing. Let's take shirts as an example. First, the clothing manufacturer plans to produce a large volume of the same shirt, say 10,000 units. Next, they buy the large amount of material needed for making them. The price of material is a lot lower if a large amount is bought at the same time, so the more shirts the manufacturer makes together, the more money they save.

After the material arrives at the factory, heavy machines cut many layers of material into the pieces of the shirt at the same time, which is very efficient. Finally, the workers make the shirts one after another, so they are able to work very quickly.

Again, this has cost advantages. If workers are paid for each shirt they make, they will work as quickly as possible because they want to earn as much money as possible. You can control the quality by not paying workers for any shirts they make that aren't made well. This generally means that producing shirts in factories results in a fairly high-quality product.

We've looked at mass-manufacturing, but are there any modern alternatives? Let's turn now to the handmade process. Despite working slowly, tailors have never completely gone away. Why is that? Well, while factories can produce items of clothing at a reasonable quality and reasonable cost, the fit is rarely perfect. You may be able to find small, medium and large items, but people come in all shapes and sizes. So even today, if you want really good quality clothes that fit you perfectly, you probably need to go to a tailor for something handmade.

A tailor who runs a small-scale shop is able to offer a real alternative to mass-produced clothing. They can offer a more flexible approach to the production of clothes, incorporating the style, measurements, time-scale and budget of the customer. You get a shirt that fits you perfectly and you can choose to have it made from the very best-quality fabric. However, both the materials and the labour cost a lot more than a factory-made shirt and you also have to invest a lot of time in getting the product made. With a factory-made shirt, you can go to a shop, try it on and buy it and wear it instantly. With a tailor-made shirt, you must go to the shop to be measured and choose the fabric. As traditional manufacturing methods, such as cutting the fabric by hand take more time than using factory machines, you then have to wait for the tailor to make the shirt. After that, you need to try on the shirt on again before it's completed and then wait for the final work to be done on it. This can take several days. However the final product is unique and made especially for the customer.

In short, mass-produced clothes will continue to dominate the marketplace, due to their low cost and high-volume, but there will always be a place for low-volume, high cost clothes for those that can afford them. Right, moving on to ...

5.2

Sewing machines were developed in the 1800s // which made the manufacture of clothing much quicker. // It was during this time // that the industrial production of clothing began.

Groups of factory workers started making identical items of clothing in high volumes // using sewing machines. // By the end of the 19th century // lots of everyday items // such as shirts, // trousers // and dresses were mass-produced.

5.3

Hello and welcome. I'm the floor manager for the plant and I'll be showing you around today and explaining the process of painting a car. Before we go in the paint shop, I'll begin by explaining a bit about what happens before this part of the car manufacturing process. Cars have to be painted after the body has been assembled, but before the engine, windows, wheels, seats or any other parts that aren't painted are attached. This is done so that we can cover the metal parts of the car body completely with paint.

Painting a car body has five steps, because the paint shop applies five coats of paint. The concept behind the different layers is to ensure that the car body is protected for its entire lifetime. If the paint is applied correctly and cared for properly, it can last for many decades. OK, let's go to the first location ...

Right, here we are at the paint section, or paint shop, of the plant. You can see over there workers are in the process of applying a base coat to a car body. This paint is designed especially for bare metal and protects the metal car body from water damage such as rust. It also helps the second coat of paint stick to the car. The entire car body is dipped into the base-coat paint. You can see here we have to have very strong machines to lift the entire car body to do this.

Moving on ... Secondly, the car is dipped into a coat of rust-protection paint. This second coat protects the base coat and increases the protection from water damage. The rust-protection coat wouldn't stick to bare metal, but it sticks to the base layer very well, which is why that goes on first.

After the base coat and the rust coat are put on, a special sealant is applied to the car, onto the places where parts of the body join together, to seal them. Here you can see one of our technicians applying this. The sealant helps ensure that the car will drive quietly and also helps keep water out of the car. This sealant is the final layer to be applied before the colour goes on. We do this so that the colour layer will cover the sealant and give a professional, smooth finish.

After this, the coloured paint is applied. This is the paint that everyone sees on the finished car. For the customer, this is probably the most important coat of paint. Obviously, the colour coat has to go on after the base coat, the rust protection coat and the sealant, because otherwise you wouldn't see it. We use many coloured paints in this plant, such as the red you can see being applied over here.

As I said, the most important layer to the customer, at least day-to-day, is the colour coat. The first three layers protect the car from rust and make it ride quietly and the fourth layer makes it beautiful. However, we need to protect the colour layer from rust from the inside, but also from scratches, sun damage, and so on from outside the car, so, last of all we put on a clear top coat. This hard, clear finish protects the coloured paint from scratches, so that the colour coat lasts longer.

Each layer of paint is applied very thinly. The bottom four layers, not counting the clear coat, use only about 3.5 litres of paint altogether, for the entire car. It takes about 12 hours to paint a car and each vehicle travels about 6.5 kilometres during painting. The paint shop produces about 40 painted car bodies per hour. That's one vehicle every 90 seconds.

After the body and the frame go through the paint shop, they go on to phase three, the assembly of the entire car. In phase three, the painted frame and painted body are assembled with the engine to make a car ...

5.4

Firstly, the client is measured. Then, the style and fabric of the suit are chosen. Next, the pieces of the suit are cut out and sewn together. When the suit is ready, the fit is checked and altered as necessary. Finally, the suit is worn.

5.5

1 The process of making coffee <u>starts</u> with boiling the water.

2 When making a cup of coffee, you have to measure the coffee carefully <u>before</u> you add it to the coffee maker.

3 If you are adding milk, or sugar, this must be added after the coffee is brewed.
4 Coffee can be put in the coffee maker at the same time as boiling the water.
5 Cups of coffee can be allowed to cool. Meanwhile, you can prepare a snack to eat with your coffee.

UNIT 6

Orangutan conservation

Narrator: Orangutans live in the rainforests of Malaysia and Indonesia.

Unfortunately, the orangutan is an endangered species. Today, there are fewer than 35,000 orangutans in the wild.

Human activities, such as logging, have destroyed the orangutans' habitat. Cutting down trees often kills adult orangutans, leaving the baby animals as orphans.

New roads and growing towns and villages have also destroyed the orangutans' habitat. More than 80% is now gone forever.

However, conservationists are working to save the orangutans. They are rescuing them and returning them to the rainforest.

This orangutan lives at a rescue centre in Indonesia.

More than 200 orangutans live in this rescue centre. The workers here prepare the orangutans for their return to the wild.

Most of these orangutans came here because their natural habitat was destroyed to create more farm land or was cut down for wood.

Some of these baby orangutans are only four weeks old. Their parents may have been killed, or captured and sold as pets. Babies normally stay with their parents until they are about six years old, so they would be vulnerable in the wild on their own.

Before the orangutans can return to the wild, they must learn basic survival skills. Every day, they are taken to the forest so they can learn and practise how to be a wild orangutan.

The orangutans love practising the skills they need to live in their natural habitat. They practise climbing, swinging and even drinking.

So while some people destroy the orangutans' habitat, others are dedicated to helping them learn the skills they need to survive.

If these beautiful and endangered animals are going to survive in the wild for years to come, they will need all the human help they can get.

Only then will orangutans survive in the Asian wilderness.

6.1

Planet Earth is dynamic and always changing. Just 10,000 years ago, about half of the planet was covered in ice. Today this is around 10%, as the Earth has been warming since that time. Part of this environmental change is due to natural, rather than human causes.

Sometimes, natural forces can destroy the environment. In 1991, a volcano in the Philippines erupted and killed many people and animals. It destroyed around 800 square kilometres of farmland and a huge area of forest. It also caused severe floods when rivers were blocked with volcanic ash.

However, humans are also responsible for a lot of habitat destruction.

There were originally 16 million square kilometres of rainforest worldwide. Only nine million remain today and deforestation is occurring at a rate of 160,000 square metres per year. In Europe, only about 15% of land hasn't been modified by humans.

In some places, habitats haven't been destroyed, but they have been broken into parts, for example, separated by roads. This is called fragmentation. If animals are used to moving around throughout the year and a road is built through the middle of their habitat, fragmentation can cause serious problems.

Humans haven't only affected the land and its animals; they have also affected the sea. Pollution from coastal cities has damaged the ocean environment and destroyed the habitat of fish and other sea life.

Habitat destruction hasn't been bad news for all animals. In fact, some species have adapted extremely well to living closely with people and benefit from living near them.

In Africa and Asia, monkeys live in cities alongside people and exploit the human environment by stealing food or eating things that humans have thrown away. In Singapore, the 1,500 wild monkeys that live in and around the city have become a tourist attraction.

In Australia, Europe, Japan and North America, foxes live in urban areas, even big cities such as London. They survive by eating a wide variety of things, from rubbish to insects and wild birds, but not everyone welcomes the foxes. They sometimes enter people's homes to steal food and they occasionally bite people.

One other animal that is as at home in both the city and in the countryside is the squirrel. In fact, squirrels are so at home in the city that the number of city squirrels has increased. Squirrels have a more limited diet than foxes and generally eat plants, though sometimes people put out nuts for them to eat.

We tend to think of human activity as always having a negative impact on the environment. However, some people feel that we can have a positive impact too.

Conservation means trying to save habitats. Ecotourism is an approach to travel and holidays where people visit natural areas such as rainforests, except rather than destroy the environment, they help to preserve it. Visitors to the La Selva Amazon Eco Lodge in Ecuador watch and learn about local wildlife, visit tribes who live in the forest and stay in an environmentally friendly hotel. Their presence doesn't damage the local environment and most guests leave the hotel as conservationists. When they experience the beauty of nature firsthand, they feel strongly that they want to protect and preserve it.

Not everyone feels that ecotourism is actually helping the environment. Tourists who travel long distances by aeroplane and resorts that use local resources such as fresh water and produce waste create pollution in the local environment.

6.2

1 Sometimes, natural forces destroy animal habitats.
2 Sometimes, natural forces destroy animal habitats.
3 Humans have changed the Earth.
4 Humans have changed the Earth.
5 Humans have changed the Earth.
6 Humans have changed the Earth.

6.3

The subject of my talk today is the decline and destruction of the world's deserts. First, I'm going to talk about the desert environment and wildlife, then we'll look at the threats to this environment. Finally, we'll talk about what is being done to save the world's deserts. Let's begin by looking at some background information from the United Nations Environment Programme. The United Nations reports in their online publication 'Global Deserts Outlook', that the Earth's deserts cover about 33.7 million square kilometres, or about 25% of the Earth's surface. Deserts are home to 500 million people, or about 8% of the World's population, but as I'll explain, people all over the world rely on things that come from this environment.

Humans have learned to exploit the resources of the desert for survival and profit by adapting their behaviour, culture and technology to its harsh environment. To give you an example, tribes such as the Topnaar, in Southwestern Africa, are known for their ability to survive in deserts due to their use of local plants and animals for food, medicine and clothing. They have a deep understanding of the natural world. The Bedouins of North Africa, who live in the Arabian and Syrian deserts, are skilled at using animals such as camels and goats to provide transport, food and clothing and also at growing basic foods around desert rivers and other water sources. The Topnaar and the Bedouins are just two examples of people who live in and rely on the desert environment for the things they need. However city-dwellers benefit from the desert, too.

Certain minerals are commonly found in deserts and they also provide a large portion of the world's diamonds together with copper, gold and other metals. They are a major source of oil and natural gas, too. These desert products are used by industries and people all over the world every day. So what I'm saying is that even though most people may not live in a desert, we are affected by changes to this desert environment.

Agricultural products are also grown and exported in deserts. Because the climate is warm and land tends to be inexpensive, desert countries are able to grow and sell foods all year. A good example of this is Egyptian cotton, famous all over the world. New methods of irrigation are currently being developed that mean desert agriculture systems can use water more efficiently. So we can see that deserts are important, not only for the people who live in them, but everyone who uses products that come from the desert environment.

That's all I have to say on that point. Moving on now to the typical desert environment. In summer, the ground surface temperature in most deserts reaches 80 centigrade and there is very little rain. Despite these harsh conditions, a wide variety of plants and animals live in and are supported by this environment. There are reportedly, for example, over 2,200 different plant species in the desert of the Kingdom of Saudi Arabia, based on research from King Saud University.

Small plants are especially important in the desert environment because they hold the soil in place so that larger plants can grow. Acacia trees can grow well in extremely hot, dry conditions, but the seed needs stable soil to begin growing. Smaller plants therefore help the larger ones and in this way, all desert plants help hold the dry soil in place, which helps to reduce dust storms.

Deserts are also an important animal habitat. One of the best known desert animals in the Arabian Peninsula is the Arabian oryx, which weighs about 70 kilograms and is about one metre tall and is the national symbol of Qatar. It rests during the heat of the day and searches for food and water when temperatures are cooler. Experts say that the oryx can sense rain and move towards it.

These examples show that the desert is an ecosystem that supports a variety of important plant and animal life. The problem is that human activity is affecting modern deserts all over the world. According to the United Nations, traditional ways of life are changing as human activities such as cattle ranching, farming and large-scale tourism grow. The process of bringing water into the desert to grow plants is making soil too salty. The construction of dams for power generation and water supply and an increase in mining have also begun to have a greater impact on the desert. Owing to the destruction of desert plants, dust storms are more likely, and desert animals therefore have less food to eat. Data from the United Nations shows that every year, nearly 2% of healthy desert landscape disappears. Today, more than 50% of the world's desert habitats are wilderness areas, but by 2050, it may be as low as 31%.

If we lose the world's deserts, we lose everything I spoke about in the first part of my talk. The Topnaar and Bedouin way of life will certainly disappear, but what does this mean for the rest of the world? Well, everyone on Earth will experience an increase of dust and dirt in the air as desert plants die. If desert soil becomes too salty to grow plants, we'll also lose a valuable source of food, and I'm talking about foods that we all eat. If we allow deserts to be destroyed, life all over the Earth will change. To put it another way, we will all be affected. Now, the big question is, what is being done about the destruction of deserts?

The United Nations Environment Programme offers two main solutions. First, we can begin to manage desert resources carefully, instead of abusing them. This means using the desert for things we need as well as not damaging it further. It might mean not allowing activities such as raising cattle in certain areas. It would also mean carefully controlling the way we use water. Secondly, we can apply technological solutions. The UN gives the example of using the latest computer technology to help forecast how climate change will affect deserts and to use that information to prepare for these changes. We can also make better use of two resources freely available in the desert: the wind and sun. These can be used to provide clean energy on a fairly small scale within existing desert cities. According to a blog called 'A Smarter Planet', scientists in Saudi Arabia are already using solar energy to produce fresh water in the desert for agricultural use.

To summarize, deserts are not only important to the people who live in them, but to plants, animals, and people everywhere, from the Bedouin tribes to city-dwellers. Human activity is causing desert habitat destruction, but there are ways in which we can help to stop this.

UNIT 7

 Changing China

Narrator: Beijing, the capital of China, is home to over 20 million people. With more than 2000 years of history, the city is of world-class architectural importance and boasts internationally famous sites such as The Great Wall, The Temple of Heaven and The Forbidden City.

The Forbidden City was built in the early 1400s and is an example of traditional Chinese palace architecture. It is a World Heritage site and listed by UNESCO as the largest collection of ancient wooden structures in the world. It is also regarded as the best-preserved palace complex in existence and attracts around 8 million visitors a year.

The Great Wall of China stretches for over 8,000 kilometres from Shanhaiguan to Lop Lake.

It crosses mountains, spans plains and passes through vast deserts. This astonishing miracle of engineering took over 2,000 years to build.

The Great Wall was built to protect the Chinese Empire against enemies, and thousands of watchtowers stretch as far as the eye can see.

These brick towers are two or three-storeys high. On the top of each one there is a small room shaped like a ship, known as the *Loulu* in Chinese. Today, the history of innovative Chinese architecture and construction lives on.

But there is increasing pressure on architects to accommodate the growing populations of large Chinese cities.

The solution is often to construct high-rise buildings, which are fast and economical to put up.

China is a county of architectural contrast, with landmarks ranging from the Forbidden City to the more recent Bird's Nest stadium, built for the 2008 Olympic Games.

Traditional housing, like the beautiful *hutongs* or the more recent *shikumen* is fortunately being preserved for future generations to enjoy.

From the ancient past to exciting modern developments ... China's architectural wonders have helped it become one of the most popular tourist destinations in the world.

Alan: Khalid, we need to talk about that warehouse the company plans to acquire in Westside.

Khalid: OK. I've just seen the pictures. I think there's a lot of potential there.

Alan: Really? I'm afraid we might be biting off more than we can chew.

Khalid: Really? Why?

Alan: Firstly, the problem is Westside area itself. Thirty years ago, it was a thriving industrial neighbourhood with a lot of businesses. Now, it's a half-empty wasteland. It's ugly. There are lots of abandoned buildings and it's not really used for anything. No one wants to go there. Secondly, the warehouse we're looking at is in terrible condition. It was abandoned about 20 years ago. The foundations of the building need some serious work; the concrete is in dreadful condition. Acquiring such an old building could be a mistake.

Khalid: Really? I think the project could be a great success. In fact, I think it's a potential goldmine.

Alan: Um, OK. Could you expand on that?

Khalid: There's been a lot of activity in Westside recently: development and regeneration going on nearby and it's really transforming the area. It's becoming popular with people who work in the financial district, which is close by. Rent is still low there and a new restaurant opens almost every week. I envisage the neighbourhood becoming really trendy. No one has spent much money there in the past 20 years, but investment in the area has increased in the past year. We're going to see a lot more improvement as well.

Alan: That may be true, but that building is more like a prison than a potential shopping centre. People would never want to go shopping there. I think the first thing we'd need to do would be knock it down, and that would cost us a lot of money.

Khalid: Have you considered doing work on the building instead of knocking it down? It has some beautiful original features.

Alan: It looks as though it's about to collapse!

Khalid: I'm not sure it's as bad as that. I think the original building has a lot of potential.

Alan: I think we really want to transform the area with something modern. Why not just start over and build a new building?

Khalid: If we designed it properly, we could maintain the old architectural features, such as the red bricks and the stone. Those construction materials would be more sympathetic to the style of some of the other buildings around it. It would reflect the character of the area. We could give the old building a new lease of life.

Alan: Maybe, but I think it would be better to transform the area with an architectural landmark; something new and contemporary. It would be more of a transformation if we built a modern structure made of materials like steel and glass.

Khalid: Couldn't we do both?

Alan: What do you mean?

Khalid: Well, we'll maintain more of a connection to the past if we include the old building as part of the new one. We could rebuild the warehouse using red bricks similar to those in the original structure and construct a new glass and steel extension. It would also create more floor space. We'd have enough room for at least two or three shops there.

Alan: I hadn't thought of doing it that way.

Khalid: Another option to consider would be putting shop units on the ground floor and flats or offices above. If we added a floor or two to the top of the building, we could definitely use glass and steel for that.

Alan: Do you mean luxury apartments?

Khalid: Maybe. We could have a modern, urban design using the old architectural materials and features.

Alan: Such as ... ?

Khalid: We could keep some of the original features as they are, such as the beams in the ceilings and the inside of the red brick supporting walls. They would then become a decorative feature.

Alan: So not traditional flats at all, then?

Khalid: No, not at all. Very modern.

Alan: It's an ambitious plan, and it could be controversial.

Khalid: We wouldn't be the first to do this sort of thing, though. We can look at some other examples around the country where the same thing has been done successfully, if you're interested in the idea.

Alan: If we make that the first phase of our planning process, we can make a better decision about how to balance the traditional and modern features of the project before we go on to the design and building phases.

Khalid: There's probably a Westside neighbourhood association or business association as well. We could meet with them and get their views.

Alan: You're right. We really should speak to some businesspeople in the area and arrange to take a better look at the building.

Khalid: Let's do it.

7.2

1 **A:** I think the original building has a lot of potential.
B: I think we really want to transform the area with something modern.

2 **A:** It has some beautiful original features.
B: It looks as though it's about to collapse!

3 **A:** Acquiring such an old building could be a mistake.
B: I think the project could be a great success.

4 **A:** It would be more of a transformation if we built a modern structure made of materials like steel and glass.
B: We'll maintain a connection to the past if we include the old building as part of the new one.

7.3

Jamal: Maria, John. Thanks for taking the time to meet with us.

Maria: Pleasure.

John: Happy to be here.

Tom: Well, we've got the first set of plans and we think you'll be really pleased with what we've put together.

Jamal: After discussing a lot of options, we now envisage building a single eight-storey apartment block.

Tom: You can see from the pictures here that we plan on fitting this into the area by using part of the wasteland behind the current housing area.

Jamal: One of the biggest benefits of this plan is that it will create accommodation for up to 80 households, or as many as 200 people.

Maria: I can't quite tell from the drawing ... what materials are you going to be using?

Tom: The outside is made of glass and steel.

John: And what's the cost of this plan?

Jamal: Around eight million dollars.

Maria: Eight million? Wow. The plan is definitely ambitious!

Jamal: Yes, we're aware that it's over the construction budget of 7.5 million, but we hope to reconsider the budget in light of some of our suggestions.

Tom: Have you got any questions?

Maria: Well, yes, a few.

Jamal: OK, we'd love to hear them.

Maria: Well, I have to say, we weren't expecting quite such a tall building.

John: Exactly. The existing buildings in the area are no higher than two storeys and you've placed the new building very close to them. I'm concerned about the other buildings on the site.

Tom: I'm not sure I follow you.

John: Well, first of all, I'm worried that this plan would block daylight from the existing homes near the site. I anticipate getting a lot of complaints from the current residents.

Jamal: We could consider using reflective glass instead then. You know, like a mirror. It's used in big cities to give a feeling of open sky.

Maria: That's a great idea, but I'm not sure it addresses the main problem. The real issue here is the height of the building. I strongly recommend that you reconsider this. After all, we originally suggested accommodation for about 100 people.

Tom: Yes, we've doubled that.

Maria: Right. Would you mind telling us a bit more about why that was decided?

Jamal: Well, our thinking was that this would increase your company's income from the building because you could sell or rent more apartments.

John: We thought that might be an option at first too, but now we realize it won't work.

Tom: Could you expand on that?

John: We've got to think about the houses that are already in the area. We want the new building to be sympathetic to the look of the area, to fit in with the other buildings.

Tom: I like that idea, but can you explain what you mean by 'fit in'? Do you mean we should copy the style of existing buildings?

John: No. We don't expect you to copy the architecture of the existing buildings, but we also don't want to completely transform the feeling of the area either. So by 'fit in', I mean that it should look as though it belongs there. Our original suggestion was that the building should reflect the size and materials of the other buildings in the area.

Tom: OK, I see what you mean.

John: I'd like to raise one other concern. You've described the natural area you'd like to build on as wasteland, but actually, that's a woodland.

Jamal: Can you tell us more about that?

John: Well, the kids who already live in the area play there and we want to maintain that open, natural area. The residents really value having access to nature nearby.

Maria: Right.

John: As it stands, this plan with the tall, single building and the loss of the natural space would be very controversial. Can I suggest we use this first design you've supplied to identify a few priorities?

Jamal: Yes, that's a good idea.

Maria: OK … first, we need to think about what will be appropriate with the existing houses. What about more, smaller, lower buildings? We could have four, two-storey buildings and following our original plan, try to accommodate 100 rather than 200 people. That might be better.

John: And while we like the idea of contemporary design, I'm not sure glass and steel is appropriate. Lots of glass is a great idea, but in my view the only viable option is to use brick, like the existing buildings.

Tom: OK. So we're talking about four, two-storey brick buildings that can accommodate about 25 people each?

John: Right.

Tom: That seems an obvious solution, but it doesn't address the issue of cost.

John: What do you mean?

Tom: Well, four smaller buildings will cost more than one larger one.

John: Well, I guess we'll have to see the actual costs to discuss that. Could we consider three buildings?

Tom: Yes, that's a possibility.

Jamal: And you mentioned having adequate green space. We hadn't realized that the area we were considering building on is regularly used by local people. We need to find a way around that. How about if we position the new buildings near the edge of the site?

Maria: Yes, that's possible. We can't acquire the land next to our site, as it's public property, but we can benefit from being near that open space. The residents would definitely be able to enjoy the views then.

Tom: I like your thinking. I agree completely.

Jamal: OK, so I think we need to go back and start over again.

John: Yes, I think you're right. My apologies, I hope you don't feel we've wasted your time.

Jamal: Not at all. I think we understand the site a lot better now and I feel confident we can come up with a suitable plan if you give us a couple of weeks. We promise to incorporate all of your comments.

Maria: We look forward to seeing what you come up with.

1 The main issue is that most retailers don't want to do business here.
2 The main issue is that most retailers don't want to do business here.
3 The main issue is that most retailers don't want to do business here.
4 The main issue is that most retailers don't want to do business here.

UNIT 8

 Water power

Narrator: California, where the majority of the USA's fresh food is grown, has perfect weather and soil for growing crops. However, the state experiences one major problem – it doesn't get enough rain.

The solution to this lack of rain has been to dam the precious few rivers and redirect them to lands thousands of miles away that get as little as 18 centimetres of rain per year.

Building dams also means creating reservoirs, which are artificial lakes. Lake Mead, in the USA, is an example of this.

The lake is 180 kilometres long. It was formed between 1931 and 1936 when Hoover Dam was built. The dam is 220 metres tall, 379 metres wide and 200 metres thick at its base.

It controls floods, provides water for farms and generates electricity from flowing river water.

The water enters the dam through these towers and falls more than 200 metres. The falling water turns the turbines inside the dam.

As the water falls, the pipes become smaller and the water flows faster.

The water is travelling nearly 100 kilometres per hour when it reaches the turbines.

The turbines turn these shafts 180 times per minute. The shafts are attached to generators, which produce massive electrical currents.

Hydroelectric power provides about 24% of the world's electricity, but dams can cause problems, too.

A quickly-formed reservoir can destroy animal and plant habitats. In hot, dry places, water can evaporate quickly from lakes, making the water saltier.

When water is stored in a reservoir its temperature also changes and when the water is released, it may be too hot for some plants and animals to survive.

Rivers are powerful natural forces.

Dams borrow some of that power, so we can turn it into electricity and power our world.

8.1

Reporter: This is Andrew Thompson, reporting from the Spanish island of El Hierro, about 400 kilometres off the coast of Africa. It's quite a distance from Madrid, Spain's capital, which is nearly 2,000 kilometres away. Today, we're going to talk to two of the 11,000 people who live here, to find out what's so special about the island. Firstly, this is Pedro Rodriguez, who owns a seafood restaurant in the village of La Restinga, on the south of the island. Hello, Pedro.

Pedro: Hello, Andrew.

Reporter: Thank you for talking with us today.

Pedro: It's my pleasure.

Reporter: So, how long have you lived on El Hierro?

Pedro: I haven't lived here for very long. I came from Madrid about five years ago.

Reporter: Don't you like it here?

Pedro: I love it here. I wish I had come a lot sooner than I did. I spent most of my life in Madrid.

Reporter: City life can be tough. I suppose island life is rather more relaxing.

Pedro: Exactly. El Hierro is my home now.

Reporter: So ... what's so great about El Hierro?

Pedro: In the city, everyone hurries everywhere. You are surrounded by traffic and you never feel like you can really relax. What's more, my career was in banking, which is an especially stressful job.

Reporter: Can you tell me more about El Hierro? What do you like about it?

Pedro: I love the sound of the sea. I love the peace and quiet and I feel free here. City life was never like that. When I was living in the city, I worked in banking, as I said. It paid well and I was able to buy my restaurant, but I should have left the city when I was a much younger man.

Reporter: So you love the quiet life on El Hierro, but is there anything else that makes it special?

Pedro: Well, for one things, El Hierro is completely energy-independent!

Reporter: Energy-independent?

Pedro: Exactly. In the past, the power on the island was provided by oil. A lot of money was paid to ship 40,000 barrels of oil over from the mainland every year. It cost the island about two million Euros a year. Now, all our own energy is created right here on the island.

Reporter: And for more about that, we'll now talk to engineer Sofia Martinez. But first, let me say thanks for talking to us, Pedro Rodriguez ...

Pedro: It was my pleasure.

Reporter: ... and we wish you many more happy years here on El Hierro.

Pedro: Many thanks.

Reporter: Sofia, hello.

Sofia: Hello, Andrew. Er ... I've never been interviewed before.

Reporter: No problem, Sofia. You'll be fine. I wonder if you could tell us about the energy generation here on El Hierro.

Sofia: Of course Andrew. Well, if you've spent a day or two here, you may have noticed we have a lot of wind on El Hierro.

Reporter: Yes. In fact, it's blowing pretty hard outside right now.

Sofia: Well, for about 3,000 hours, or for about 30% of the year, the wind here blows hard enough to turn wind turbines, which can provide electricity.

Reporter: Does El Hierro rely completely on wind to power the island?

Sofia: No. The island's wind turbines have a capacity of about 11 megawatts, about enough to power 3,500 homes, but nevertheless we need more power than that. The bigger problem is that the wind doesn't blow all the time, so the power source isn't consistent.

Reporter: So you need another energy source on windless days?

Sofia: Of course. That was the challenge; to create an energy generation system, or a network of systems, that could supply enough energy for the island all the time.

Reporter: And that's ...

Sofia: Hydroelectric power.

Reporter: But doesn't hydroelectric power require a river and a dam? Isn't El Hierro too small for a river?

Sofia: A river with a dam is the usual way of producing hydroelectric power, but really, all you need is water that can move from a high place to a lower place to get energy from the water.

Reporter: OK ...

Sofia: At the centre of El Hierro is a dormant volcano: a volcano that is no longer active. In the middle of the volcano, we built a reservoir that holds 500,000 cubic metres of water, at a height of 1501 metres, 700 metres above sea level. So that's our water in a high place.

Reporter: But you don't get much rain here. What happens when all of the water runs out of the reservoir?

Sofia: Well, I mentioned the wind turbines. The wind power and the hydroelectric power are in a network together. When the wind is blowing, energy from the wind turbines pumps water up into the reservoir.

Reporter: So the wind turbines power the pumping station?

Sofia: Right. We also use the wind power for all of our electrical needs, when it blows. Then when the wind stops, we let water run out of the reservoir and through some turbines. The turbines turn generators and we have hydroelectric power we can access.

Reporter: So the water flows in a cycle – it's pumped up the hill by the wind, then released when it's needed.

Sofia: Yes, that's right. In addition to this, the system also provides our drinking water and water for use in agriculture.

Reporter: But where does the water come from?

Sofia: We use seawater.

Reporter: But you can't drink salt water...

Sofia: We have a desalination plant to take the salt out of the seawater so it can be used in agriculture and as drinking water. We're constantly adding new water and taking stored water out of the cycle as we need to use it. In fact, I've just come from the desalination plant, where we're having some problems today. Something isn't working properly and the replacement parts haven't arrived yet. We're a long way from the mainland. So delivery of anything takes at least a few days. If they don't come soon, we may have to ask people to use less water for a few days.

Reporter: You're a long way from everything out here, aren't you? It must be difficult sometimes.

Sofia: Well, it's a real challenge living here. On the other hand, ... we all love it. It can be a hard life, but I wouldn't live anywhere else.

See script on page 146.

See script on page 146.

Jane: As you all know, there's been a proposal that we should try to reduce our energy consumption here in the office, both to save money for the business and to help the environment. The function of this meeting today is to get your ideas on how to do this and to hopefully come up with a plan to take forward. Would anyone like to start? What are your views? Yes, Zara.

Zara: Well, if we really want to do something to save on electricity costs long-term, why don't we consider an alternative energy source? We could install some solar panels on the roof. That would generate plenty of environmentally-friendly electricity.

Jane: That's not a bad idea. Would anyone like to add to Zara's comments? Allen?

Allen: It's true that we could go for a big solution like solar power generation. Even so, I think we could consider some rather simpler, smaller-scale ideas too, like changing over to low-energy light bulbs. There's a lot of potential to save energy there.

Jane: I think that's a great point, Allen. Abdul, would you like to expand on that?

Abdul: Yes. Allen's light bulb idea is a really good one. Energy-efficient bulbs aren't hugely expensive to install. In addition, they pay for themselves quickly.

Jane: Pay for themselves?

Abdul: They don't use much energy, so they're cheap to run. It means they will soon save us more money than the cost of the new bulbs. Although these energy-efficient bulbs are expensive, we would save enough money in one year to pay for them.

Jane: I see. Do you have any other ideas?

Abdul: Yes. Some of the ideas are very simple: cleaning our dirty windows, for example. As a result of that, we'll allow more natural light in. Furthermore, we can turn off our computer screens when we get up from our desks.

Jane: Yes, Zara.

Zara: We could also consider turning off the air conditioning when it isn't quite so hot, so we can use less energy.

Jane: Great idea.

Zara: We could get rid of one of our photocopiers, too, as we don't really need two. The current machines use energy even when they're on stand-by.

Jane: Also a good plan. Now, I'd like to go back to Abdul. Abdul, you said we should consider smaller-scale solutions to our energy consumption here. Are you saying you're against installing a solar-energy system?

Abdul: No, I really like that idea, because once it's installed, the system will have a low operating cost and it's an environmentally friendly ways to generate electricity, which are two big positive points, but, there are other considerations. For example we'd have to look at the generating capacity of the system. It's very expensive to buy and install and if it doesn't produce a lot of power, it'll end up costing rather than saving us money, at least for the first few years. The challenge is to choose ways of saving energy that also save money right now.

Allen: Yes, I agree with that. The other real environmental problem we have here in the office is rubbish. Most of us buy our lunch in plastic containers that have to be thrown away. It's a disgrace. We really should try to reduce the volume of rubbish we create here in the office.

Jane: Sorry, but that's not really what we're discussing right now. We can deal with waste and recycling later. Right now we're talking specifically about energy use.

Allen: Ok, fine. Sorry about that.

Zara: So, I was talking about turning off computer screens and turning off the air-conditioning, but I don't think we should forget about installing solar panels, or a solar water heating system.

Jane: But there are some downsides to that, such as the installation cost, which Abdul mentioned.

Abdul: Right, and there's also the problem of ...

Simon: Can I just say, by the way ...

Jane: Sorry, but could you hold that thought until Abdul has finished, please?

Simon: Sure. Sorry.

Abdul: The fact is, the systems Zara mentioned are technically complex and expensive to install. There's also the problem of maintenance, as we'd need to pay a technician to travel to make repairs if anything went wrong or expensive parts needed to be replaced. There could be a real decline in the amount of money we save if we ran into operational problems.

Jane: Can I just clarify something here? Abdul, is this experimental technology, or have alternative-energy generation systems been successful in other office environments?

Abdul: Well every small-scale system is different, because every building is different. The technology would have to be specially designed for our building.

Allen: I can't help but feel that a solar project would be too ambitious. There would probably be technical limitations about the sort of system we could install on the office roof. I'm not sure it's even possible, or if the local government would let us.

Jane: I can assure you that the company wouldn't do anything unsafe or illegal.

Zara: It could be good publicity though. We could market ourselves as a complete 'green' business.

Simon: Maybe we should have some of our marketing people look at that. I think ...

Jane: We're getting sidetracked. Can we stick to the main points of the meeting? We should probably move on to the next part of the agenda, so I'd just like to summarize the key points so far. First of all, we want to immediately start making the simple energy-saving changes mentioned, such as cleaning the windows, turning off computer screens and installing energy-saving light bulbs. Second, we want to look into possible larger-scale alternative energy systems such as solar panels or a solar water heating system. However, we need to do a lot of research in that area to see if we could get permission to install a system on the roof. A positive to installing a larger-scale project would be that it could generate good publicity for the company. Have I missed anything out?

Abdul: You didn't mention ...

Jane: So to summarize the key points so far; we agree that we want to reduce energy consumption and we want to consider an alternative energy source. Does anyone have anything to say about a solar energy system?

Simon: I'm more concerned about the amount of people who drive to the office.

Abdul: Sorry, but that's not really what we're discussing right now.

See script on page 154.

UNIT 9

Narrator: At one of the busiest road junctions in Mexico City stands a giant yellow sculpture.

It is called *El Caballito* and it is the work of Mexican artist Sebastián.

When Sebastián was a child, he collected crystals. The crystals inspired him to make sculptures using basic geometric shapes and bold, bright colours. He uses geometry and colour to express human feelings and emotions.

Some of his sculptures are small and easy to display in galleries. Others are large and require more space.

Sebastián is travelling to a mine near his childhood home in Chihuahua, Mexico. Recently, the miners made an amazing discovery. Today, Sebastián is going underground to see it with his own eyes.

Three hundred metres underground, nature has created amazing, natural sculptures.

Giant crystals – the biggest ever discovered – grow up from the floor towards the ceiling. Some of them are 15 metres long.

The crystals formed thousands of years ago when the cave was filled with mineral-rich water. A volcano heated the water to about 58 degrees centigrade – perfect for growing crystals.

Sebastián has never seen anything like it – he is deeply impressed with these sculptures created by nature.

The sculptor cannot stay in the cave for long because of the intense heat, but he has remained long enough to find inspiration for his next great work of art.

Sebastián is now designing a sculpture that will be as tall as a 12-storey building. When he has completed the design the construction of the sculpture can begin.

Like *El Caballito*, this new work will stand at a major road junction in Mexico City.

This area of the city is very flat, so the sculpture will be visible from a long way away.

Some of the pieces of the sculpture weigh two tonnes.

Each piece must be lifted with a crane and carefully joined to the other pieces of the sculpture. It takes a huge team of people to construct a sculpture of this size.

Like the giant crystals, Sebastián's sculpture slowly rises from the earth. Inspired by nature, the sculptor's work is truly amazing.

Host: Hello from the city centre. Overnight, the area's mystery graffiti painter has struck again. Although the identity of the painter remains unknown, their work is having an impact on the community. This large image has been painted on the side of an office building. A lot of people in the street on their way to work are stopping to look at it. Let's talk to a few of them and find out what they think of this latest spray-painted image.

Hello, excuse me?

Neighbour: Yes?

Host: I'm reporting on the recent increase in street art in the city centre. Can I ask you a few questions?

Neighbour: Sure, no problem.

Host: So, what do you think of this new artistic addition to the neighbourhood?

Neighbour: This street art? I think it's great. It's something interesting to look at and it's well done, isn't it? I live round the corner so this is on my doorstep.

Host: What do you like about it?

Neighbour: I just think it's cool – it has a distinctive style. At first glance, it looks as if the painting has been done in a few minutes. But in fact, it's not just spray painting; it's the work of a talented artist. It really decorates the area and I think it makes quite an ugly neighbourhood a lot better looking.

Host: Does everyone in the area like it?

Neighbour: Most of my neighbours do. We think this kind of thing could become a special feature of the area. It's a real shame that it's going to be covered up before many people have a chance to see it.

Host: Covered up?

Neighbour: The police are going to paint over it soon, because street art is illegal.

Host: Oh, right. Yes, we'll come back to that in a minute. Thanks for talking to us.

Neighbour: No problem.

Host: Clearly some people really like the painting. However, there's also already been some criticism of the piece. Let's see what more we can find out about this side of the story. Hello, excuse me?

Woman: Yes?

Host: I'm finding out what people think of street art in this area. Can I ask you a few questions?

Woman: I'm just on my way into the office so you'll have to be quick.

Host: What do you think of this painting?

Woman: I don't really like it. It's just graffiti, isn't it?

Host: What do you mean?

Woman: The people who own this building didn't ask for this, did they? I mean, what right does this person have to spray paint their message here? If somebody wants to express themselves in this way, they should get permission. I'd be really angry if someone did this in my neighbourhood.

Host: Do you think it's a work of art?

Woman: No, not at all. Art is an exhibition in art museum. This is just somebody spraying paint onto a wall in the middle of the night. Like I said, it's just graffiti.

Host: Yes, I see what you mean.

Woman: Sorry, I have to go. My boss is looking out of the window at me!

Host: Thank you. I think it would be a good idea to get a professional view on this now. I have a local police officer with me …

Hello, and thanks for talking with me today.

PO: Hi, no problem.

Host: What's your view on the latest work of the mystery painter?

PO: Well, to be honest, as a piece of art, I actually quite like it, despite the fact that it's illegal. However, I also completely agree with the person you just spoke with. We can't have this sort of thing. It *is* vandalism, and it *is* against the law.

Host: I'm very interested to hear you call this piece of vandalism a work of *art*.

PO: It is artistic, though, isn't it? I couldn't paint that. The person who did this, especially very quickly and at night, is very creative. This painting is really expressive, but I have to stress that it's illegal and therefore we're going to paint over it later today. All graffiti should be completely removed by law.

Host: What would you recommend for people who want to express themselves through street art?

PO: My recommendation? Well, if this artist wants to paint where everyone can see the artwork, he or she should get permission. We can work with street artists to create art that people have chosen to have in their community.

Host: So you mean you can give someone permission to do graffiti?

PO: Yes, well, sort of. However they have to apply for a permit and get approval and so on. This makes it a legal activity rather than vandalism.

Host: Thanks a lot for talking with us.

PO: My pleasure.

Host: Next I've got an art critic with me, who agrees with some people about the quality of the latest street painting. This is Simone James, an art gallery owner and collector. Hello, Simone.

Simone: Hello.

Host: Simone, could you comment on the latest creation of our illegal painter?

Simone: Many people think that the painting is just rough spray painting. However, the fact of the matter is the artist has created a very expressive piece of artwork using very basic tools and materials. The colour scheme and the composition work very well together. It's a strong piece. If this artist were to exhibit and sell their work, I think he or she could make a lot of money.

Host: Do you have any idea who the artist might be?

Simone: I have no idea at all, but technically, the work really is very good, so I'd like to find out!

Host: Thank you very much. Finally, there's one more person I'd like to speak with. This is Joseph, who's 13. Joseph, what do you think of the mystery artist's latest painting?

Joseph: I wish I'd done it! I think it's really good.

Host: What do you like about it?

Joseph: I think this type of art is a really good way of expressing your ideas. I don't know who did it, but I guess he's a young person like me and by doing his art in this way, on the streets, he's communicating a message about how young people feel. I think it's really cool.

Host: OK, thanks Joseph. So we've had a full range of responses to the latest street art in the town centre. However the true identity of the graffiti painter remains a mystery.

 9.2

1 decorate – decoration
2 compose – composition
3 communicate – communication
4 create – creation
5 exhibit – exhibition
6 recommend – recommendation
7 permit – permitted
8 artist – artistic

9.3

A: ... Right everyone, are we ready to get back to business? The next item to look at today is the proposed sale of the sculpture that stands in City Park. We've recently had to spend a lot of money repairing and restoring the sculpture because vandals have broken parts of it. We've also spent a lot of time and money removing graffiti from it. The city accounting office has confirmed that the total bill for cleaning and repairs has come to more than £5,000 this year. There's been a proposal that we sell the sculpture and use the money to pay for a new leisure centre. Would anyone like to comment on this?

B: Yes, I'd like to say something.

A: OK, go ahead.

B: Personally, I'm not really sure that constantly cleaning and restoring a piece of art is an appropriate way to spend public money. We take it for granted that we should do this, but in reality, it's costing us a lot of money and the sculpture doesn't really benefit the city's population. A lot of people simply don't appreciate the sculpture. The truth of the matter is, more people would use and benefit from a leisure centre.

A: If I understand you correctly, you're saying that we shouldn't spend money more maintaining the sculpture?

B: Well, yes. I think public art is a waste of money.

C: I see what you mean, and I'm not an expert, but it's been said that art, and appreciating art, is an important part of any culture. OK, it's true that some people say we're wasting money taking care of this sculpture, but the fact of matter is that art is an important part of any culture. Art can help make us proud of our city and a lot of people really enjoy looking at it. We had 400,000 visitors to our art museum last year, so people are interested in art.

E: That's true. Research has demonstrated over and over again that art can have a very positive effect on people.

D: One other thing to remember is that, although many people think that the sculpture is worth a lot of money because it's by a famous artist, we don't actually know how much money we can get for it yet. Since it's been damaged and repaired so much, it may be difficult to sell to a private collector.

A: OK, thank you both for your comments. I think we need to find out what the sculpture is worth. We'll have to get an art expert to analyze it and find out about the market for this sort of thing.

Would anyone else like to make a comment?

E: If we remove the sculpture, we'll need to put something in its place.

B: I don't think we'll be able to find anything that everyone likes.

D: You say that, but I think we could choose something that would be popular enough. We'd need to talk to a lot of people to gather data and opinions, but this might reveal some really good ideas we haven't thought of.

A: Yes, I think that's right. Let's put together a proposal. This will include three or four ideas about what we can do with the site if we remove the sculpture. Then we can get people to look at it. Is there anything else anyone would like to say?

F: For me, there's a public safety issue here. The police reports have shown that kids climb on the sculpture almost every night and they're breaking it and graffiting it. This sculpture really is a danger to the public.

C: You may be right, but I wonder if it's the location of the sculpture rather than the sculpture itself that's the problem.

B: In other words, you think we should move it?

C: I think moving it might solve the vandalism problem. It seems as if the sculpture is just costing us money for cleaning and repairs. If we were to display it in a different position, we probably wouldn't have these problems.

D: I agree with that. I think we could consider moving the sculpture to the front of City Hall, next to the hospital or possibly even inside the main shopping centre. In fact, the shopping centre has already expressed that they would be interested in this because they believe the sculpture could be a tourist attraction. If we planned it properly, we could get people to see the sculpture and do some shopping at the same time!

B: So what you're saying is you'd definitely rather keep the sculpture rather than sell it?

D: Yes, that's right.

A: OK, yes, those ideas make sense. I think we need to do more research here. First, we need to focus on identifying some places that the sculpture could go. We need to reject any places where we feel vandals would be likely to damage the piece. Second, we need to consider the cost of moving the sculpture.

D: There's one other point I'd like to raise.

A: OK.

D: This sculpture is public art, right? Does the government actually have the right to sell it? It belongs to the people.

B: You have a point, but the money would be put back into a public project, like a leisure centre as we discussed, which reflects what people really want.

C: Well, a leisure centre is a good thing, but it isn't art. I think our children need to see art in public places – especially the work of a famous artist, right here in our city. We need to have a balance of investment in sporting activities and public art in the lives of our children.

A: OK, I think we need to look into this. We need to find out whether the government can legally sell this sculpture and use the money for sport.

Are there any other comments on this topic? No? OK. We'll move on, then ...

9.4

1 Personally, I'm not really sure ...
2 I'm not an expert, but ...
3 All I know is ...
4 For me, ...

5 You could say that, however actually ...
6 That's true in part, but I think ...
7 You may be right, but I wonder if ...
8 I see what you're saying, but maybe ...

UNIT 10

 Taking care of the family

Narrator: This is Ali. Like many children in Egypt, he works hard to support his ageing parents.

Cairo is one of the most densely populated cities in the world with an approximate population of 17 million.

Ali was sent to work in Cairo from his home in the south when he was just seven years old.

He has worked at this bakery for ten years now.

Ali delivers bread to people. He is the only member of his family who works. Twenty percent of the population in Cairo live in poverty.

Families where older members find it hard to secure employment often rely on the younger relatives to provide income for food and household bills.

It is often more cost-effective for shops and businesses to employ children. As a result, older generations can find themselves unemployed.

Starting at dawn, Ali works all day, earning up to six dollars. Keeping just one dollar for himself, he sends the rest back home to help his parents and younger brothers in his village.

Ali works for up to ten hours every day. It's gruelling work.

He lives with a group of boys who also work every day in Cairo. Far away from home and missing their families, the boys have become good friends. They don't go to school but the money they send home may mean that their younger brothers and sisters can.

Ali hasn't seen his family for ten months, but today is a holiday and he's returning to his village. Eighty-one percent of all children working in Cairo are from rural areas, like Ali.

Everyone in the village is pleased to see him. His mother and father are thankful for the money he has sent home to provide for his family. They are unable to find work in their own village and would be unlikely to find work elsewhere.

Although Ali is unable to go to school, the money means his younger brothers can attend and will therefore have a better chance of getting a good job when they are older. Thirteen percent of children in Egypt have never been to school.

For now, Ali and his family all enjoy the reunion and the little time they share together, as he will soon return to the bakery.

But, unless the employment situation in Egypt changes, the question remains as to whether Ali and his brothers will experience the same economic problems as their parents when they grow older ...

Host: Hello and welcome to the Money and Finance Podcast. I'm your host, Ian Brown, and today's topic is retirement. In the past, giving up work at 60 or 65 signalled the end of an active, exciting life. It was seen as a time for staying at home, doing the gardening and being very careful with money. Twenty years ago, most people planned to leave a large sum of money to their children on their death and didn't spend a lot on themselves once they started to receive a pension.

But times have changed. People nowadays don't think of 65 as old. People who have exercised and eaten a good diet throughout their lives have plenty of energy to enjoy life after work. Many of today's older people see retirement as a reward for a lifetime of hard work, and rather than saving their money to give to their children, they're spending it: on luxuries, travel, new cars, and meals out, and because they worked hard and saved hard for their retirement, they have plenty of money to spend. As a group, the over-60s in the UK have 500 billion pounds in assets: property, money in the bank, investments and so on. Last year, they spent 240 billion pounds on leisure, accounting for more than 60% of all consumer spending. This included 345 million pounds on meals out and 535 million pounds on travel.

Rick and Nadia Jones are typical of this new approach to retirement. I asked them to share their thoughts.

Nadia: Well, in my working life I was a banker and Rick was in business. We both retired at 62 and since that time, we've travelled a lot and have had years of excitement and fun. A lot of our friends are doing the same. We're still healthy and we love travelling, so why shouldn't we? I had to persuade Rick to agree to the idea at first. It just wasn't like that for our parents. However, we've managed to save enough money to permit us to live the life we've always wanted, and I think we've earned it.

Rick: We've been to New Zealand and South Africa – and Nadia loves the weather in Dubai! We've been there three times.

Host: According to one survey, 20 years ago, most of today's older people believed they would work in the garden, read and babysit their grandchildren. However, retired people now want to do more exciting things! Do you agree with this?

Nadia: I do, I think. We worked hard during our careers and made sure our two daughters had a good education. They're both married and working now. I want to be involved in my children's lives, but I do also want adventure! We live close to both our daughters and offer to babysit our grandchildren regularly, but we're not free childminders!

Rick: Exactly. Our daughters need to work hard and save their money just as we've done. Our savings allow us to live the life we've always wanted. This is our chance to have some fun and we don't want to stay at home all day gardening and watching television. Our daughters have agreed to support our choices and we're going to encourage them to do the same.

Nadia: I think our parents' generation thought it was really important to save for the next generation, to give money to their children, but our generation doesn't think that way.

Rick: We've talked to our daughters about it. They understand that the money is ours to spend. They also understand that as long as we're fit and healthy we might as well enjoy life. Our home is also worth about 400,000 pounds. We are not planning on selling it, so they'll get that eventually.

Host: Recent research shows that about two-thirds of older people agree with Rick and Nadia, and plan to leave their home to their children, and no money, but what about the next generation? Today's working generation is probably facing a more difficult retirement than their parents. Pensions are getting smaller and the average age of retirement is increasing. According to the United Nations, about 18% of Europeans aged 65 and over are still working, but that number is increasing. By the year 2030, more than 20% of European people age 65 and over will still have regular jobs. So should these parents be doing more? Rick?

Rick: I think we both feel we've done our part as parents. We have many happy, healthy years ahead of us and still have other things we want to do with our lives, and now we're doing them. I'd advise everyone else to do the same.

See script on page 182.

Fahad: Hello. My name is Fahad and I'd like to talk to you today about changes in the situation of elderly people in Egypt. First, I'm going to explain a bit about the Egyptian concept of family. Then I'll present some figures about how the Egyptian population is changing. Finally, I'll explain one way that the Egyptian government is preparing for the population changes over the next decades.

I'll begin by explaining the importance of the family bond in Egyptian culture. For Egyptians, family is a huge part of our identity and our main source of social support. Household members assist each other and feel responsible for the welfare of both the nuclear and extended family. When children are young, their parents support them. The father is usually the provider as the children grow up, but as they become older, the parents' ability to provide for their children declines. Eventually this leads to the child's role changing from being a dependent to supporting the family, providing for the parents and other family members in their old age.

Throughout life, family members cooperate closely to ensure everyone's welfare. Let me give you an example from my own household. In addition to our nuclear family, my father's aunt lives with us because she never married and it is my father's role to support her. When my two older sisters married, my father also bought each of them a flat in our apartment building. He has supported them financially, but it will also result in a benefit for my parents: when they are older, my sisters will be living in the local community, to provide support in return.

In the 21st century, this traditional way of caring for elderly people is slowly changing. If you look at the line graph, you will see that the current population of Egypt is about 85 million, but it's expected to be around 100 million people by the year 2050. The population increase stems from the fact that people are living longer. The fertility rate in the country is an average of 2.7 births per woman, which contributes only slightly to population growth. According to United Nations figures, today, 4.7 per cent of the population is over 65. By 2050, this will steadily increase and could be as high as 16.8%. This increase will result in more elderly people that need care and fewer young people to care for them.

Of course many elderly people will continue to be cared for by their family, but people without children will have to live in institutions for the elderly, provided by the Egyptian government. According to an article by Dr. Mohsen Gadallah, there were 37 homes for the elderly in Egypt in 1982. However, by the year 2000, the number of homes shot up to around 80, and since that time, there has been a steady increase in the number of institutions. As the population continues to age, it is expected that the number of homes for the elderly will increase to meet the demand …

Mika: Hello. My name is Mika. I'd like to begin by thanking Fahad for his interesting talk. I'm going to discuss similar issues, relating to Japan. I'll begin by explaining the importance of family in Japan and present some figures that explain how the population is changing. Finally, I'll talk about the way Japanese government is dealing with the ageing population. As in Egypt, family in Japan is very important. However, where the extended family is very important in Fahad's country, the focus in Japan is on what we call the 'family line'. This is the bond between children, parents, grandparents and so on, right back to our ancestors. Of course this means that in many cases, when elderly people can no longer look after themselves, they move in with their children.

Japan has one of the highest life expectancies in the world. Its population is about 127 million. If you look at the data I've provided, you will note that the UN reports that there are about 29 million people over the age of 65 in Japan today, nearly 23% of the population. This is much higher than the 4.7 % figure for Egypt. By 2050, Japan's population will be about 106 million, and 35% of the population will be over 65, which is much higher than the 16.8% predicted in Egypt. The population of children aged four and under is expected to fall from about 6 million now to under 5 million in 2020, and just 4 million in 2050. This can be traced back to a low fertility rate, which has plummeted to just 1.5 children per woman. Young Japanese people are waiting longer than their parents' generation to get married and when they do, they're having fewer children. Young people now enjoy a lot of free time in their 20s and 30s, but this also results in the same issues that Egypt is facing: more and more elderly people to take care of, with fewer younger people to take care of them.

As in Egypt, the Japanese government has taken steps to deal with the situation. Most Japanese people between the ages of 40 and 65 pay a 1% income tax that goes to help those over 65. The over-65s don't get the money directly, but the government supports them. Even elderly people living at home with family have a care worker who makes sure they have everything they need. Some elderly people go to a daycare centre a few times a week, where they can share meals and participate in social activities. Those elderly people who don't live with family generally live in institutions, with about nine people living in one home. Each has a bedroom and they share a living room and kitchen. This enables them to have some independence and to feel cared for at the same time ...

Ahmet: My name is Ahmet. Thank you Fahad and Mika for your interesting presentations. My topic today is how elderly people are cared for in Turkey. First I'll give some background on how the elderly are usually cared for. After that, I'll talk about some of the drawbacks and benefits of this system and I'll finish by explaining the challenges ahead.

Fahad and Mika explained that it is becoming more and more common in both Egypt and Japan for elderly people to live in institutions when their ability to care for themselves declines. Moving old people into nursing homes allows the younger generation to continue their lives without having to worry about daily care for an ageing parent. However, in Turkey, 80% of households have an older person in them. Many families see this as the natural solution to dealing with old age. As parents, we devote ourselves to our children. In turn, as adults, we devote ourselves to our ageing parents. Most people my age have a grandparent living at home.

The system has drawbacks, both for the families caring for elderly people and for the elderly people themselves. Those responsible for the welfare of an elderly person can feel that they aren't free to do as they like in their own home. The older people being cared for may also not feel completely free and dislike the way things are done by their carers. Living closely together in forced circumstances can give rise to tensions. However, there are many benefits to these arrangements. In many households, older people contribute to the family by participating in domestic jobs and helping with childcare. This gives them something to do and a sense of responsibility.

Turkey's population is nearly 80 million today. If you look at the graph I've provided, you will see that more than 5 million people, or around 6.4%, are over 65. This is only slightly higher than the number for Egypt and much lower than Japan's 23%. UN projections indicate that by 2050, Turkey's population will reach 92 million and about 18 million people, or 20% of the total, will be over 65. This is higher than the 16.8% figure that we heard for Egypt, but much lower than Japan's 38%. So we can see that in the long-term, the same challenges lie ahead for Turkey as for Egypt and Japan. However, for now, the solution is for Turks to continue caring for the elderly at home.

10.4

1 Today, the over-65s make up 2.5% of Country A's total population. This figure is smaller than the figure of 7% for Country B.

2 The population of Country B will be 77 million in 2050. This number is much larger than the population figure of 1.4 million for Country A in 2050.

3 By 2050 Country A's population will have risen to 1.78 million people. The population for Country B also peaks in 2050 with 92,000 people.

ACKNOWLEDGEMENTS

Author acknowledgements
I'd like to thank the team at Cambridge University Press for their excellent research and for developing the series on a solid pedagogical footing. Special thanks to Fran Disken and Caroline Thiriau for bringing me on board, to Kate Hansford for managing the project with a firm hand and cool head and to Jenna Leonard for her readiness to discuss editorial matters.
Lewis Lansford

Publisher acknowledgements
The publishers are extremely grateful to the following people and their students for reviewing and trialling this course during its development. The course has benefited hugely from your insightful comments and feedback.

Mr M.K. Adjibade, King Saud University, Saudi Arabia; Canan Aktug, Bursa Technical University, Turkey; Olwyn Alexander, Heriot Watt University, UK; Valerie Anisy, Damman University, Saudi Arabia; Anwar Al-Fetlawi, University of Sharjah, UAE; Laila Al-Qadhi, Kuwait University, Kuwait; Tahani Al-Taha, University of Dubai, UAE; Ozlem Atalay, Middle East Technical University, Turkey; Seda Merter Ataygul, Bursa Technical University Turkey; Harika Altug, Bogazici University, Turkey; Kwab Asare, University of Westminster, UK; Erdogan Bada, Cukurova University, Turkey; Cem Balcikanli, Gazi University, Turkey; Gaye Bayri, Anadolu University, Turkey; Meher Ben Lakhdar, Sohar University, Oman; Emma Biss, Girne American University, UK; Dogan Bulut, Meliksah University, Turkey; Sinem Bur, TED University, Turkey; Alison Chisholm, University of Sussex, UK; Dr. Panidnad Chulerk , Rangsit University, Thailand; Sedat Cilingir, Bilgi University, Istanbul, Turkey; Sarah Clark, Nottingham Trent International College, UK; Elaine Cockerham, Higher College of Technology, Muscat, Oman; Asli Derin, Bilgi University, Turkey; Steven Douglass, University of Sunderland, UK; Jacqueline Einer, Sabanci University, Turkey; Basak Erel, Anadolu University, Turkey; Hande Lena Erol, Piri Reis Maritime University, Turkey; Gulseren Eyuboglu, Ozyegin University, Turkey; Muge Gencer, Kemerburgaz University, Turkey; Dr. Majid Gharawi and colleagues at the English Language Centre, Jazan University, Saudi Arabia; Jeff Gibbons, King Fahed University of Petroleum and Minerals, Saudi Arabia; Maxine Gilway, Bristol University, UK; Dr Christina Gitsaki, HCT, Dubai Men's College, UAE; Sam Fenwick, Sohar University, Oman; Peter Frey, International House, Doha, Qatar; Neil Harris, Swansea University, UK; Vicki Hayden, College of the North Atlantic, Qatar; Ajarn Naratip Sharp Jindapitak, Prince of Songkla University, Hatyai, Thailand; Joud Jabri-Pickett, United Arab Emirates University, Al Ain, UAE; Aysel Kilic, Anadolu University, Turkey; Ali Kimav, Anadolu University, Turkey; Bahar Kiziltunali, Izmir University of Economics, Turkey; Kamil Koc, Ozel Kasimoglu Coskun Lisesi, Turkey; Ipek Korman-Tezcan, Yeditepe University, Turkey; Philip Lodge, Dubai Men's College, UAE; Iain Mackie, Al Rowdah University, Abu Dhabi, UAE; Katherine Mansfield, University of Westminster, UK; Kassim Mastan, King Saud University, Saudi Arabia; Elspeth McConnell, Newham College, UK; Lauriel Mehdi, American University of Sharjah, UAE; Dorando Mirkin-Dick, Bell International Institute, UK; Dr Sita Musigrungsi, Prince of Songkla University, Hatyai, Thailand; Mark Neville, Al Hosn University, Abu Dhabi, UAE; Shirley Norton, London School of English, UK; James Openshaw, British Study Centres, UK; Hale Ottolini, Mugla Sitki Kocman University, Turkey; David Palmer, University of Dubai, UAE; Michael Pazinas, United Arab Emirates University, UAE; Troy Priest, Zayed University, UAE; Alison Ramage Patterson, Jeddah, Saudi Arabia; Paul Rogers, Qatar Skills Academy, Qatar; Josh Round, Saint George International, UK; Harika Saglicak, Bogazici University, Turkey; Asli Saracoglu, Isik University, Turkey; Neil Sarkar, Ealing, Hammersmith and West London College, UK; Nancy Shepherd, Bahrain University, Bahrain; Jonathan Smith, Sabanci University, Turkey; Peter Smith, United Arab Emirates University, UAE; Adem Soruc, Fatih University Istanbul, Turkey; Dr Peter Stanfield, HCT, Madinat Zayed & Ruwais Colleges, UAE; Maria Agata Szczerbik, United Arab Emirates University, Al Ain, UAE; Burcu Tezcan-Unal, Bilgi University, Turkey; Dr Nakonthep Tipayasuparat, Rangsit University, Thailand; Scott Thornbury, The New School, New York, USA; Susan Toth, HCT, Dubai Men's Campus, Dubai, UAE; Melin Unal, Ege University, Izmir, Turkey; Aylin Unaldi, Bogaziçi University, Turkey; Colleen Wackrow, Princess Nourah bint Abdulrahman University, Riyadh, Saudi Arabia; Gordon Watts, Study Group, Brighton UK; Po Leng Wendelkin, INTO at University of East Anglia, UK; Halime Yildiz, Bilkent University, Ankara, Turkey; Ferhat Yilmaz, Kahramanmaras Sutcu Imam University, Turkey.

Special thanks to Peter Lucantoni for sharing his expertise, both pedagogical and cultural.

Text and Photo acknowledgements
The authors and publishers acknowledge the following sources of copyright material and are grateful for the permissions granted. While every effort has been made, it has not always been possible to identify the sources of all the material used, or to trace all copyright holders. If any omissions are brought to our notice, we will be happy to include the appropriate acknowledgements on reprinting.

Maplecroft for the map 'Pandemic Risk Index – Risk of Spread' on p. 54.

United Nations for the text on pp. 211–212 adapted from 'Global Deserts Outlook' edited by Ezquiel Ezcurra, Denmark, *United Nations Environment Programme: UNEP*, 2006. Reproduced with permission.

p.12:(1) © Eric Limon/Shutterstock; p.12: (2) © szefai/Shutterstock; p.12: (3) © Steven Vidler/Eurasia Press/Corbis; pp.14/15: © Macduff Everton/Corbis; p.18:Bloomberg/Getty Images; p.22: © Yadid Levy/Alamy; p.23(TL): © George Steinmetz; p.23(TR): © Ed Darack/Science Faction/Corbis; pp.32/33: © Wunkley/Alamy; p.35: RGB Ventures LLC dba/Superstock/Alamy; p.37: © Tim Pannell/Corbis; p.40: © Christophe Lehenaff/Photononstop/Corbis; p.43: © Jamie Grill/Tetra/Corbis; pp.50/51: © Yuan Xue Jun/Redlink/ Corbis; p.59: © Julie Hiebaum/Alamy; p.61(TR): Tetra Images/Corbis; p.61(TL): Blend Images/Shutterstock; p.63(TL): MBI/Alamy; p.63(TR): Bonkers About Pictures/Alamy; pp.68/69: AFP/Getty Images; p.72: © Brian Madhaven/Arabia/Alamy; p.76: © Greg Pease/Getty Images; p.78(TL): Itanistock/Alamy; p.78(TC): OJO Images Ltd/Alamy; p.78(TR): Cultura Creative/Alamy; pp.86/87: AFP/Getty Images; p.88: © Oliver Leedham/ Alamy; p.90(CL): Tetra/Corbis; p.90(CR): © Ryan Pyle/Corbis; p.95: © Monty Rakusen/Cultura/Corbis; p.98: Thinkstock; p.99(TL): Thinkstock; p.99(TC): Thinkstock; p.99(TR): © Carol Yepes/Getty Images; pp.104/105: © Cyril Russo/J H Editorial/Minden Pictures/Corbis; p.107: WEDA/epa/ Corbis; pp.122/123: © Jacobo Zanella/Getty Images; p.130: West Yorks Images/Alamy; pp.140/141: © Paul Souders/WorldFoto/Corbis; p.144: © Werner Dieterich/Alamy; p.148: Ssuaphotos/Shutterstock; p.149: Hacohob/ Alamy; pp.158/159: Getty Images; p.162: © Klaus Hackenberg/Corbis; p.173: © Richard Cummins/Robert Harding World Imagery/Corbis; pp.176/177: Flickr Vision/Getty.

All videos stills by kind permission of © Discovery Communications LLC 2014

Illustrations
Oxford Designers & Illustrators pp.96, 126, 132, 142.

Dictionary
Cambridge dictionaries are the world's most widely used dictionaries for learners of English. Available at three levels (Cambridge Essential English Dictionary, Cambridge Learner's Dictionary and Cambridge Advanced Learner's Dictionary), they provide easy-to-understand definitions, example sentences, and help in avoiding typical mistakes. The dictionaries are also available online at dictionary.cambridge.org. © Cambridge University Press, reproduced with permission.

Corpus
Development of this publication has made use of the Cambridge English Corpus (CEC). The CEC is a multi-billion word computer database of contemporary spoken and written English. It includes British English, American English and other varieties of English. It also includes the Cambridge Learner Corpus, developed in collaboration with Cambridge English Language Assessment. Cambridge University Press has built up the CEC to provide evidence about language use that helps to produce better language teaching materials.

Picture research by Alison Prior.

Typeset by emc design ltd.

Contents

■ Henry VIII – A Magnificent Monarch ■

HENRY VIII OF England was the king with six wives. He was also, for a long time, a king without a son. The need for an heir to the throne spurred Henry to his first divorce. To gain it, he separated the Church of England from the Roman Catholic Church and so established the Protestant Reformation in England. This was not what he had intended.

HENRY'S LIFE

1491 *Born*
1509 *Henry becomes king. Marries Catherine of Aragon.*
1516 *Henry's daughter Mary is born.*
1533 *Divorces Catherine of Aragon and marries Anne Boleyn. Henry's daughter Elizabeth is born.*
1534 *Henry declares himself the Supreme Head of the Church in England.*
1537 *Henry's son Edward is born.*
1547 *Henry dies.*

Henry reigned at a time of great change: the Renaissance brought new ideas that changed art and science; the Reformation changed religion and the church; and even the world changed, as explorers found new lands overseas. England was changing too, from a country dominated by noble landowning families into a modern nation state in which parliament played a larger role. And stamped on the English nation was Henry VIII's larger-than-life personality. Despite all his faults, he played the part of a real king – a magnificent monarch who inspired in his people awe, fear, loyalty and confidence.

HENRY'S WIVES

1. Catherine of Aragon, born 1485, married 1509, divorced 1533, died 1536.
2. Anne Boleyn, born 1507, married 1533, beheaded 1536.
3. Jane Seymour, born 1509?, married 1536, died 1537.
4. Anne of Cleves, born 1515, married 1540, divorced 1540, died 1557.
5. Catherine Howard, born 1521?, married 1540, beheaded 1542.
6. Catherine Parr, born 1512, married 1543, died 1548.

▼ **Henry VIII's signature.**

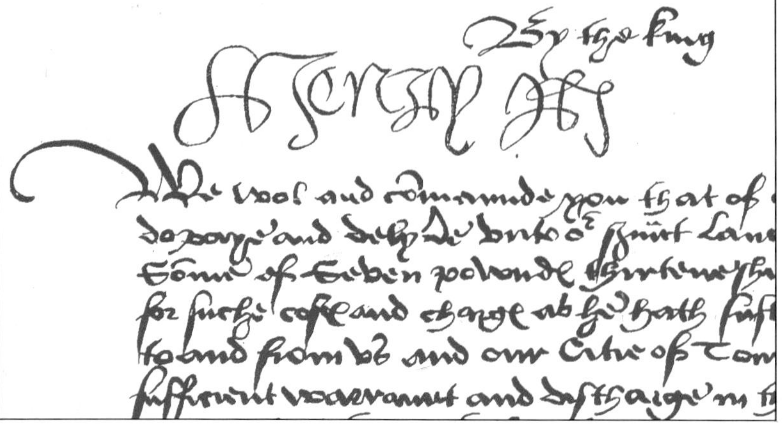

QUOTES

'Hitherto small mention has been made of King Henry, whereas for the future the whole world will talk of him,' declared a Venetian living in London.

The Italian writer Machiavelli never met Henry but heard of him as *'rich, ferocious and eager for glory'*.

As the holly groweth green
And never changeth hue,
So I am, ever hath been,
Unto my lady true.
From a poem said to be by Henry VIII, written around 1515.

◀ Henry aged about 45 and at the height of his power. This superb portrait is from the school of Holbein.

▪ A TUDOR PRINCE ▪

THE BOY WHO became King Henry VIII was born at Greenwich near London on 28 June 1491. He was the second son of Henry VII, who had won the English throne in battle. The family had come from Wales and its name was Tudor.

Henry VII proved a strong and able king. He saved money, made himself rich and kept the English nobles under control. He wanted to leave his son a secure kingdom, with no rivals for the throne. He also wanted Spain on his side to face the

▲ **Henry as a young boy. At the age of 10, on the death of his brother Arthur, he became heir to his father's throne.**

EVENTS

1491 *Henry VIII born.*
1492 *Christopher Columbus sails to America.*
1494 *Treaty of Tordesillas divides New World discoveries between Spain and Portugal.*
1495 *Henry VII's daughter Mary born.*
1497 *John Cabot reaches North America.*
1498 *Vasco da Gama, a Portuguese captain, sails to India.*
1499 *Vespucci explores the north-east coast of South America. Erasmus, the Dutch scholar, first visits England.*
1500 *Wynken de Worde sets up a printing press in Fleet St, London.*

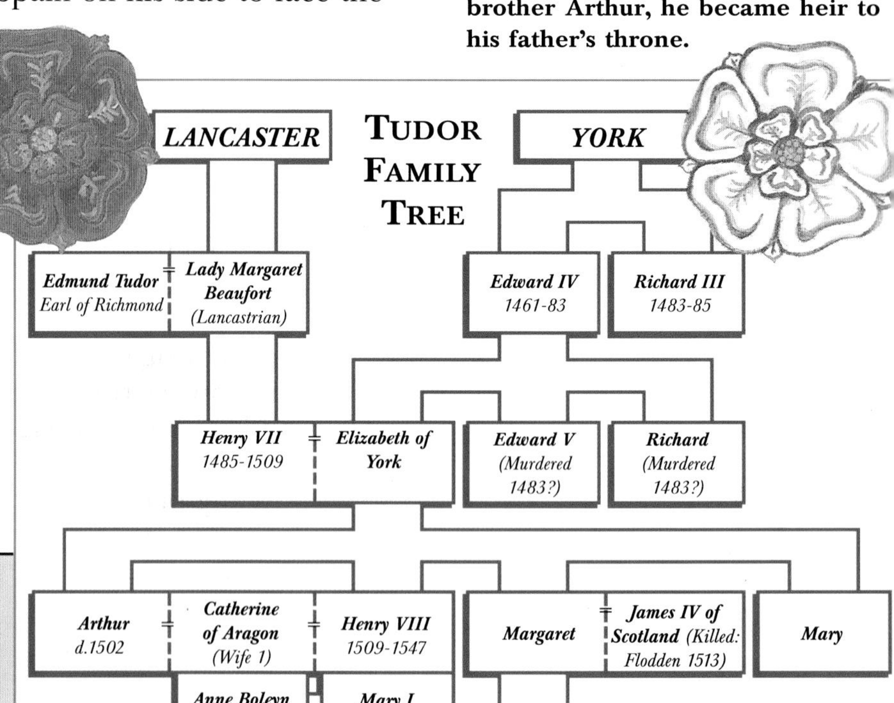

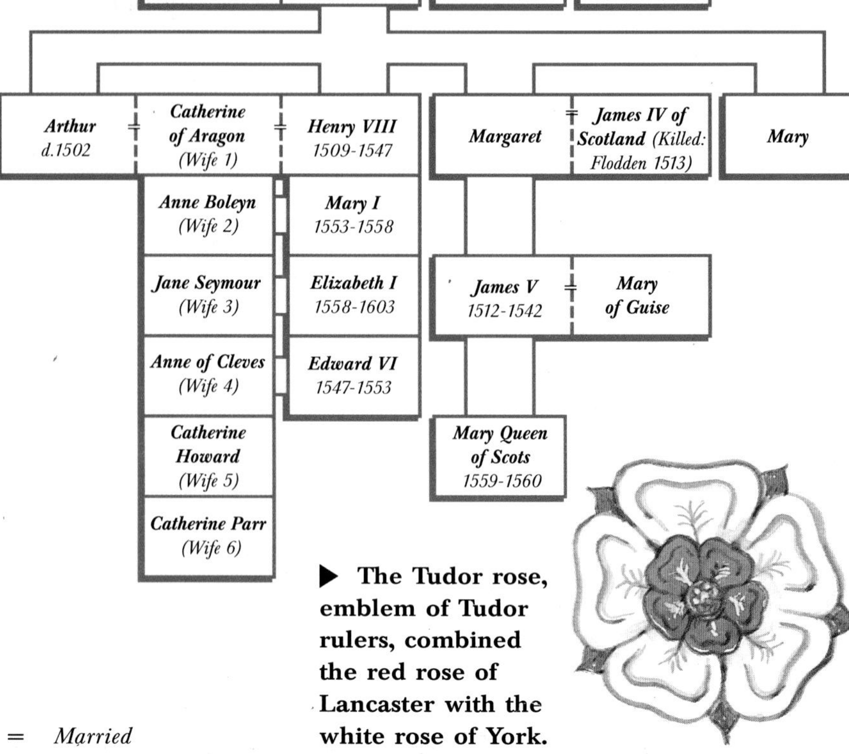

▶ **The Tudor rose, emblem of Tudor rulers, combined the red rose of Lancaster with the white rose of York.**

WARS OF THE ROSES

ENGLAND'S nobles were battle-weary. For years, two families had claimed the crown. One – Lancaster – had a red rose as its badge; the other – York – had a white rose. In 1485, the last battle of their Wars of the Roses was fought, at Bosworth Field. There, Henry Tudor led Lancaster to victory against King Richard III. The king was killed and Henry took his crown as Henry VII. He then married Elizabeth of York. So the two warring sides were joined and England was at peace.

▲ **Henry VII, father of Henry VIII. As Henry Tudor of Lancaster, he defeated King Richard III of York in battle at Bosworth in 1485 and became the first Tudor monarch.**

growing power of England's old enemy, France. So he chose the Spanish princess Catherine of Aragon as a bride for his first son, Arthur. But a few months after the wedding in November 1501, Prince Arthur died. His 10-year-old brother Henry would now be England's next king – and Catherine's new husband, since Henry VII still wanted to keep this link with Spain.

◀ **Elizabeth of York, mother of Henry VIII. Before the battle of Bosworth, Henry Tudor made a promise that, if he won, he would marry Elizabeth of York, so uniting the families of Lancaster and York.**

A NEW WORLD WAITING

Henry was born into a world that was growing. In his lifetime, sailors from Europe found their way to America and ships from Europe first sailed all round the world. Before he died, Spain ruled Mexico and much of South America. Portugal controlled the seaways round Africa to India, China, Japan and the spice islands of the East. Henry VII sent John Cabot across the Atlantic Ocean in 1497. He landed in Newfoundland (Canada), bringing back news of its rich fishing grounds. Cabot's son, Sebastian, later made maps for Henry VIII.

PROTESTANTS AND REFORMATION

EUROPE WAS split by new ideas in religion. The head of the Christian church in western Europe was the pope in Rome. But many people did not like the way the church was run. It seemed too worldly and corrupt. The German priest Martin Luther was among those who protested at what they saw was wrong with the church. The 'Protestant' movement to change, or reform, the church was called the Reformation.

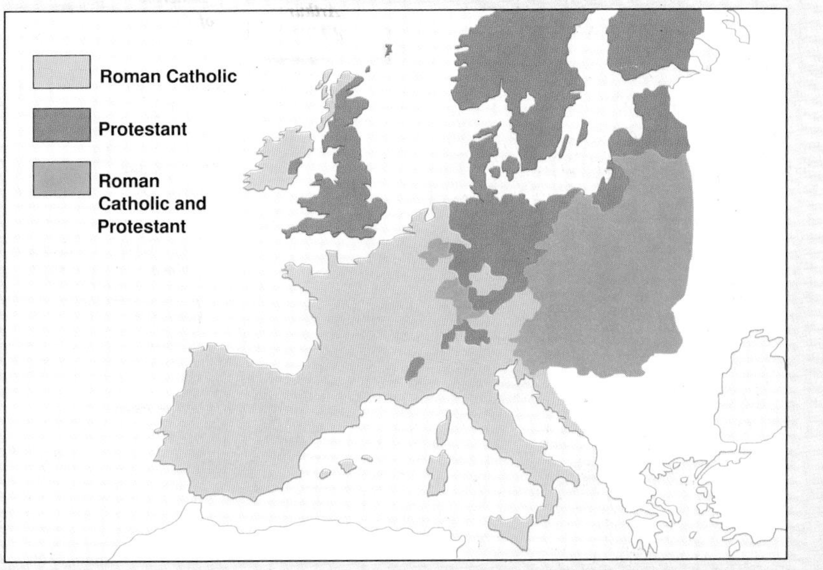

THE YOUNG HENRY

HENRY VIII WAS one of seven children, but only he and two sisters outlived their parents. One sister, Margaret, married King James IV of Scotland. The other, Mary, married King Louis XII of France, who died soon afterwards.

Henry grew up a tall and strong young man with reddish hair 'combed short and straight in the French fashion'. He was clever, good at lessons and at sports such as tennis, riding and hunting. A skilled marksman with a bow and arrow, he also loved to take part in mock fights called jousts. Knights in armour, mounted on horseback, charged at each other with pointed lances to knock their opponent to the ground.

A TALENTED YOUNG MAN

Henry loved dancing, as well as playing the lute and singing. The

EVENTS

1501 *Catherine of Aragon arrives in England and marries Henry VII's son Arthur.*
1502 *Prince Arthur dies. First Africans arrive as slaves in America.*
1503 *Henry VII's daughter Margaret marries James IV of Scotland. Italian artist Leonardo da Vinci paints the* Mona Lisa.
1507 *Martin Luther ordained a priest.*
1508 *Michelangelo begins painting the Sistine Chapel in Rome.*

THE PRICE OF WOOL

ENGLAND'S towns and merchants grew rich from selling wool and cloth abroad. Wealthy farmers wanted more land to raise more sheep and began to shut off – or 'enclose' – the common land where villagers grazed their own animals. Less land was used for growing food and fewer farmworkers were needed. Farms (right) could not supply enough food for the growing population and so many families went hungry. Laws were passed to stop a person owning more than one farm or keeping more than 2000 sheep.

young prince had a lively mind. He was interested in religion and in the new learning of the Renaissance which he discussed with the famous Erasmus and other scholars. He liked mathematics and astronomy. When he was king, Henry roused his councillor Sir Thomas More from his bed to look at the stars from the palace roof!

RICH MAN, POOR MAN, BEGGAR MAN . . .

When Henry was crowned king on 24 June 1509 (four days before his eighteenth birthday), people had high hopes. He was well educated, handsome, with a commanding, graceful air and a strong personality.

His kingdom had grown richer with peace. It was a land of forests, villages and small farms. There were towns, too, which were small but growing. But, as trade grew, rents and food prices went up. A huge rise in England's population took place during Henry's reign. Many people had no work, and no money. Bands of beggars roamed the countryside, frightening the law-abiding.

THE PALACES OF NONSUCH AND GREENWICH

THOUGH THE king had many palaces, he built new ones around London, where he spent most of his time. The old palace at Greenwich stood beside the river Thames, where the Royal Naval College stands today. Building was started in 1428 by a brother of Henry V, but the Tudors made it into a royal palace. Henry VIII, who was born there, added a banqueting hall, an armoury and a tiltyard for jousting. It was at Greenwich that he married Catherine of Aragon, Anne Boleyn and Anne of Cleves. His daughters Mary and Elizabeth were also born there. Henry's most magnificent palace, Nonsuch (left), built in Surrey during the 1540s, was later demolished.

▲ Henry playing the harp. All his life he loved music. He had a fine singing voice and composed well. Standing beside Henry in the picture is his jester, Will Somers.

■ A Planned Marriage ■

AS HE LAY DYING, Henry VII told his son to marry Catherine of Aragon. The Spanish princess was 23, six years older than Henry. She was small, dainty and graceful, as well as dignified and sensible. Six weeks after Henry became king, the two were married at Greenwich and later crowned at Westminster Abbey. There was much merry-making. Henry had plenty of money, carefully saved by his father. He threw lavish banquets, dances and tournaments.

EVENTS

1509 *Henry VII dies. Henry VIII becomes king and marries Catherine of Aragon. St Paul's School founded in London by John Colet.*
1511 *Spain ships first slaves from Africa to Cuba. Prince Henry is born to Catherine of Aragon but lives only six weeks.*
1512 *Henry joins Spain in the Holy League against France and in support of the pope.*
1513 *Vasco Nunez de Balboa of Spain is the first European to see the Pacific Ocean. The Italian Machiavelli writes a book called* The Prince *about how princes (and kings) should rule. Henry VIII leads an army across the Channel to France. English army defeats invading Scots at Flodden, where James IV of Scotland is killed.*

Feasts but no thanks

Although clever, Henry was lazy. He found writing 'tedious and painful' and was happy to leave day-to-day government to others – so long as they did what he wanted. Henry also wanted to be popular. Early in his reign, he executed two of his father's hated tax-collectors, even though they had filled the royal treasury with gold. Henry rarely showed thanks to those who served him well.

▲ Bringing news of the battle of Flodden (1513). The Scots, allied with England's enemy, France, had invaded England while Henry was fighting in France. The defeat of their army was a great blow to the Scots. They lost their king, James IV, and 10,000 men.

QUEEN CATHERINE

CATHERINE of Aragon was born in 1485, the daughter of Ferdinand and Isabella, rulers of Spain. When her first husband, Prince Arthur, died in 1502, Catherine stayed in England. Her marriage to Arthur's brother Henry needed special permission from the pope, for it broke church rules. She and Henry were happy at first. But of six babies born between 1510 and 1518, all except Mary died young. Prince Henry, born in 1511, lived only six weeks. The king wanted a son to succeed him. When Catherine failed to give him one, he looked for a new queen.

WARS AND GLORY

The new king sought fame and glory. He loved the idea of leading soldiers in battle. In 1513 he led an army across the Channel to fight against France. While he was away, the Scots (allies of France) attacked England, but were beaten in a fierce battle at Flodden. The Scots king was killed, leaving a baby son. The baby's mother, Margaret, was Henry's sister and now ruled Scotland for her young son.

▼ Queen Catherine watches from the stand as Henry takes part in a tournament to celebrate the birth of their son, Prince Henry, in 1511. But the baby prince died a few weeks later. Princess Mary, born in 1516, was the only child of Catherine to survive.

■ MEN OF POWER ■

HENRY SOON found a man to run his government. Thomas Wolsey was the son of an Ipswich butcher and had risen high in the church, becoming archbishop of York in 1514. As adviser to the king, Wolsey had organized Henry's war in France. Though the war cost a lot and won little, Wolsey had negotiated an advantageous peace treaty.

Wolsey did more and more for the king, leaving Henry free to enjoy himself. In 1515 the pope made Wolsey a cardinal and in the same year the king made him lord chancellor. Nobody in England was now richer or more powerful – except the king. Wolsey's aim was to be pope. But he did little to reform the church. Indeed, many ordinary people saw in Wolsey all the things that were wrong with it.

EVENTS

1514 *Henry's sister Mary marries Louis XII of France. Thomas Wolsey becomes archbishop of York and begins to build Hampton Court Palace.*
1515 *Wolsey is made lord chancellor of England and a cardinal of the church.*
1516 *Thomas More's book* Utopia *is published. Henry's daughter Mary is born.*
1517 *Martin Luther protests against wrongs in the church by nailing a list of complaints on a church door in Germany. Thomas More becomes a councillor to the king.*
1519 *Birth of Henry's illegitimate son Henry Fitzroy. Charles V of Spain is elected to rule the Holy Roman Empire. Leonardo da Vinci, artist and scientist, dies. In Mexico, Spanish soldiers capture Montezuma, king of the Aztecs. Magellan sets out to sail round the world.*
1520 *Henry meets Francis I of France at the Field of Cloth of Gold.*

▼ **The Field of Cloth of Gold (1520) was a dazzling meeting between Henry VIII and Francis I.**

HAMPTON COURT

IN 1514, Thomas Wolsey began to build the largest house in England. It grew bigger as he grew richer, with living space for a household of over 400 people and 280 rooms for guests! Such a display of wealth angered Henry. It is said that the cardinal gave Hampton Court (below) to the jealous king in 1526 to try to save himself. Four of Henry's wives lived there and Jane Seymour died there. Much of the building remains. The palace has a tennis court built by Henry in 1529.

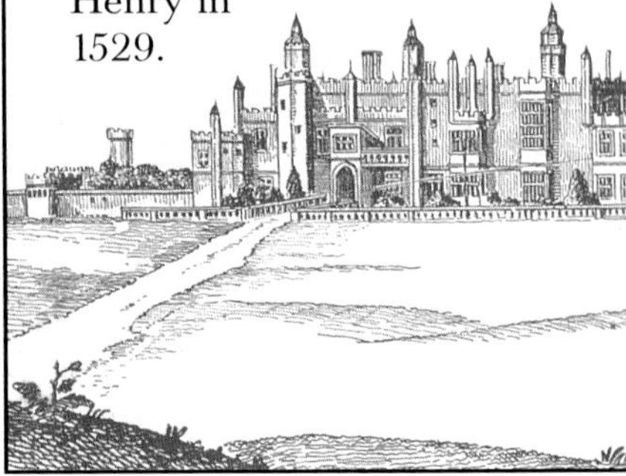

Thomas Wolsey was cardinal, ıancellor and the richest man ı England after the king. He ;as Henry's right-hand man ıntil he fell from power in 1529.

A Field of Gold

Two other new kings had come to power in Europe. One was Francis I of France. The other was Charles V, ruler first of Spain and then of the Holy Roman Empire. Wolsey hoped to play them off against each other to the advantage of England and its king. He organized a meeting between Henry and Francis near Calais in June 1520. Here, to gain the English king's support against Charles V, Francis put on a show of midsummer splendour. The two kings camped in dazzling tented palaces. They held banquets and tournaments celebrating the 'rebirth of chivalry'. Finally, they signed a treaty. But it meant little, for Henry soon met Charles V and signed another treaty with him.

Emperor Charles V

THE MOST powerful man in Europe was Charles V (below). His many lands included Spain, the Netherlands, and some of France, Italy and Germany. He fought the king of France over parts of Italy which they both claimed. He fought the Turks, who were France's allies. For a time, he held the pope prisoner. The explorers Cortez and Pizarro added more to his empire in America. But in his German lands, Protestant and Catholic groups caused problems. In the end, Charles left his empire for others to rule and went to live in a monastery.

▪ The King at Court ▪

HENRY VII'S COURT had been dull and gloomy. His son wanted brilliant people around him, to create a magnificent court as famous for art and learning as for music and sport. It was during the reign of the Tudors that the Renaissance flowered in England.

The Renaissance

The great movement called the Renaissance, or 'rebirth', had begun in Italy in the 1300s and spread across Europe in the 1400s. Renaissance scholars, artists and scientists looked anew

Tudor Schools

TUDOR TOWNS had grammar schools set up by townsmen and craft guilds (associations of skilled workers). Churches and monasteries also ran schools. Wolsey founded a school in Ipswich. Some famous public schools, such as Harrow, were begun for 'the poorest sort, if they shall be apt'. Boys worked from 6 to 11 am in the morning and from 1 to 6 pm in summer; two hours less in winter. They learnt a lot of Latin, the language used by the church and scholars. Girls were taught at home or not at all.

Events

1520 *Death of Raphael, one of the greatest Renaissance artists. Suleiman the Magnificent becomes ruler of the Ottoman (Turkish) empire.*

1521 *Magellan is killed in the Philippines but one of his five ships completes the first voyage round the world a year later. Martin Luther is excommunicated (expelled) from the Catholic church. Cortez captures Tenochtitlan, the capital of the Aztecs, in Mexico. Henry writes a pamphlet supporting the church against Luther and is given the title Fidei Defensor (Defender of the Faith) by the pope.*

▶ The king at the opening of parliament in 1515. Cardinal Wolsey is on the king's right (beneath the cardinal's red hat). At top right are members of the House of Commons who have been called to hear the king's speech. In the centre, judges sit on woolsacks.

A schoolmaster teaches a ild the alphabet from a *rnbook*, which hung from the upil's belt.

The family of Sir Thomas More, ne of the king's councillors and ter lord chancellor, was painted y the court painter Hans Holbein e Younger (1497-1543), who also ainted Henry's family and court. he original painting is now lost but is copy hangs in the National ortrait Gallery in London.

at the books and art of ancient Greece and Rome, using these ancient examples as models for their own work. Henry VII had invited Italians to his court, where they encouraged English scholars to study ancient 'classical' books. Among such scholars was John Colet, who in turn inspired the Dutch scholar Erasmus and Sir Thomas More. They were known as humanists because they acknowledged the prime importance of human beings.

THE KING AND HIS GOVERNMENT

Sir Thomas More became one of Henry's councillors in 1517. By now, people had grown unhappy. There were riots against priests, foreign merchants, tax-collectors and landlords. To make matters worse, plague struck the country. Trade was bad, yet the king was spending huge sums of money to equip armies for foreign wars. The king and Wolsey tried to bring in a new tax to raise money. To do this, Henry had to ask parliament to agree. But there was such an outcry that the idea was dropped. During Henry's reign, parliament gained a stronger voice in England's government.

Henry also spent lavishly on new palaces, magnificent clothes and jewels, banquets and entertainment. As he moved from palace to palace, the king's servants and court moved with him. His closest courtiers were rich lords and landowners who attended him in his private apartments.

■THE WORLD IN TURMOIL■

THE NEW IDEAS of the Renaissance, and those of the Protestant reformers, had spread to England with the aid of printing. But in church matters, England so far remained loyal to the pope. Henry himself wrote a book defending the church against Martin Luther's attacks, earning from the pope the title 'Defender of the Faith'. Nevertheless, many people in England were critical of the church and its priests. Scholars such as Erasmus and Colet pointed out the errors of its ways.

EVENTS

***1522** Anne Boleyn returns to England from serving as maid of honour to Henry's sister Mary in France.*
***1523** Holbein paints portrait of Erasmus. Thomas More elected speaker of House of Commons.*
***1525** About this date, the first turkeys are brought to Europe from America. At the battle of Pavia, Francis I of France is defeated and captured by Charles V of Spain.*
***1526** Babur founds new Mogul dynasty in India. William Tyndale's English translation of the New Testament published in England.*

THE HUMANISTS

Erasmus stayed in England with his friend Thomas More, another humanist scholar. More was a loyal churchman, who in 1516 published a book called *Utopia,* which described an ideal world. While not what they intended, the questioning ideas of the humanist scholars led the way for Protestant views to spread in the universities, among lawyers, and in the city of London.

THE PRINTED WORD

All over Europe, books poured from the printing workshops. By 1520 there were more than 200 different editions of the Bible. For the first time, people could read the scriptures in their own languages. Martin Luther wrote dozens of books and in one year (1523) more than 900 books were published in Germany, the centre of the religious revolution.

▶ Martin Luther started the Reformation by pinning his '95 theses' to the door of the castle church in Wittenberg, Germany. Henry strenuously opposed his views. His break with Rome was prompted by his desire for a divorce – not for Protestantism.

▲ The title page of Coverdale's Bible of 1535, the first to be printed in English.

ERASMUS

ERASMUS (1466?-1536) was a Dutch scholar. For a time, he supported Martin Luther and other Reformation leaders as they pointed out what was wrong with the church. But Erasmus did not want the church divided and refused to take sides. He visited England several times, teaching Greek at Cambridge and meeting Thomas More and John Colet. These learned men were called humanists, because their interest – unlike that of the scholars of the Middle Ages – lay in human thought and action.

▶ This portrait of Henry VIII was painted around 1535. The Latin words on the scroll are from St Mark's gospel: 'Go ye into all the world and preach the gospel to every creature'. The distribution of Bibles printed in English gave ordinary people access to the scriptures for the first time.

▼ Many new ideas of the Renaissance clashed with the views of the church. An example was the theory, stated in 1543 by the Polish astronomer Copernicus, that the earth moves round the sun.

PROTESTANT EUROPE

Sweden and Denmark were among the first countries in Europe to become Protestant. The French preacher John Calvin moved to Switzerland, where he made the city of Geneva a centre of a new strict Protestantism. Calvin's ideas (Calvinism) spread to the Netherlands, to England and to Scotland, where his writings were read eagerly by John Knox. This former Catholic priest became the fervent spokesman for the new beliefs in Scotland.

▪ THE KING'S GREAT MATTER ▪

BY 1527 IT WAS clear that Catherine would have no more children. There was no son to carry on the Tudor line, and Henry began to think this was God's punishment for marrying his dead brother's wife. Besides, the king had fallen in love with Anne Boleyn, one of the ladies at court, and wished to marry her. From now on, Henry's thoughts were directed to this 'great matter'.

To be rid of Catherine, Henry asked the pope to say that she had never been his lawful wife – even though the pope had given special permission for the wedding to take place! Catherine, too, asked the pope for help. Her nephew, Charles V, had the pope in his power. The pope said 'no' to Henry.

EVENTS

***1527** Henry signs treaty with France against Charles V. Rome sacked by troops fighting for Charles V and the pope surrenders to them. Henry applies to Rome to end his marriage.*
***1529** Wolsey falls from power. Thomas More becomes lord chancellor.*
***1530** Pope crowns Charles V Holy Roman Emperor. Wolsey dies.*
***1532** Thomas More resigns as lord chancellor. Thomas Cromwell gains control of the king's council.*
***1533** Thomas Cranmer becomes archbishop of Canterbury.*

▲ **The lively and witty Anne Boleyn was 'not one of the handsomest women in the world' but had eyes that were 'black and beautiful'. She had many admirers. By divorcing Catherine in order to marry her, Henry broke from the pope's authority. Anne and Henry had a baby girl – the future Queen Elizabeth. The marriage lasted only three years. In 1536 Anne was executed.**

THE FALL OF WOLSEY

Henry blamed Wolsey for not getting his way and in 1529 stripped the cardinal of all his powers. A year

◀ **This gold half-sovereign shows Henry majestically seated on his throne.**

THOMAS CRANMER

THOMAS Cranmer (1489-1556) became in 1533 the first Protestant archbishop of Canterbury, the leading churchman in England. He advised Henry to let university scholars, not the pope, rule on the royal marriage. He let churches use prayers in English, rather than Latin, and is remembered for his *Book of Common Prayer*. Cranmer did what he was told to bring about the royal divorces but he was a kindly man who tried to save the lives of Thomas More and Anne Boleyn. In 1556 Henry's daughter Mary had him burned as a heretic (right).

▲ Despite the political upheavals caused by his divorce, Henry still found time for court entertainment. This frieze of musicians, painted about 1585, is in Gilling Castle, Yorkshire.

▲ Henry Fitzroy, the illegitimate son of Henry VIII, was created Duke of Richmond in 1525 by his father, who hoped to make him his heir. But the young duke died in 1536.

later Wolsey was arrested for treason, but died before a trial could take place. His job as chancellor went to Sir Thomas More. More was a lawyer, who by 1518 had become a councillor and ambassador abroad for Henry. For a time, he was speaker of the House of Commons. More tried hard to keep Luther's Protestant ideas out of England, but a tide of feeling against priests and church was swelling in the country. Nobles, country landowners and wealthy merchants who sent members to parliament all wanted to curb the privileges of the church.

THE RISE OF CROMWELL

The king's new adviser, Thomas Cromwell, said that for the royal marriage to end lawfully, England must break free from the authority of the pope. Parliament agreed. Together, king and parliament began passing laws to bring this about. As a result, Henry became the Supreme Head of the Church in England.

▶ Thomas Cromwell was once Wolsey's assistant and, like him, later lord chancellor. Ruthless and clever, he modernised the government and civil service and helped Henry gain his divorce.

▪ A Son to Succeed ▪

THE KING NOW had his wish. In 1533 he secretly married Anne Boleyn and some months later the new archbishop of Canterbury, Thomas Cranmer, cancelled the first wedding to Catherine of Aragon. In September at Greenwich, a child was born to Anne and Henry. It was not the longed-for son, but a girl – Elizabeth. Catherine was banished from court with a few servants. She had little money and died, lonely and wretched, in 1536. To celebrate the news, Henry wore an outfit of yellow.

EVENTS

1531 *Pizarro begins conquest of Inca Empire in South America.*
1533 *Cranmer becomes archbishop of Canterbury. Henry marries Anne Boleyn. Ivan the Terrible becomes ruler of Russia, aged three.*
1534 *Henry declared Supreme Head of the Church in England. Ignatius Loyola founds the Society of Jesus (the Jesuits) as part of the revival in the Roman Catholic church known as the Counter-Reformation.*
1535 *The French explorer Jacques Cartier claims Canada for France. Sir Thomas More is excecuted.*

The end of More

Cromwell, with Henry's approval, began to modernise the workings of government and parliament. Meanwhile, the king wanted all his subjects to show that they agreed with his actions over the divorce. One who did not was Sir Thomas More, who gave up his job as chancellor in 1532 because he could not support the king.

When More would not swear the Oath of Supremacy stating that Henry ranked above the pope, he was arrested for treason, tried on false evidence and beheaded in 1535.

Tudor medicine

THE KING'S doctors could do little to save Jane Seymour. Many women in Tudor times died in childbirth, as did many babies. Children also died from diseases easily cured today, and people of all ages dreaded catching smallpox, plague, or any of the other epidemics that spread through crowded, dirty towns. But doctors were learning more about the human body. The first book on anatomy was published in Italy in 1543. There was a new interest in surgery, too. In 1518 Henry granted a charter to the new Royal College of Surgeons in London, which still exists today.

▶ Catherine of Aragon had numerous miscarriages before Mary was born. Banished from court, she died sad and lonely in January 1536 four months before Anne Boleyn went to the block.

▼ The royal nursery. The king visits his children, little Edward (centre), Mary (right) and Elizabeth (left).

Two queens die

A year later, Anne Boleyn followed More to the execution block. The charge was treason, for being unfaithful to the king. Henry, now desperate for a son, at once married one of Anne's ladies-in-waiting. This third wife, Jane Seymour, at last gave birth to a son – Edward – in 1537, but died a few days later. Henry mourned the loss of the fair, pale Jane, who had acted as peacemaker between him and his daughter Mary. His baby son was made Prince of Wales, as a sign of the union between England and Wales, which became law in 1536.

Thomas More

SIR THOMAS More was a lawyer, scholar, writer and lord chancellor of England. He was known for his merry wit and enjoyed family life. More supported the Catholic church, and the king as far as he was able. But he could not accept Henry in place of the pope. For this, he was executed on 6 July 1535, dying 'the king's good servant – but God's first'. The Catholic church declared More a saint in 1935.

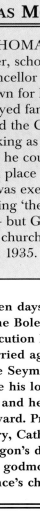

▶ Ten days after Anne Boleyn's execution Henry married again – Jane Seymour, who bore his longed-for son and heir, Edward. Princess Mary, Catherine of Aragon's daughter, was godmother at the prince's christening.

■ Henry the Tyrant ■

▲ **Henry in 1536, aged 45. In this year he took part in his last tournament. Injured in a fall, he afterwards suffered from headaches**

HENRY'S NEW CHURCH laws established the Reformation in England and made him head of the church in his own realm. But he was still short of money. Now the king and Cromwell eyed the rich lands and treasures of the monasteries to supply them with more. Many monasteries in England had fallen into decay. Fewer people joined them as monks or nuns and few of these lived up to the high standards of work and behaviour expected from them. Cromwell made a survey of all church lands and monasteries. Then they were sold off; first the smaller ones and then the large. By 1540 all were gone. Their property and treasures went to the crown.

EVENTS

***1536** Catherine of Aragon dies. Anne Boleyn is executed. Henry marries Jane Seymour. The dissolution of the monasteries begins. Pilgrimage of Grace uprising in the north. Union of England and Wales declared. Henry Fitzroy dies.*

***1537** Henry's son Edward born. Jane Seymour dies.*

Plain Anne

Cromwell and Cranmer furthered the Reformation in England. (Cromwell, for example, decreed that every parish should have a Bible in

▲ Holbein's portrait of Anne of Cleves persuaded the king to marry her, but the bride turned out to be plain and not to Henry's taste.

English.) Meanwhile, looking for a Protestant ally abroad, Cromwell steered the king towards marrying Anne of Cleves, a German princess. Henry saw Holbein's flattering portrait of her and agreed. But the marriage proved Cromwell's downfall, for the plain Anne was not to Henry's taste. Their wedding took place in 1540. Divorce quickly followed.

The End of Cromwell

The king, who hated looking foolish, blamed the disaster on Cromwell. The minister's many enemies at court convinced Henry that he was a traitor, trying to make England a Protestant country. In 1540 Cromwell was arrested and beheaded without trial. Before long, Henry realised how much he missed his clever and able adviser. Having executed his wisest counsellors, he now ruled alone. He was growing old, fat and ill. He trusted nobody and was unpredictable.

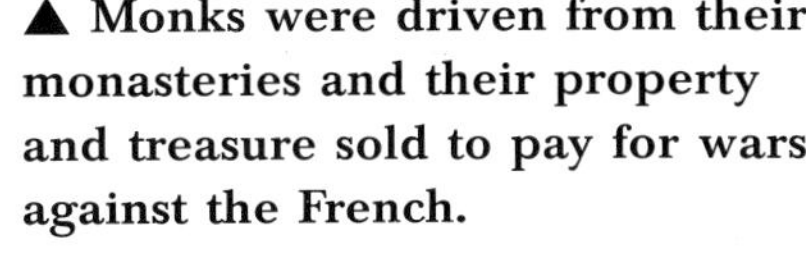

▲ Monks were driven from their monasteries and their property and treasure sold to pay for wars against the French.

On the Block

BEHEADING is said to have been brought to England by William the Conqueror, who had a Northumbrian earl beheaded in 1076. It was a sentence kept for nobles and important people such as Cromwell and More, whose execution is shown here, along with that of other victims. (The events, though shown together, took place on different dates.) Usually an axe was used. A scaffold was kept on London's Tower Hill in Henry's time, but Anne Boleyn was put to death within the Tower walls on the green near St Peter's Chapel. Her head was struck off with a sword, not an axe, by an executioner specially brought from France.

▼ This engraving shows Henry, now head of the church, trampling on the pope, helped by Cranmer and Cromwell.

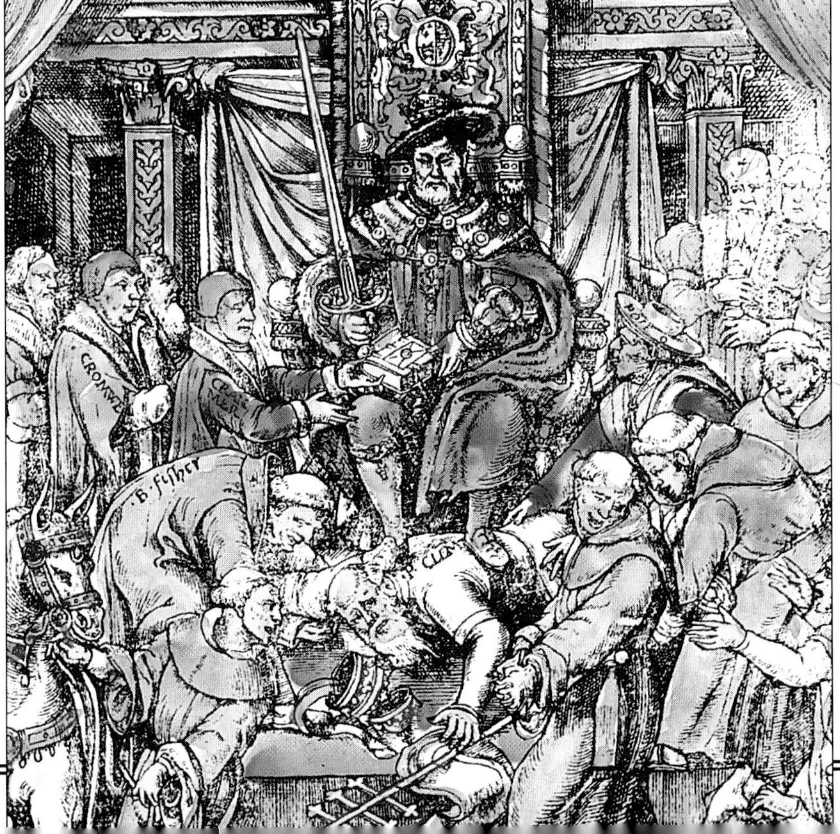

■ WAR AND REBELLION ■

HUGE CHANGES had taken place in Henry's kingdom. Not everybody liked them, and some rebelled. The most serious uprising was the Pilgrimage of Grace, which took place in the north in 1536 in protest against the dissolution of the monasteries.

In 1540 the king married again, secretly, a young lady-in-waiting to Anne of Cleves called Catherine Howard. Anne Boleyn had brought Protestant influence to court. Catherine Howard saw the Catholic cause rise. Henry always considered himself a Catholic. But the new queen, like Anne, was accused of being an unfaithful wife and was beheaded two years after her marriage.

EVENTS

__1540__ Henry marries Anne of Cleves and then divorces her. He marries Catherine Howard. Thomas Cromwell is executed for treason.
__1542__ Catherine Howard is executed. Henry joins Charles V against the French, who are supported by the Scots. At Solway Moss the English defeat the Scots. Portuguese sailors arrive in Japan.

A SHOW OF STRENGTH

The pope had called on other rulers in Europe to attack Henry after his break with Rome. To strengthen his kingdom, Henry built castles and a

▲ This suit of armour was worn by Henry in tournaments at the Field of Cloth of Gold in 1520.

▼ The use of firearms grew during Henry's reign. Armour gave little protection against artillery – guns and cannon – and so fell out of use.

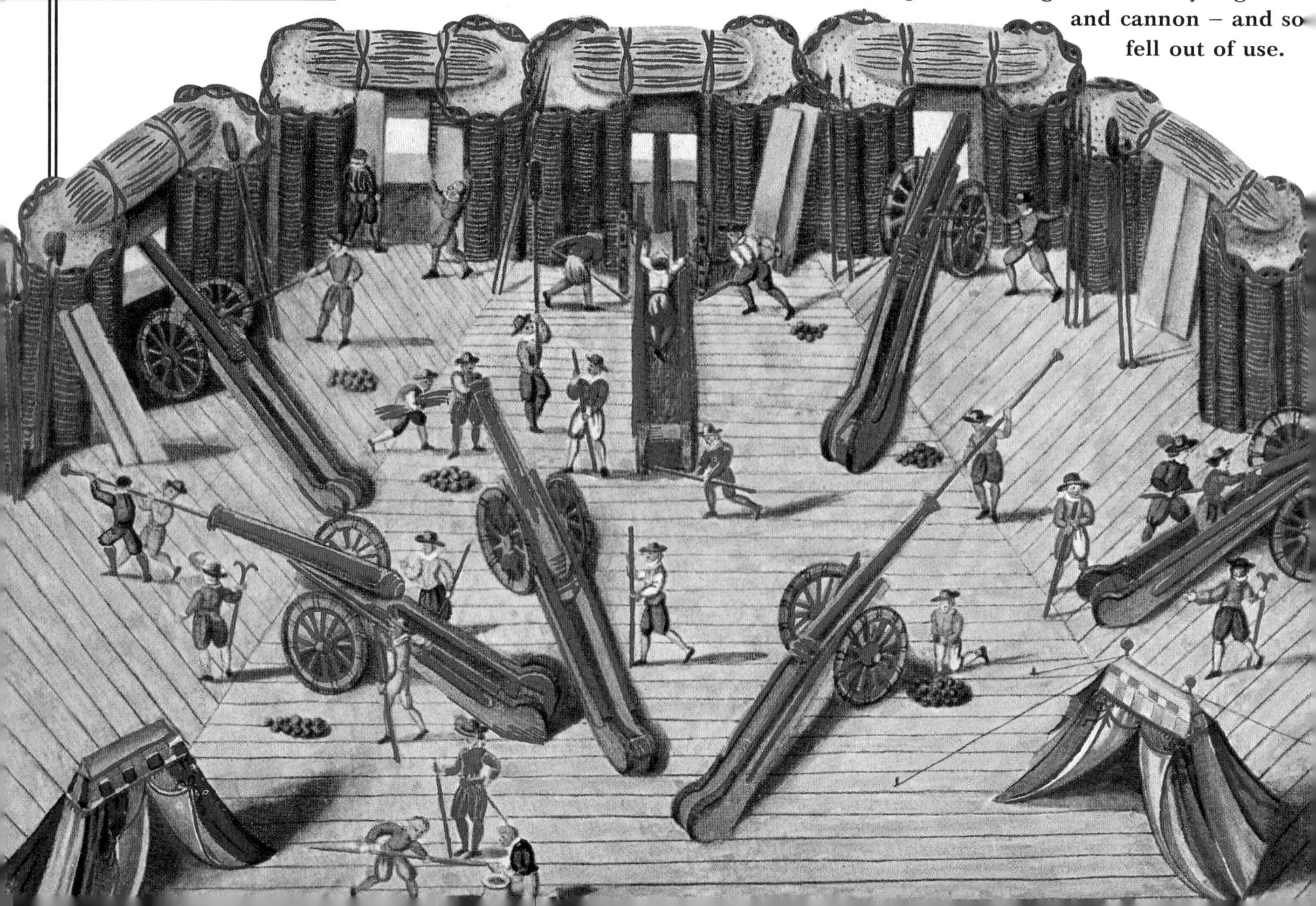

Pilgrimage of Grace

THE REBELLION called the Pilgrimage of Grace (right) began in the north in 1536. It was a protest both against the closing of the monasteries and against the enclosure of common land that led to such hardship for people in the countryside. About 30,000 rebels took over York, but the uprising collapsed when the king promised to look into the rebels' grievances. Instead, their leaders Robert Aske and Lord Thomas Darcy were arrested for treason and executed.

strong navy. With money from the monastery sales, he sought glory in battle once more. First he needed to be secure at home, to spread English influence further in Wales and Ireland and see off the threat from Scotland.

Neighbours but not friends

The union of England and Wales had been declared in 1536. Henry also called himself king of Ireland, though there was little English influence outside the city of Dublin. The Irish chiefs held real power. Scotland was always ready to ally itself with France and Henry feared the pope's influence through Ireland or Scotland.

In 1542, the Scots fought a much smaller English army at Solway Moss and were defeated. Their king, James V (Henry's nephew), died soon after hearing the terrible news, leaving his baby daughter Mary as queen of Scotland. In 1543 Henry again joined Spain in wars against France that lasted until 1546. They gained nothing but cost the fortune that Henry had seized from the monasteries.

▲ Prince Edward, who succeeded his father at the age of 10. His education was entrusted to the best scholars.

▶ Catherine Howard, Henry's fifth queen, was a Catholic. Young and lively, 'the very jewel of womanhood', she was beheaded in February 1542 for being unfaithful to the king.

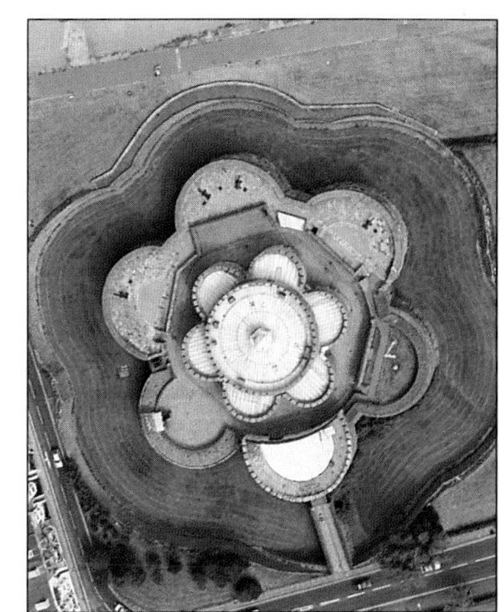

▶ Deal Castle, Kent, is shaped like a Tudor rose. It is one of some 20 forts that Henry built along the south coast.

■ ENGLAND AT SEA ■

ENGLAND NEEDED a strong navy to defend its shores and to fight the French. Henry VII had formed the first real English navy. Now Henry VIII built even bigger fighting ships. Old warships had been like floating castles, crammed with soldiers carrying spears and bows. Henry's new ships were armed with cannon and had openings called gunports in their sides, through which cannon could be fired. These were the most powerful warships of their day.

EVENTS

1497 *John Cabot, sailing under Henry VII's flag, discovers the Grand Banks fishing grounds off the coast of Newfoundland.*
1507 *Portuguese capture Mozambique in East Africa.*
1510 *Portuguese control Goa in India.* Mary Rose *built.*
1512 *Sebastian Cabot becomes Henry VIII's mapmaker.*
1514 Henry Grâce à Dieu *built.*
1522 *First voyage around the world, by survivors of Magellan's expedition*
1544 *Sebastian Cabot makes a map of the world.*

NAVAL GIANTS

In 1510 shipbuilders in Portsmouth finished the great warship *Mary Rose*, built at Henry's command. Two years later, the new ship was at war against the French. Even bigger was the 1000-tonne *Henry Grâce à Dieu*, known as the 'Great Harry'. Launched in 1514, this huge ship had 186 guns. Most were small, but the biggest cannon could fire an iron ball of 22 kilograms some distance.

◀ Sebastian Cabot, son of the Italian navigator and explorer John, became a mapmaker for Henry VIII. A famous map that he made of his and his father's discoveries is preserved in Paris.

▶ Henry can be seen on board his flagship, the *Henry Grâce à Dieu* (second ship from right), at Dover in May 1520, as his fleet prepares to sail to meet the French king at the Field of Cloth of Gold.

THE *MARY ROSE* RISES

THE *MARY ROSE* sank into the mud of the Solent by the Isle of Wight, and remained there for 400 years. In 1982 the remains of the ship were raised and the *Mary Rose* can now be seen at the Naval Dockyard in Portsmouth. Many fascinating objects from the ship, including

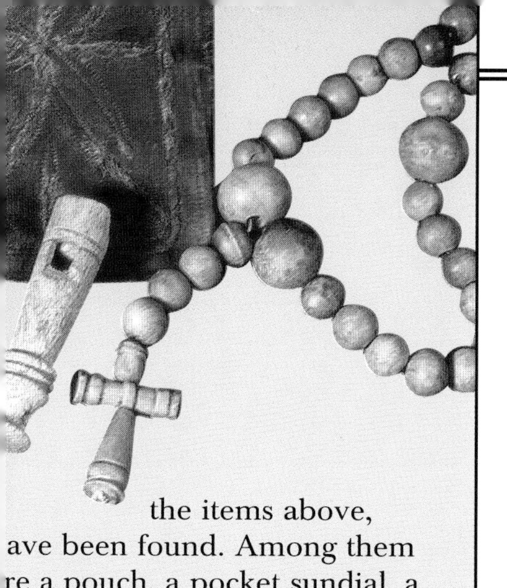

the items above,
ave been found. Among them
re a pouch, a pocket sundial, a
histle, a comb and a rosary,
s well as musical instruments,
rass guns and a large number
f bows and arrows. When it
ink, the great ship was
reserved, like a time capsule,
howing us what life was like
r the men of Henry's navy.

All wooden sailing ships needed constant repairs, because seawater rotted their timbers. The *Mary Rose* and *Henry Grâce à Dieu* were rebuilt in 1536. More guns were added, making the ships still heavier.

Sea disaster

In 1545 a French fleet of 200 or more ships sailed to raid the south coast of England. Henry rode down to Portsmouth to watch his fleet drive them off. Four enemy galleys rowed to attack the English flagship, the *Henry Grâce à Dieu.* The *Mary Rose* moved to help, its guns out ready to fire and its decks packed with soldiers. Suddenly, the great ship lurched over on to its side. Water rushed in through the open gunports. Guns broke loose and rolled across the deck. Men weighed down by heavy armour were swept into the sea. The *Mary Rose* sank, and most of the 800 people on board were drowned.

Henry watched in dismay from the shore. Despite the tragedy, the French fleet failed in its attack. King Henry's navy had done its job.

▪HENRY'S LEGACY▪

IN 1543 HENRY married for the last time. Catherine Parr was 31 and twice a widow. She had Mary, Elizabeth and Edward all brought to court, claiming it as 'the greatest joy and comfort' to care for the king and his children. The new queen also took much interest in their education and encouraged Henry to found Trinity College, Cambridge.

The last years of Henry's reign saw a struggle between powerful nobles who each wanted to rule as regent for the young Prince Edward after the king's death. Henry did not live to see Edward grow up. His will left the crown to each of his children in turn, with no one person as regent. A ruling council was to direct affairs for Edward.

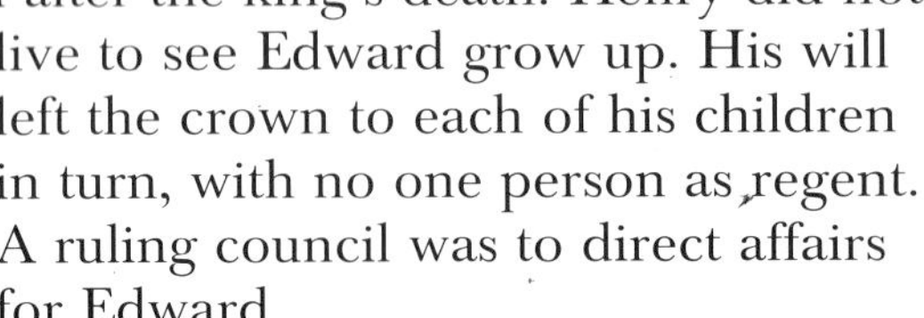

Henry died at Whitehall in January 1547, with Cranmer beside him. His nine-year-old son, a Protestant, lived for just six more years. Afterwards Mary, a devout Catholic, became queen, and then Elizabeth. None had children. The Tudor line – which Henry VIII had moved heaven and earth to try to create – ended with Elizabeth.

EVENTS

__1543__ Henry marries Catherine Parr. Copernicus states that the earth moves around the sun. Vesalius publishes his book on human anatomy.
__1544__ Henry and Charles V send troops to invade France, but have little success.
__1545__ Council of Trent (in Italy) meets to reform the Roman Catholic church.
__1546__ Martin Luther dies.
__1547__ Henry dies.

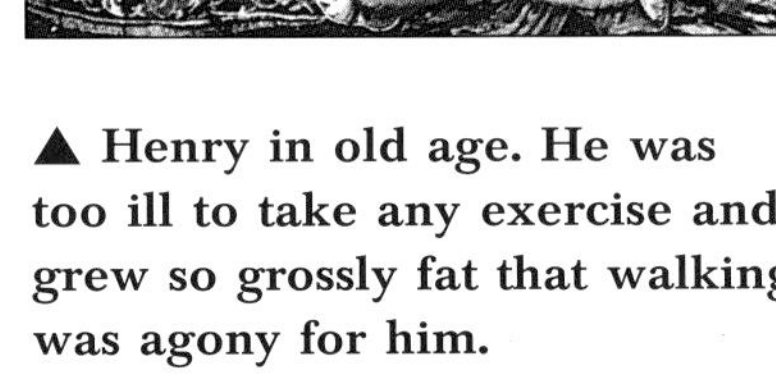

▲ Henry in old age. He was too ill to take any exercise and grew so grossly fat that walking was agony for him.

▶ Catherine Parr, Henry's sixth wife, was nurse and companion to the aging king. A kind and loving stepmother, she reunited Henry's family and directed the education of the royal children.

▼ Henry in his youth was a keen sportsman. He played a form of indoor tennis called *court* tennis or *royal* (or *real*) tennis. The court he built at Hampton Court is still used today.

▲ Mary I, Catherine of Aragon's daughter, rarely saw her father. She ruled England after her half-brother, Edward VI, and tried to make it a Catholic country again.

▲ Elizabeth I was Anne Boleyn's aughter and 25 when she ucceeded her half-sister Mary as ueen. She was a rotestant, head of he Church of ngland – and the ast of the Tudor line.

Few kings have left such a strong impression on their country as Henry. He promised more than he achieved, yet he left an English nation that felt itself independent and strong. He left his great houses and palaces, schools and colleges. More land was in the hands of landowners, after the sale of the monasteries – an act which halted the ancient monastic tradition and destroyed many treasures. Parliament grew in importance, a strong navy was built. Under its larger-than-life and sometimes terrifying king, Tudor England enjoyed new vigour at home and importance abroad.

▼ The ruins of Fountains Abbey, Yorkshire – one of the medieval monasteries closed by Henry VIII. During his reign, England moved from the Middle Ages to the modern world.

■ Glossary ■

Alliance An agreement between countries to work or fight together.

Ambassador An official sent abroad to represent his or her country.

Archbishop A bishop ranking above other bishops. In the Church of England the archbishop of Canterbury is the most senior of all bishops.

Armoury Place where weapons, or arms, are kept.

Artillery Large guns, such as cannon.

Calvinism Teachings of the Protestant religious reformer John Calvin.

Cardinal A senior bishop in the Catholic Church who acts as the pope's adviser and who elects new popes.

Catholic Roman Catholic; a Christian whose religious leader is the pope in Rome.

Chancellor See lord chancellor.

Councillor Member of a council that gives advice.

Counsellor An adviser who gives counsel; may also be a councillor.

Court 1. A place where trials are held – a court of law. 2. The household of a king or queen and the people who work for the monarch.

Courtier Person, usually of high rank, who attends the monarch.

Classical Describes the art and writing of ancient Greece and Rome.

Counter-Reformation Movement in the Roman Catholic Church to reverse the Protestant Reformation.

Dissolution The act of dissolving, undoing or breaking something up, particularly the monasteries during Henry VIII's reign.

Emperor The ruler of a territory made up of separate states.

Enclose In Tudor times and later, taking into private farms the open fields and common land formerly shared by villagers.

Flagship Ship that carries an admiral and flies his flag.

Galley A long ship with one deck that is propelled only by oars or by oars and sails.

Grammar School Originally a school in which grammar, especially Latin grammar, was taught.

Guild A group of people following the same trade or craft who act together to protect their business and personal interests.

Heretic Originally someone who disagreed with the official beliefs of the Christian church. Now it applies to anyone who dissents from the authorised teaching of their religion.

Holy Roman Empire Name given to the empire, founded by Charlemagne in 800 AD, of lands which are now part of Germany and France.

Humanist Person devoted to human, rather than divine or supernatural, interests, particularly the classical scholars of the Renaissance.

Illegitimate Outside the law; once commonly used to describe a child born to unmarried parents.

Jester A person at court or in a noble household employed to amuse people.

Joust Combat between two mounted knights with lances blunted to avoid serious injury.

Lord Chancellor The monarch's chief adviser.

Monastery A place where monks live, work and worship together.

Ottoman Belonging to the Turkish empire founded around 1300 by Osman.

Parliament A council who meet to advise the monarch and pass laws. It consists today of two houses: the House of Lords (nobles and important churchmen) and the House of Commons (members who have been elected).

Pilgrimage Journey made to some sacred place as an act of religious devotion.

Plague A highly infectious and once incurable

disease that is passed to humans by flea-ridden rats.

Privilege A special right or advantage given to one person or a selected group of people.

Protestant A member of a part of the Christian church that separated from the Roman Catholic Church in the 16th century.

Public School Originally a school set up by wealthy people for the free education of ordinary children. Today a school for fee-paying pupils.

Reformation The religious movement in Europe in the 16th century to reform the Roman Catholic Church and which led to the establishment of Protestant churches.

Regent A person who rules a country while its monarch is a child, absent or otherwise unable to govern.

Renaissance Period in Europe from the 14th to the 16th century when learning and scholarship underwent a revival thanks to the rediscovery of the works of ancient Greece and Rome.

Sovereign 1. Supreme ruler, or monarch.
2. Gold coin (no longer in use) worth £1.

Speaker Parliamentary official who speaks impartially on behalf of all members and keeps order.

Succeed To follow on; one monarch succeeds to the throne after another.

Taxes Money paid to the church, nobles, and the king and parliament to pay for running the country.

Theses A collection of theories or statements to be proved by argument. Martin Luther proposed 95 theses that opposed the teaching and practices of the church.

Tiltyard A place where knights tilted, or charged, at each other with blunted lances. The enclosure was divided into lists, narrow lanes separated by rails to keep the horses apart.

Tournament A competition in which knights on horseback fought with blunted lances and swords.

Treason The betrayal, usually of a ruler, by a trusted servant or adviser. It is punishable by death.

Places to Visit

Anne of Cleves House,
Lewes, Sussex.
Home of the queen after her divorce.

Compton Wynyates,
Warwickshire.
Tudor house.

Deal Castle,
Kent.
Example of Henry VIII's coastal forts.

Greenwich,
London.
Birthplace of Henry VIII, where the Royal Naval College and Maritime Museum now stand, and Greenwich Park, where he hunted.

Hampton Court Palace,
London.
The great palace that belonged to both Cardinal Wolsey and Henry VIII.

Hever Castle,
Kent.
Girlhood home of Anne Boleyn.

Mary Rose,
Portsmouth.
Ship of Henry VIII's navy.

Museum of London.
Many Tudor exhibits.

Royal Armouries Museum,
Leeds.
Tudor arms and armour.

Tower of London.
Armour of Henry VIII. Prison and site of executions.

Walmer Castle,
Kent.
Coastal fort of Henry VIII.

Westminster Abbey,
London.
Henry VII's Chapel.

Westminster Hall,
Houses of Parliament, London.
Scene of Sir Thomas More's trial.

Yarmouth Castle,
Isle of Wight.
Example of a fort built by Henry VIII.

INDEX